GLOBAL MICROECONOMIC PERSPECTIVES

Jagdish N. Sheth
Brooker Professor of Research
Graduate School of Business
University of Southern California

Abdolreza Eshghi
Associate Professor of Marketing
Bentley College

GN66AA
SOUTH-WESTERN

ISBN: 0–538–81065–3

1 2 3 4 5 6 7 M 5 4 3 2 1 0

Library of Congress Catalog Card Number: 90–60603

Printed in the United States of America

PREFACE

A number of exogenous forces are reshaping the microeconomic concepts of supply and demand. For example, technology advances such as computerized design and manufacturing, just-in-time operations, and flexible factories are reorganizing economies of scale and scope concepts. Similarly, global competition is restructuring industry concentration and pricing policies. At the same time, firms are seeking market access for growth as domestic markets mature and stagnate. Finally, and perhaps most importantly, changing government policy is restructuring markets. For example, economic integration of Western Europe (EC 1992) is reshaping global competitiveness of European firms and industries. Similarly, many governments are abandoning the role of the public sector and encouraging market processes by privatization, deregulation, and liberalization of infrastructure industries such as transportation and telecommunications.

This volume is somewhat unorthodox in its selection and concept. Instead of focusing on the traditional international aspects of microeconomics such as international trade policy, comparative advantage, and balance of payments, it focuses on the supply and demand and how five resources firms that acquire globally; capital, human resources, technology, products (including raw materials), and information. Furthermore, it describes how multinational firms tend to operate in a global economy with respect to allocation of its resources.

This volume is designed to supplement standard textbooks on microeconomics for required courses in the MBA program. It is intended to fulfill the accreditation requirements for internationalizing the core courses in business schools.

A number of criteria were utilized in selecting the papers for this volume:

- They must have a managerial economics perspective.
- The authors must be well recognized for their contributions to the field.
- The authors must represent a worldwide perspective in addition to the U.S. perspective.

Although this volume is primarily designed to supplement the required course in managerial economics at the MBA level, it can also satisfy the needs of the Executive MBA programs, as well as corporate executive seminars on international economics.

The editors and the publisher are grateful to the authors and publishers who granted permission to reprint articles in this volume.

Jagdish N. Sheth
Abdolreza Eshghi

CONTENTS

INTRODUCTION

Supply of, and demand for, a firms's resources (products, technology, people, capital and information) are becoming increasingly global in scope. For example, many U.S. firms have significant offshore procurement, manufacturing, and marketing operations. This is especially true for firms in other nations that are (or must be) export-oriented because of small or less developed domestic markets, such as in Germany, France, the United Kingdom, Japan, Korea, Taiwan, Denmark, India, and China.

Unfortunately, traditional microeconomic theories of supply and demand are anchored to a domestic economy orientation. This has been augmented by theories of international economics such as comparative advantage, trade policy, economic development, economic integration, and balance of payments. However, it seems that exogenous forces shaping the theory and practice of the firm in recent decades, especially since the 1960s, have become powerful enough to suggest that we need a new perspective in microeconomics.

Need for Global Microeconomics Perspectives

A number of exogenous forces are creating the need for a global microeconomic perspective. This is summarized in Figure I.1.

Figure I.1
FORCES SHAPING THE NEED FOR GLOBAL MICROECONOMIC PERSPECTIVES

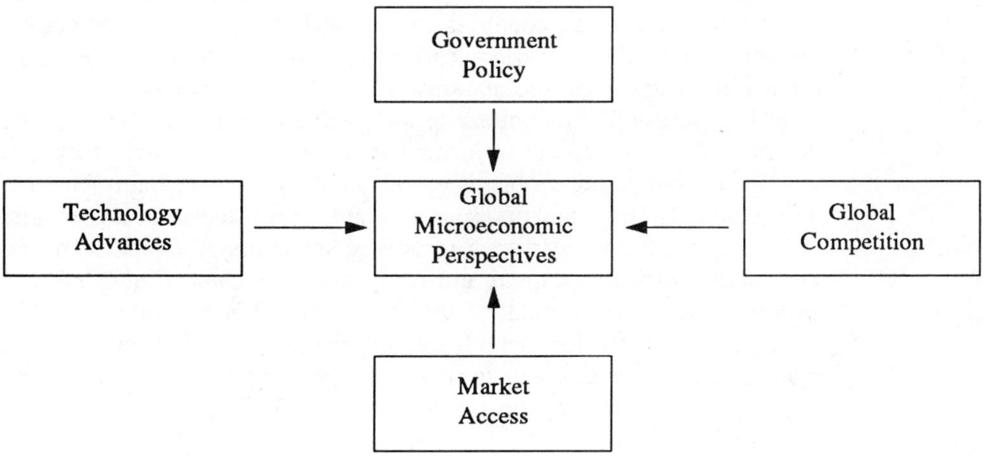

Perhaps the single most powerful exogenous force shaping the supply and demand aspects of firms in an industry is the changing government policy. Governments are changing in at least three respects. First, governments are allowing and often encouraging, even in the socialist nations of the Soviet Union and Eastern Europe, market competitive processes to shape the competitive structures and strategic operations of firms in a given industry. Recent examples include the privatization of public sector monopolies such as telecommunications, transportation, and financial institutions in both the United Kingdom and Japan. Second, governments, as the largest single buyer in any nation, have decided to procure products and services from offshore vendors in order to contain costs or increase efficiency among domestic suppliers. Even in countries with strong nationalistic feelings such as West Germany, Japan, and France, we increasingly see the evidence of this. Finally, governments have decided that economic cooperation among nations beyond trade and technology transfer policies are extremely critical to their future political and social influences. They have agreed to develop regional economic integration such as the ASEAN block, and perhaps the most significant recent example is European Community's regional integration by the end of 1992. Industry restructuring as a consequence of the changing government policy is simply massive and often unprecedented.

A second major exogenous force shaping the need for a global perspective in microeconomics is the emergence of global competition. Industry after industry are facing global competition whether it is in basic industries such as steel, aluminum, chemicals, and semiconductors or in finished products such as electronics, automobiles, and garments. Global competition is increasing in numerous services industries where traditionally the microeconomic concepts of supply and demand dominated local markets and local production. Examples of increasing global competition in services include banking, insurance, retailing, and many professional services. How does a domestically oriented industry get restructured? and, consequently, How does a firm in that industry respond to global competition? are issues for which we need new perspectives.

Third, market access has become increasingly important in microeconomics. As industries in advanced countries mature and the growth in domestic gross national product (GNP) slows, it becomes increasingly important to explore market opportunities outside the domestic markets. There are a number of significant factors related to market access. First, contrary to the traditional economic views, the less developed countries (LDC's), except in a few cases, have not provided market opportunities as imagined. Look at the problems encountered by firms in Latin America, China, India, and Africa. These nations present a number of obstacles to a firm attempting to successfully transfer its resources (products, technology, capital, and people) including lack of infrastructure capital and ready markets. On the other hand, most advanced nations seem to have markets that are both willing to buy and able to pay. It is, therefore, important for firms from both developed and developing nations to ensure market access and to compete in some of the most advanced nations such as Japan, West Germany, France, the United Kingdom, and the United States. A firm has to think differently in its competitive strategies and resource allocations if it must compete in the highly competitive markets of advanced nations as opposed to pioneering new markets in less developed nations.

A second and more recent market access dimension is related to the opening of East Europe and Soviet Union markets. While the market potential seems enormous, it is likely to require more innovative economic concepts to manage different managerial, cost accounting, pricing, and market development issues as Western firms enter those socialist markets. In other words, how do you measure profits when cost allocation formulas and currency exchange rates are either undefined or radically different? Finally, global market access in the future will require strategic alliances with archrival competitors as evidence by General Motors and Toyota, Ford and Mazda, or Chrysler and Mitsubishi, just in the automobile industry. And this pattern is replicated in electronics, basic materials, and many industrial finished goods. We have no theory in microeconomics that provides guidelines for cooperation with competitors except the oil concepts of industry collusion and price-fixing. But what is manifested goes way beyond price-fixing; it entails joint R & D, joint manufacturing or marketing, and often the formation of separate companies jointly owned and operated by archrival competitors.

Finally, technological advances in electronics and especially in computing and telecommunications have revolutionized a firm's research and engineering, manufacturing, marketing, and business operations in general. Technology's impact on the economic behavior of the industry and the firm are critical to examine. For example, time-based competition, distributed manufacturing, demand-driven manufacturing, and computerized on-line linkages with customers and suppliers are making the traditional single location-based economy of scale and economy of scope concepts less and less useful. We believe economists in the next decade will focus on the impact of technology on the theory of the firm and on demand theory anchored to the basic concepts of marginal analysis and utility.

Supply and Demand of Firm's Resources

What we need is a new conceptual framework that is capable of accommodating the influences of the exogenous factors described above while building on the traditional concepts of supply and demand in microeconomics.

One way to approach this is to suggest that the fundamental objectives of a firm are survival and growth. Survival is often achieved by profit maximization through the principles of marginal analysis (marginal cost equals marginal revenue). However, it can also be achieved by other means including partnering with competitors, mergers, and acquisitions. Similarly, survival is not the only objective of a firm. It has a twin objective of growth, which enables a firm to separate its short-term survival objective from its long-term and more strategic growth objective. In other words, a firm has both short-term and long-term objectives that are distinct in their definition, measurement, and implementation.

Furthermore, the short-term survival objective and the long-term growth objectives are sequential and cyclical in nature. In the early stages of a firm's evolution, survival is extremely critical and it drives the behavior of the firm at the expense of its growth potential. In other words, short term dominates over the long term. On the other hand, when a firm is a successful ongoing business, growth objective is critical and it is achieved often at the expense of short-term survival or profit objective. The following Figure I.2 reflects this cyclical and sequential phenomenon.

Figure I.2
SURVIVAL VERSUS GROWTH OBJECTIVES OF THE FIRM

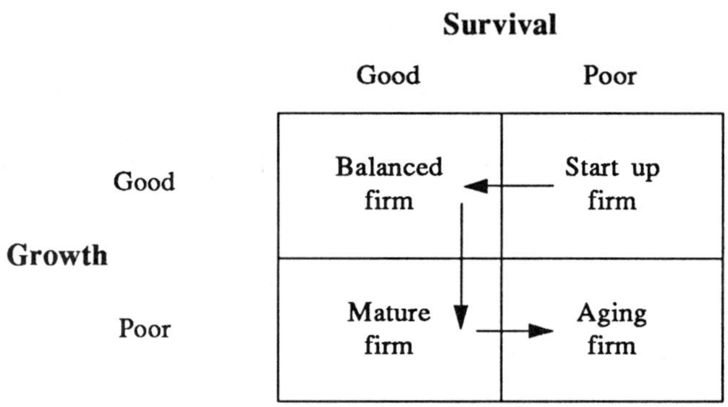

When a firm is survival oriented, it needs to *import* its resources, and when a firm is growth oriented it needs to *export* its resources. In other words, resources (factors of production) for a new entrant in an industry are insufficient, and the firm is constantly searching for them from outside sources, these include technology, human resources, capital, management, and products (including raw materials). The firm needs worldwide access to these resources in order to organize them on the principles of marginal analysis and earn a profit. If these resources are not available, the firm tends to engage in other survival strategies that require co-opting with competitors through joint ventures, mergers, and acquisitions.

At the maturity stage, however, the firm tends to have excess resources: people, management, technology, products, and money. It must learn how to export its resources to the outside world. It must learn how to reduce its excess capacity without jeopardizing survival. The most common strategy is increasing the market scope, especially in the global arena. However, if market access is a problem, it can still achieve growth through joint ventures, mergers, and acquisitions.

Ideally, a firm must be balanced between its import and export resource streams. To the extent that it is able to balance them, it makes no trade offs between the short-term survival objective and the long-term growth objective. Unfortunately, this is more easily prescribed than carried out. In general, a firm is either profit driven or growth driven at a point in time. This creates the sequential and cyclical evolution of a firm in an industry.

At the microeconomic level, it is important for a firm and for an industry to match supply of and demand for the resources (capital, people, technology, management information, and products including raw materials). Unfortunately, a number of exogenous factors intervene in the process of matching supply and demand of these resources on a global basis. Figure I.3 depicts these forces. We will review each of these forces in the following pages.

Figure I.3
PROBLEMS OF MATCHING SUPPLY AND DEMAND OF RESOURCES

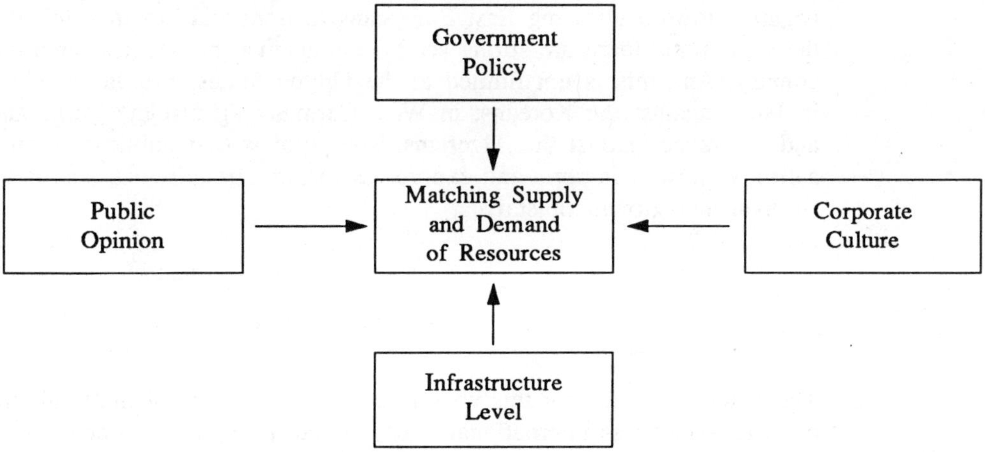

Government policy, as a consequence of its political, social, and cultural agenda, often does not permit free flow of resources between national boundaries. For example, technology flow is often impeded by national security issues, human resources flow by brain drain issues, and capital flow by risk–return issues. A firm as to either suboptimize its resource matching process or learn to influence government policy through lobbying, political intervention, or bribery and corruption. In fact, most multinational corporations have experienced this dilemma and have either learned to live with it, or have decided to exit specific foreign markets.

A second and equally important factor is the corporate culture or management attitudes. Most firms tend to be ethnocentric and their mind-sets lag behind their market shares when it comes to global orientation. It is not common to see either the board of directors or top management team of a large multinational proportionately represented by nationalities of geographic markets they serve. And this is not limited to U.S. multinationals. It is also true of the German, Indian, Chinese, French, and especially the Japanese multinationals. Import and export of a firm's resources (people, money, technology, information and products) are, therefore, not in line with the firm's objectives.

A third factor impeding optimal flow of resources is lack of infrastructure. Poor infrastructure with respect to transport, telecommunications, energy, training, and travel often results in less than ideal inflow or outflow of resources, especially in and out of less developed nations. Therefore, nations with excellent infrastructure tend to have a strong competitive advantage for their industry and their firms.

Finally, public opinion also impacts the flow of a firm's resources across national boundaries. This is particularly true for people and capital resources. Recent anti-Japanese sentiments in the United States demonstrates that. It is interesting to note that while the largest foreign private investment in the United States is from the United Kingdom and The Netherlands, very little negative public opinion is expressed about those countries; and at the same time, the Japanese are criticized for their investment in the United States. Similarly, it would appear that public opinion would be less negative toward allowing East Europeans to immigrate to the United States; and at the same time, there are strong sentiments against the Mexican immigration into the country. And this is not limited to the United States. Similar public opinions exist in Japan against the Koreans; in West Germany against the Turks and the Italians; and in France against the Algerians. The point is that public opinion will influence a firm in how it imports and exports its resource requirements as it tries to achieve survival and growth objectives.

Book Summary

The articles selected for this volume are not reflections of the traditional microeconomic areas such as international trade, private foreign investment, and economic development. We have selected papers from well-known scholars who are concerned with *unique* issues firms experience as they manage import and export of their resources. Part I deals with intra-industry and intra-firm trade in light of economic integration and balance of payment problems. Part II reflects on cultural and structural issues related to flow and transfer of technology across national boundaries. Part III discusses new forms of investments in developing nations and cultural influences multinationals manifest with respect to debt and equity ratios in private foreign investments. It, therefore, discusses problems and challenges related to the flow of capital across national boundaries. Part IV is specific to human resource issues. The two papers included in this section focus on the challenge of transforming an ethnocentric firm to a geocentric or a global firm in its selection, development, and management of human resources. Finally, Part V focuses on flow of information within and between firms across national boundaries. It discusses the infrastructure issues of compatibility of standards, privacy issues, political and national sovereignty threats, as well as economic issues associated with the private networks operated by the multinationals on a global basis.

I THE GLOBAL FLOW OF GOODS

1. INTRA-INDUSTRY TRADE, INTRA-FIRM TRADE AND EUROPEAN INTEGRATION: EVIDENCE, GAINS AND POLICY ASPECTS

DAVID GREENAWAY
University of Nottingham

1. Introduction

The concepts of intra-industry trade and economic integration have been closely associated for many years. This is largely a consequence of the fact that the earliest studies of intra-industry trade began as studies of the trade effects of European integration. Ironically, the prevailing wisdom of customs unions theory at that time led to the expectation of increased *inter*-industry specialization among the original six. In the event, Balassa (1965), Dreze (1960) and Verdoorn (1961) identified evidence of increased intra-industry specialization following integration.

Since the early/mid 1960s, research on intra-industry trade has grown to an impressive degree. A great deal of information has now been accumulated with regard to the growth and extent of the phenomenon, and we now know quite a lot about the determinants of this growth. (See Greenaway and Milner, 1986.) Among the determinants which have been examined, and for which some evidence can be adduced, is economic integration. There would appear to be a causal association between economic integration and intra-industry trade. Moreover, there also appears to be a link between intra-firm trade and intra-industry trade.

This contribution considers various aspects of the links between economic integration, intra-firm trade and intra-industry trade. Section 2 examines various theoretical perspectives. Section 3 provides an overview of evidence with particular reference to experience in the EC. This comments more on intra-industry trade than intra-firm trade since the evidence on the latter is somewhat sparse. Section 4 comments upon possible welfare implications and Section 5 considers policy aspects of particular relevance to the European Community. Finally, section six offers some concluding comments.

2. Integration, Intra-Firm Trade and Intra-Industry Trade: Theoretical Effects

A number of commentators have pointed to a possible connection between economic integration and intra-industry trade. Several studies have provided corroborative evidence for such a connection (e.g. Willmore, 1974, and Balassa, 1979, for the Central American Common Market and Latin American Free Trade Area; Balassa, 1965, and

Reprinted from the *Journal of Common Market Studies*, 26:2, 1987, pp. 153–72 by permission from the publisher.

Grubel and Lloyd, 1975, for the EC). Despite the accumulation of work suggesting such a connection, little by way of systematic theoretical analysis of links between the two exists. It is not difficult to explain why this is so. Traditional (Vinerian) customs union theory, with its stress of three country, two commodity and two factor models cannot easily accommodate preference diversity, multiple products and imperfect competition. Ethier and Horn (1984) ably demonstrate the difficulties of incorporating such market imperfections into customs union theory. Despite the absence of a clearly articulated and widely accepted theoretical point of reference it is possible to establish a number of possible causal connections between economic integration and intra-industry trade in particular.

Trade Liberalization

One of the most distinctive features of an integration arrangement is the liberalization of tariff barriers among the integrating economies and (in the case of a customs union) the erection of a common external tariff against *'outside'* countries. One could argue that trade liberalization is likely to promote intra-industry trade on the grounds that liberalization is likely to promote trade expansion in general. Whilst it seems reasonable to suppose that discriminatory trade liberalization is likely to promote intra-community trade expansion (whether this be of a trade creating or trade diverting type), there are no *a priori* reasons why trade liberalization *per se* should stimulate the growth of intra- as opposed to inter-industry trade. To put this another way, why should discriminatory trade liberalization be expected to affect the growth of intra-industry trade to a greater extent than multilateral trade liberalization? There is in fact no *a priori* reason for believing that it should, unless perhaps we argue that, in principle anyway, customs union formation should result in a reduction of both tariff *and* non-tariff barriers. Trade liberalization will as a result be more extensive. Again, however, this will only impact upon the extent of any trade expansion and will not necessarily alter the relative importance of intra- *vis-a-vis* inter-industry trade.

In order to find reasons why economic integration may stimulate intra-industry exchange to a greater degree than inter-industry exchange one needs to focus more closely on features of the pre-union market structures.

Preference Diversity and Overlapping Demands

Theoretical analysis suggests that the distribution and intensity of preferences has an important bearing on the potential for intra-industry trade. Other things being equal, the more evenly preferences are distributed across a given product spectrum, the greater the potential for intra-industry exchange. Moreover, it is not only the horizontal product spectrum (i.e. diverse preferences for alternative combinations of a given set of attributes) which is relevant, but also the vertical spectrum (i.e. diverse preferences for alternative quality gradings). In addition, as Lancaster (1980) and Greenaway (1982) demonstrate, the extent of any taste overlap between potential trading partners is relevant. Other things being equal, the greater the overlap of preferences, the greater the potential scope for intra-industry trade. Thus, if the pre-integration economies have similar preference structures, and produce similar, but differentiated, commodities, a greater stimulus will be given to intra-industry exchange than would be the case with multilateral liberalization. If it is predominantly countries with similar factor endowments, similar per capita incomes and similar demand structures which form customs unions, this will be an important basis for intra-industry exchange.

Decreasing Costs in Production

In general, the demand factors discussed above are necessary but not sufficient conditions for the emergence of intra-industry trade. In a world of zero set-up costs and constant marginal costs, customization would be costless and any amount of preference diversity could be catered for domestically. Thus, decreasing costs over the relevant range of output is the sufficiency condition. It is this which results in the equilibrium number of firms in the market, and the equilibrium number of differentiated goods, being finite. This condition is quite general and applies to free entry models which result in a large numbers solution, as well as blocked entry models which result in small numbers solutions. Of course, the nature of the scale economies available affect entry conditions and therefore the equilibrium number of varieties. It has often been argued that one of the principal benefits stemming from customs union formation is that producers are able to lengthen their production runs and in effect *'exchange'* scale economies. Thus, overlapping demands together with decreasing costs in the production function can facilitate intra-industry specialization.

Factor Movements and Intra-Firm Trade

Liberalization of capital flows tends to be a concomitant of economic integration. The conventional wisdom on the relationship between factor movements and trade in goods is that they are substitutes rather than complements (Mundell, 1957). This proposition, however, derives from the structure of the Heckscher-Ohlin model, and in particular the assumption that initial factor endowments differ (since this leads to complementarity in production structures). Markusen (1983) argues that this may be a result which is peculiar to the Heckscher-Ohlin model, and as such may be the exception rather than the rule. It is argued that, in many circumstances, factor movements and intra-firm trade may be complementary. For example, Agmon (1979) argues that where intra-industry trade is concerned, it is likely that factor movements and trade will be complementary. The vehicle of transfer turns out to be the transnational corporation which engages in foreign direct investment in order to specialize in different varieties in different countries. Foreign direct investment followed by intra-industry trade allows the firm to exploit the rents associated with firm specific advantages, as well as providing a means for reconnaissance of foreign markets. In turn, the latter facilitates a new product development and further expansion.

This horizontal specialization is not the only mechanism whereby foreign direct investment leads to intra-firm trade which is then recorded as intra-industry trade.

Vertical specialization may also be a contributory factor. In other words, firms may *'peel off'* parts of the production process in order to take advantage of the opportunities offered by further division of labour in a larger market. Some commentators have argued that this is in fact the principle explanation of recorded intra-industry trade (e.g. Pomfret, 1986). It need not necessarily result in intra-firm trade; this depends on whether the requisite O-L-I preconditions exist. It is probable, however, that for a given set of OLI advantages the probability of FDI occurring which results in intra-firm trade is higher in a common market than in a non-integrated market. This follows from the greater ease of movement of capital within the integrated market. Thus there are sound *a priori* reasons for expecting the potential for intra-firm trade, which may be recorded as intra-industry trade, to be greater in an integrated market than in a non-integrated market.

There are therefore a variety of channels which might be expected to lead to a deterministic link between economic integration and intra-industry trade. What of the empirical evidence in the case of the EC?

3. Integration, Intra-Firm Trade, and Intra-Industry Trade: Some Evidence for the EC

As noted at the outset, work on intra-industry trade and the trade effects of economic integration in Europe have been intimately connected. As a result quite a large amount of evidence is now available on this subject. Before considering this evidence, a few brief remarks on the measurement of intra-industry trade and intra-industry specialization are in order.

Measuring Intra-Industry Trade and Intra-Industry Specialization

The terms intra-industry trade and intra-industry specialization are often used interchangeably. Insofar as trade can result in specialization, there are good reasons why this is so. They are, however, conceptually separable concepts which should be measured quite differently.

Intra-industry trade refers to the simultaneous export and import of commodities from a given industry, and is generally expressed as a proportion of total trade in the relevant commodity. Thus, using the Grubel-Lloyd (1975) index, intra-industry trade in product j would be defined as:

$$B_j = \left[1 - \frac{|X_j - M_j|}{(X_j + M_j)} \right] .100 \qquad (1)$$

where,
$0 \leq Bj \leq 100$

This index[1] could alter without any necessary concomitant alteration in specialization. Changes in an industry's product mix could lead to changes in intra-industry trade across several activities, without altering either the overall level of output or factor requirements in the industry. In these circumstances, changes in intra-industry trade would not result in intra-industry specialization.

Although there is a strong presumption that intra-industry trade and intra-industry specialization will go hand in hand, in principle the latter should be measured by reference to production side changes. Hufbauer and Chilas (1974) rely on a Grubel and Lloyd type index to measure changes in specialization patterns. This is done by expressing net or gross trade in a given industry relative to industry output. A more ambitious approach has been adopted by Glejser et al. (1979), (1982) and Glejser (1983). Here, specialization on the supply side (exports) and the demand side (imports) is identified by reference to whether a country exports or imports more in particular product lines than comparable countries. The index of export specialization is defined as:

$$e_t = \frac{1}{n} \sum_{j=1}^{n} \log \left[\frac{X_j}{\Sigma X_{ij}} \Bigg/ \frac{\Sigma X_j}{\Sigma X} \right] = \frac{1}{n} \sum_{j=1}^{n} e_{jt} \qquad (2)$$

whilst that for demand specialization is defined as:

$$u_t = \frac{1}{n} \sum_{j=1}^{n} \log \left[\frac{M_j}{\Sigma M_{ij}} \Bigg/ \frac{\Sigma M_j}{\Sigma M} \right] = \frac{1}{n} \sum_{j=1}^{n} u_{jt} \qquad (3)$$

where,

X_{ij} (M_{ij}) = intra-group exports (imports) of country j by country i
ΣX_{ij} (ΣM_{ij}) = total intra-area exports (imports) across all industries of country i.
ΣX_j (ΣM_j) = total intra-area exports (imports) of industry j excluding country i
ΣX = total intra-area exports (imports) by group of countries across all industries excluding country i.

If, inter-industry specialization dominates, then $X_{ij}/\Sigma X_{ij}$ ($M_{ij}/\Sigma M_{ij}$) will diverge from $\Sigma X_j/\Sigma X$ ($\Sigma M_j/\Sigma M$). If intra-industry specialization dominates, the ratios will approach zero. Although the measures can be shown to have similarities with the Balassa (1965) index of specialization,[2] and although a production side *'numeraire'* is absent, the index is still used as an index of specialization.

Evidence on the EC can be adduced using both Grubel and Lloyd and Glejser type indices.

Table 1
AVERAGE LEVELS OF INTRA-INDUSTRY TRADE IN SELECTED EC COUNTRIES

Country	1959	1967	1977	1980
Belgium-Luxembourg	53	63	69	63
Netherlands	55	56	67	65
West Germany	39	46	64	57
France	45	65	76	65
Italy	35	42	58	50
UK	35	69	72	60

Sources: Data for 1959 and 1967 from Grubel and Lloyd (1975). Data for 1977 and 1980, own calculations.

Intra-Industry Trade in the EC

Table 1 reports details of average (third digit) levels of intra-industry trade in the original six members of the European Community plus the United Kingdom. The table reports point estimates for 1959, 1967, 1977 and 1980. These figures suggest that intra-industry trade increased in importance from the late 1950s through to the late 1970s in all of the countries concerned. A reduction in average levels is then recorded for 1980. Of course, this only provides evidence to support the proposition that intra-industry trade has increased in EC countries. In the absence of information on what would have occurred in the absence of integration it is impossible to judge from this whether the growth of intra-industry trade is faster than it would have been otherwise. In this regard it is interesting to note that the greatest proportionate increase between any two points applies to the United Kingdom between 1959 and 1967, i.e. during a period when she was *not* a member of the EC but was a member of EFTA. Since this is a free trade area rather than a fully fledged customs union, it at least poses a question mark against the strength of integration effects on intra-industry trade. Moreover, it is also true that during this period all countries benefited from multilateral trade liberalization under the auspices of the GATT. It is difficult to disentangle the effects of this liberalization from the effects of regional liberalization, especially in view of the fact that, as Hufbauer and Chilas (1974) have argued, multilateral liberalization among developed market economies may have been biased towards intra-industry trade in order to minimize costs of adjustment.

More penetrating insights into possible integration effects can be gleaned from two other avenues, first by examining intra-bloc intra-industry trade relative to total intra-industry trade, and secondly by comparing the experience of countries which are party to integration arrangements with that of comparable countries which are not party to any such arrangements. Some evidence on the former has been adduced by Grubel (1967), Balassa (1966), Grubel and Lloyd (1975) and Drabek and Greenaway (1984).

These studies suggest that intra-EC, intra-industry trade grew more rapidly than total EC intra-industry trade in the 1960s and 1970s. With regard to the latter possibility, the evidence is less conclusive. As we have already seen, intra-industry trade appears to have grown more rapidly in Britain than in the original six Members of the EC during the period 1959-1967, though not between 1967 and 1977. Against this, Grubel and Lloyd (1975) and Drabek and Greenaway (1984) offer evidence in support of the proposition that intra-industry trade has grown more rapidly in EC countries than in comparable non-EC countries (specifically Austria, Switzerland, Sweden and Norway).

Intra-Industry Specialization in the EC

As we have already seen, the notion of using the experience of comparable countries to comment on EC experience was followed by Glejser et al. (1979, 1982) to identify trends in intra-industry specialization in the EC. Basically they used the ratios presented in equations (2) and (3) to estimate export and import specialization in the EC relative to a group of comparable countries. They then used information on the variance of the specialization indices around their mean values. (The attractiveness of computing the variance is that one can administer an F test in order to establish whether changes in specialization appear to be statistically significant or not.)

Some results from applying the Glejser index are presented in Table 2. This reports variance measures for all (post second enlargement) EC countries. It will be recalled that a reduction in the measure implies increased intra-industry specialization, whilst an increase implies increased inter-industry specialization. In the event, all changes are in a downward direction with the exception of export specialization in France and import specialization in Ireland. It should be noted that only a few of these changes turn out to be statistically significant at the 5 per cent level. Notwithstanding this, the changes do provide strong presumptive evidence to the effect that intra-industry specialization increased in the EC between 1973 and 1979.

Table 2
INTRA-INDUSTRY SPECIALIZATION IN THE EC, 1973–1979

Country	Export	Specialization	Import	Specialization
	1973	1979	1973	1979
Belgium-Luxembourg	0.185	0.184	0.041	0.039
Denmark	0.577	0.314	0.063	0.037
France	0.066	0.070	0.035	0.026
West Germany	0.076	0.065	0.049	0.029
Ireland	0.261	0.189	0.069	0.075
Italy	0.276	0.244	0.102	0.098
Netherlands	0.175	0.099	0.040	0.033
United Kingdom	0.139	0.122	0.059	0.044

Sources: Adapted from Glejser (1983) Table 1.

Econometric Analysis

Some analysts have endeavoured to elicit evidence of integration effects in cross section studies of intra-industry trade. Very few studies have yet been completed. Those which have find evidence to support a positive *'integration effect'* (see Pagoulatos and Sorensen, 1975, Havrylyshyn and Civan, 1983 and Balassa, 1986). The main problem with this work is that the integration proxies are invariably *'catch all'* proxies and could be picking up distance factors, taste overlap factors and so on.

Overall, then, although the evidence is far from conclusive, it does suggest that European integration has been linked to the growth of intra-industry trade. To what extent is this a reflection of intra-firm trade?

Intra-Firm Trade and Intra-Industry Trade

A number of commentators have argued that the increase in recorded intra-industry trade may in large measure be a reflection of increased intra-firm trade (see Casson, 1986, Pomfret, 1986, Helleiner, 1981). It is certainly true that the two phenomena have increased simultaneously. It is also true that we can establish sound *a priori* reasons for believing them to be related. There is, however, a very real problem in finding empirical evidence to support this link. This is so first because of the limited information on intra-firm trade *per se*, and, second, because of the even more limited information linking intra-firm trade and intra-industry trade.

The only systematic information available on intra-firm trade is that produced by the U.S. Department of Commerce and U.S. Bureau of Census. Where the EC is concerned, only limited information for specific years is available from a few of the Member States. At the global level, it has been suggested that around 40 per cent of total trade is intra-firm trade (Clairmonte and Cavanagh, 1982). The information which is currently available for EC countries is summarized in Table 3, from which it can be seen that the share of total MNE trade which is intra-firm trade increased between the 1960s and 1970s for both Belgium and West Germany, and accounts for a substantial proportion of total MNE trade. Moreover, this evidence also suggests that the share of intra-firm trade in national trade may also be substantial—23 per cent of 1976 exports in Belgium, 30 per cent of 1980 exports in the United Kingdom. It might be noted parenthetically that the more extensive evidence available for the U.S. also reveals that intra-firm trade is becoming increasingly important, and that it accounts for a substantial proportion of national trade (see Van Den Bulcke, 1985).

Thus, what (admittedly sketchy) evidence is available suggests that intra-firm trade is becoming increasingly prevalent in the EC. What, however, of empirical evidence on the link between intra-firm trade and intra-industry trade? Unfortunately, the empirical evidence here is remarkably thin. Very little information exists, but a few studies have been carried out. Caves (1981) examines the relationship in a multi-country, multi-industry study. In analysing the determinants of intra-industry trade in the principle OECD countries he includes a variable recording the exports to majority-owned affiliates and imports of U.S. parents from majority-owned foreign affiliates, divided by total U.S. exports. This turns out to be positively and significantly related

Table 3
EVIDENCE ON INTRA-FIRM TRADE IN THE EC

Country	Share of Intra-Firm Trade in Total MNE Trade (%)	Share of Intra-Firm Trade in Total National Trade (%)
West Germany	1966: Exp. 34	
	1974: Exp. 44	n.a.
	Imp. 27	
Belgium	1968: Exp. 37	
	Imp. 57	
	1976: Exp. 53	1976: Exp. 23
	Imp. 48	Imp. 15
United Kingdom	1976: Exp. 29	: Exp. 30
	Imp. 31	

Sources: Van Den Bulcke (1985) Table 1. Panic and Joyce (1980)

to the pattern of intra-industry trade across countries. This study is unique in including a proxy which directly measures intra-firm trade in a study of intra-industry trade. Other studies have related multinational activity and intra-industry trade and established a positive association between the two, for example Wickham and Thompson (1986), whilst other case studies have provided evidence on intra-firm trade in particular industries where intra-industry trade is prevalent (Casson et al., 1986, and Kol and Rayment, 1986). Thus, although some evidence which is consistent with a positive association between intra-firm trade and intra-industry trade does exist, it is rather thin, and, in places, tenuous.

4. The Gains from Trade and Adjustment to Trade Expansion

The welfare effects of customs union formation were first analyzed systematically by Viner (1955). According to Viner, the net effects of customs union formation depended upon the relative importance of trade creation and trade diversion. The former concept refers to the replacement of relatively expensive domestic production by relatively cheap imports from the partner country(ies). Trade diversion, on the other hand, describes a phenomenon whereby relatively low cost imports from a non-partner country are replaced by higher cost imports from the partner. Viner held trade creation to be generally beneficial, and trade diversion harmful. Whether or not a given customs union yielded net benefits for the members depended upon the relative magnitude of the two effects.

The Vinerian reference case has been extended in a number of ways. First, as Gehrels (1956) recognized, there is a role for consumption effects. Lipsey (1957) demonstrated that these could be positive even when trade diversion dominated. Second, economics of scale in production could be important. Thus the wider market associated with the customs union may facilitate the lengthening of production runs, allowing domestic producers to undercut non-partner suppliers. Such a development would have both trade and welfare effects. Finally, there may be dynamic effects related to capital accumulation.

It is extremely difficult to estimate the gains resulting from customs union formation, largely because of the problems of identifying a credible antimonde—we can never be sure what would have occurred in the absence of the customs union. Nor can we be certain about the impact and magnitude of policy changes induced by membership. As Winters (1986) demonstrates, this is difficult enough for one country entering a union, let alone a group of countries forming, or entering, a union. In the context of the EC, empirical work has adduced evidence of both trade diversion (primarily in agricultural trade), and trade creation (primarily in manufactures). The consensus appears to be that the benefits from trade creation have exceeded the costs of trade diversion. (See Mayes, 1978, Winters, 1987.)

One question which can be posed, however, is whether the potential gains are likely to vary with the relative importance of intra *-vis-a-vis* inter-industry trade. To put this another way: since there is evidence to suggest that increased intra-industry trade may have been linked to European integration, are the gains associated with this likely to have been greater or less than would have the case had inter-industry specialization and trade dominated?

This is very much an open question. Research on the theory of intra-industry trade does indicate that the gains from trade are likely to be qualitatively different from those generally associated with inter-industry trade. With regard to the latter, it is usual to distinguish between gains from specialization and gains from exchange. The same distinction could be made in a setting of intra-industry trade. However, the gains from exchange might be largely attributable to the widening of consumer choice, whilst the gains from specialization probably accrue largely from the exploitation of scale economies. *A priori* one cannot say whether these are likely to exceed or fall short of the gains resulting from inter-industry trade. Empirical estimates for the EC do not distinguish between the two. Several pieces of circumstantial evidence can, however, be adduced. First, the major gains so far appear to have been associated with increased trade in manufactures where the potential for intra-industry trade is greatest. Second, several studies of the welfare effects of trade expansion have offered *'guesstimates'* of the possible order of magnitude of gains associated with scale economies *vis-a-vis* deadweight gains from specialization and exchange (e.g. Cline et al., 1979). These studies conclude that the gains from scale economies far outweigh the deadweight gains. Again, since intra-industry trade appears to be associated with the opportunities for increased exploitation of scale economies, this might provide grounds for arguing that potential gains from intra-trade exceed those for inter-trade. Finally, Cox and Harris (1985) recently simulated the impact of trade liberalization in a general equilibrium model of the Canadian economy. The estimated gains from trade expansion were substantially in excess of those associated with expanded opportunities for intra-industry trade.

The total gains from trade are also influenced by the ease with which adjustment to trade expansion takes place. Some commentators have argued that adjustment to trade expansion will be easier when that expansion takes the form of an increase in intra-industry trade rather than an increase in inter-industry trade (e.g. Balassa, 1965; Aquino, 1978). The rationale behind this argument is that differences in factor proportions between the expanding export sector and the contracting import substitute sector are likely to be more similar in a setting of intra-industry trade. In the extreme case where intra-industry trade is predominantly intra-firm trade, then adjustment would largely occur within the enterprise. In principle, this would result in greater ease of adjustment than the case where expansions and contractions are centred on different enterprises. If this is the case, then it could be a further reason for believing that the gains from intra-industry trade exceed those from inter-industry trade. (This particular argument assumes of course that adjustment costs should be deducted from the potential gains from trade; some commentators would argue that this should not necessarily be done, on the grounds that adjustment frictions are rarely *directly* attributable to trade expansion.)

The case for relative ease of adjustment is far from conclusive. As yet little work of a systematic nature has been completed. As Greenaway and Milner (1986) argue, it very much depends on the institutional features of product markets and, more important, factor markets. The similarity in factor requirements across activities is clearly of crucial importance. This, together with any geographical segmentation, fashions the speed with which resources can be reallocated from one activity to another. The question of occupational and geographical mobility of labour is ultimately an empirical question. *A priori* there is no reason to expect greater flexibility in this respect where intra-industry specialization is concerned. With regard to factor requirements, this, too, is an empirical question. Lundberg and Hanssen (1986) have recently argued that there is greater variability in factor requirements between industry groups (i.e. third digit SIC categories) in Sweden than between them. Evidence to the contrary has however been adduced by Rayment (1976) for the United Kingdom and Finger (1975) for the United States.

Few direct studies of adjustment have been completed to date. Two notable exceptions are Cox and Harris (1985) and Adler (1970). Cox and Harris (1985) explored the effects of unilateral and multilateral liberalization in Canada. In both scenarios, intra-sectoral resource reallocation dominated inter-sectoral resource reallocation, in some cases by a significant amount. This led the authors to conclude that, due to the relative importance of intra-industry trade in Canada, the adjustment consequences of trade liberalization would not be significant. This can be viewed as evidence in support of the propostion that adjustment to trade expansion is smoother in a setting of intra- as opposed to inter-industry trade. One other piece of evidence which can be cited is the study by Adler (1970). He examined changes in steel production and trade across the original six members of the European Coal and Steel Community (ECSC). Vinerian customs union theory had led to the expectation that there would be significant adjustment difficulties in this sector as West Germany rose to pre-eminence at the expense of France and Italy. Interestingly, Adler's study reveals that this did not materialize. Significant increases in intra-industry specialization and trade occurred between the formation of the ECSC in 1952 and the mid-1960s. Country specialization could be detected in the majority of product lines examined. Adler is in no doubt that adjustment was easier and less costly as a consequence of this intra-industry specialization. In a wider context, Hufbauer and Chilas (1974) have argued that adjustment frictions among the original six Members of the EC were minimized due to the predominance of intra-industry specialization.

Some empirical evidence does therefore exist to support the proposition that adjustment to trade expansion will be smoother in a setting of intra- than inter-industry trade. Unfortunately, this work is of somewhat limited coverage. The entry of Greece, Spain and Portugal into the Community should provide an interesting basis for further exploration of this issue. It would seem that differences in factor proportions between these entrants and the existing members are more exaggerated than such differences within the original six, or between the original six and the new entrants of the first enlargement. *A priori*, therefore, one would anticipate a greater degree of inter-industry specialization and resource reallocation and, in principle at least, greater potential adjustment frictions.

5. Commercial Policy, Industrial Policy and Policy Co-Ordination

The effects of commercial policy and industrial policy interventions in the context of intra-industry trade and, more generally, markets which are imperfectly competitive have been extensively explored.[3] A number of interesting insights have been gained. Some of the basic postulates of intervention have been challenged; for instance, those relating to the ability of small open economies to engage in welfare-improving interventions, and the ability of a single instrument of intervention both to restrict imports and expand exports.[4] The detail of all of these arguments need not concern us here. The issue which is of interest in the present context is the implication of this work for commercial policy and industrial policy in customs unions, with particular reference to the EC. In this regard, there are at least three issues to be considered. First, the possibility of strategic intervention to redistribute income away from non-union firms towards union firms; second, the possibility of using commercial policy simultaneously to encourage import substitution within the union, and export promotion outside the union; and third, the possibility of using commercial policy to redistribute profits from non-union multinationals towards the union. Each of these will be briefly considered.

Rent Snatching Intervention

The possibility of using export subsidies to snatch rents from foreign firms has been demonstrated by Spencer and Brander (1983) and Brander and Spencer (1984). They consider a market where a domestic and foreign monopolist compete in a third market. Each firm has a Cournot mentality. In other words, it takes its competitor's output as given and does the best it possibly can for itself. If firms behave in this way, a determinate price and output equilibrium can be established. Moreover, this price and output equilibrium will be stable. Neither firm can threaten to increase its output to capture market share from its rival, simply because such a threat would not be credible. In such a situation, however, the provision of an export subsidy by the home government to the home firm constitutes a credible threat. The export subsidy allows the domestic firm to expand its output, and its foreign rival realises that any threat on the part of the domestic firm is credible because it is backed by government action. Faced with this, the best the foreign firm can do is contract its own output. As a result the domestic firm expands its output and its profits increase. Rents have been shifted from the foreign firm to the domestic firm. Moreover, under certain circumstances, the rents which are captured will exceed the cost of the export subsidy so that the home economy is better off as a consequence of the intervention.

This type of story tends to be told in the context of the aerospace industry. Here is an industry which is arguably a natural oligopoly, the market for wide-bodied jets can be supplied by a few large firms. If a given domestic government supports its own firm via industrial policy, this will shift profits from some foreign rival(s) and may deter entry by other potential rivals. Clearly, this can be seen as a justification for Airbus Industrie receiving protection *vis-a-vis* its American rivals. To generalize the argument, one could contend that since the European Community can support such *'large'* producers in other markets (e.g. semi-conductors, consumer electronics and so on), these should be supported to allow them to challenge effectively American (and Japanese) rivals. Because these markets are imperfectly competitive, profits can be redistributed from the foreign firms to the domestic firm, leaving the Community better off as a result. It ought to be noted, however, that the gains from such intervention may be limited. Little by way of systematic empirical evidence has so far been produced. However, Krugman (1987), on the basis of implausibly generous estimates, suggests that potential losses to the United States associated with successful rent snatching by Japanese firms would amount to no more than a once and for all reduction in GNP of 1 per cent. Venables (1987) simulates the effects of intervention in a general equilibrium model of the European domestic electrical appliance industry and concludes that, although the redistributional effects of intervention may be substantial, the net welfare gains are likely to be relatively small.

Neo-Infant Industry Protection

A second, and related, line of argument, applies to the possibility of neo-infant industry protection. It is argued that in some industries there are significant learning economies and spill-over effects. These serve to act as an entry barrier to potential firms, in part because of the initial cost disadvantage, and in part because the spill-over effects may create first-mover disadvantages. Providing potential entrants and/or actual market incumbents with a protected market thus becomes a worthwhile policy. This permits domestic firms to invest and to move down the scale curve. Moreover, under certain circumstances, the cost savings associated with capturing a larger share of the domestic market can be translated into greater competitiveness in foreign markets. In this setting, import protection becomes export promotion (Krugman, 1984).

Arguments of this kind underlie some of the recent pressures for *'Europrotectionism'* (Hager, 1982). It is claimed that a protected European home market would provide a sufficiently wide base to benefit from the learning effects necessary in order for European firms to compete effectively with Japanese and American firms—in their markets, in the European market and in third markets. It is further claimed that the argument is especially applicable to the *'high-tech'* industries in general and semi-conductors in particular. Moreover, it is argued that it is just this kind of strategy which has underpinned Japanese success in foreign market penetration.

Taxing Multinationals

A third possibility which has not yet been widely explored relates to the opportunities which may exist to use commercial policy as a means of redistributing profits from foreign multinationals operating in the European Community. In examining the effective protection concept in the context of intra-industry specialization, Greenaway and Milner (1987) demonstrate how non-zero input tariffs directed at intermediates used by foreign-based multinationals can be welfare improving. Tariffs on inputs are, of course, taxes on value added. When directed at foreign-based multinationals which are earning pure profit, such taxes effectively redistribute rents from foreign firms to the domestic treasury—in the European context, directly to the Commission. The extensive presence of multinationals in the manufacturing sector means that the circumstances under which this particular argument is applicable may be quite widespread.

General Arguments or Special Cases?

There is at least a possibility that the prevalence of intra-industry trade in the EC could be used as a basis for arguing that the grounds for intervention identified above are general, and widely applicable. This is an important issue. After all, policy formulation should be guided by general arguments rather than special cases. It can be argued that, although the phenomenon of intra-industry trade is widespread, the circumstances in the EC under which welfare-improving intervention is feasible are in fact somewhat limited. If, for example, we examine the rent snatching argument more closely, we find that the results of that particular model are simply not robust. The prediction that export subsidies result in welfare improvement is in fact very sensitive indeed to the assumptions of the model. If we alter the number of firms assumed in the market, alter our assumption regarding the manner in which they behave, alter assumptions regarding entry conditions and so on, we find that the predicted outcomes alter.[5] Given this sensitivity, the model provides a fragile basis for policy recommendations. Moreover, the policy being proposed is *explicitly* predatory. The home firm gains at the expense of the foreign firm(s). Clearly, in such a situation there must be a high probability of retaliation. If retaliation follows, both parties lose.

Similar observations can be made with regard to neo-infant industry protection. Results here are again sensitive to variations in model specific assumptions. In addition, even where clear spill-over effects can be identified it will rarely, if ever, be appropriate to react by providing import protection. As the theory of optimal intervention demonstrates, some form of subsidy intervention will invariably be superior to a tariff. Finally, again retaliation is clearly a potential problem.

Reaping gains by taxing multinationals appears to be a more robust result. A major problem again, however, is that this is explicitly a predatory strategy and as such can be accounted a high risk policy.

In sum, the prevalence of recorded intra-industry trade, together with the proliferation of models where welfare-improving intervention appears to be feasible has created the impression of a more general case for protection. In fact, however, the circumstances where these arguments can be applied may not be very general and may, in fact, be highly specific. Moreover, for a large open economy, which the EC as whole can be thought of, the dangers of retaliation are self evident. One important deduction which can be made from the literature, however, is that the case for (commercial) policy coordination is stronger than in a setting of inter-industry trade. This follows because, if the EC can establish arguments for strategic intervention, so too can rivals (i.e. Japan and the United States). A classic prisoner's dilemma problem therefore exists, with the likelihood being that a (sub-optimal) tariff-ridden equilibrium results. This being so, the case for policy co-ordination to avoid such an outcome is enhanced.

6. Intra Firm-Trade and EC Policy

The previous section was concerned with the implications of intra-industry trade for EC policy *vis-a-vis* non-Members. Since, as we have seen, there is a strong presumption that intra-industry trade and intra-firm trade are closely correlated, what are the implications of this for intra-EC policy?

Some commentators have argued that an increase in the relative importance of intra-firm trade increases the prospects of effective market cartelization. For example, according to Schwamm (1980), "As a result of their special structure, these corporations can practice a thousand and one forms of restrictions designed to ensure for them a dominant position in markets where they have their operations . . ." (p.24). If this is so, and the evidence here tends to be circumstantial rather than rigorous, it argues for a more effective competition policy than currently exists in the EC, as well as greater clarity with regard to the division of responsibility as between EC and national arrangements.

Related to this point is the issue of transfer pricing. The potential which exists for transfer pricing within MNEs is well known. The incidence of the phenomenon is less well documented. Nevertheless the identification of a few spectacular cases of transfer pricing and super normal profits within the EC indicates that it does exist. A prerequisite for the phenomenon is differences in fiscal arrangements between countries. If it is felt that the potential for transfer pricing is increasing because of an increase in intra-firm trade, then the appropriate policy response is clearly greater fiscal harmonization.

This raises a further point with regard to industrial policy. Often, differences in fiscal arrangements are a policy response to footloose MNEs. Governments compete to attract investment by MNEs by offering fiscal inducements. This kind of policy competition is well documented with regard to Less Developed Countries. There are also many examples of the practice within the EC. Clearly such competition has an impact upon the distribution of the gains from MNE investment, redistributing income from host country tax payers to MNE shareholders. It is, thus, understandable, in a situation where MNEs are becoming increasingly important potential, that host governments are likely to become increasingly competitive. If the objective of policy from the standpoint of host governments is to minimize the cost to taxpayers of attracting FDI then clearly this too can only be accomplished by greater policy coordination.

Concluding Comments

This contribution has been directed at considering the growth of intra-industry trade and intra-firm trade in the EC; the factors behind their growth; the economic effects of that growth and some possible policy implications. We have seen that links between economic integration and intra-industry trade can be established, as can links between these and intra-firm trade. In some cases these links are somewhat tenuous; nonetheless, causal connections do appear to exist. Moreover, the evidence suggests that European integration has been associated with a growth of intra-industry trade and intra-firm trade. Ultimately, however, we can never be sure whether this growth is greater than it would have been in the absence of integration. Nevertheless, the prevalence of intra-industry and intra-firm trade does make the policy implications of considerable interest. From the perspective of EC policy *vis-a-vis* non-Member States it was noted that the circumstances in which opportunities for welfare-improving intervention exist may appear to be relatively widespread. However, the policy rules for intervention do not turn out to be robust. In fact, since the EC is a large open economy, the probability of retaliation to such intervention is relatively high. This being so, the case for policy co-ordination is probably strengthened. This conclusion also carries over to intra-EC policy if it is desired to reduce distortions which may be associated with intra-firm trade, such as restrictive practices, transfer pricing and the dissipation of potential gains from MNE investment.

Notes

1. There are measurement problems associated with the use of the Grubel and Lloyd index. These relate to the impact of overall imbalance on the index, and the inappropriate grouping of activities in a given industry. On the former see Aquino (1978) and Greenaway and Milner (1981). On the latter see Greenaway and Milner (1983).
2. See Kol and Mennes (1986).
3. See Greenaway (1985) and Venables (1985).
4. See Krugman (1984).

5. For example, the rent snatching argument assumes Cournot behaviour. If, instead, Bertrand behaviour is assumed the optimal policy becomes an optimal tariff rather than an optimal subsidy.

References

Adler, M. (1970), "Specialization in the European Coal and Steel Community," *Journal of Common Market Studies* 8, pp. 175-91.

Agmon, T. (1979), "Direct investment and intra-industry trade: substitutes or complements?" in Giersch (1979).

Aquino, A. (1978), "Intra-Industry trade and intra-industry specialization as concurrent sources of international trade in manufactures" *Weltwirtschaftliches Archiv*, 114, pp. 275-95.

Balassa, B. (1965), *Economic Development and Integration* (Mexico, DF: Centro de Estudios Monetarios Latino Americanos).

Balassa, B. (1966), "Tariff reductions and trade in manufactures among industrial countries" *American Economic Review* 56, pp. 466-73.

Balassa, B. (1986), "Intra-Industry Trade among exporters of manufactured goods" in Greenaway and Tharakan (1986).

Brander, J. A. (1981), "Intra-industry trade in identical commodities" *Journal of International Economics* 11, pp. 1-14.

Brander, J. A. and Krugman P. (1983), "A reciprocal dumping model of international trade" *Journal of International Economics* 13, pp. 313-21.

Brander, J. A. and Spencer, B. J. (1984b), "Trade warfare: tariffs and cartels" *Journal of International Economics,* 16, pp. 227-42.

Casson, M. et al. (1986), *Multinationals and World Trade* (London: Allen and Unwin).

Clairmonte, F. and Cavanagh, J. (1982), "TNCs: The Ever Grasping Drive" *Development Forum.*

Cline, W. R., Kronsjo, N., Kawanabe, T. and Williams, T. (1978), *Trade Negotiations in the Tokyo Round: A Quantitative Assessment* (Washington: Brookings Institution).

Cox, D. and Harris, R. (1985), "Trade liberalization and industrial organization: some estimates for Canada" *Journal of Political Economy* 93, pp. 115-45.

Drabek, Z. and Greenaway, D. (1984), "Economic integration and intra-industry trade: the CMEA and EC compared" *Kyklos* 37, pp. 444-69.

Dreze, J. (1961), "Les exportations intra-CEE en 1958 et al position Belge" *Recherches Economiques de Louvain* (Louvain), 27, pp. 717-38.

Ethier, W. and Horn, H. (1984), "A New Look at Economic Integration", in Kierzkowski (1984).

Finger, J. M. (1975), "Trade overlap and intra-industry trade" *Economic Inquiry,* 13, pp. 581-9.

Giersch, H. (ed.) (1979), *On the Economics of Intra-Industry Trade* (Tübingen: J. C. B. Mohr).

Glejser, H. (1983), "Intra-Industry trade specialization: trends and cycles in the EC (1973-1979)", in Tharakan (1983).

Glejser, H., Goossens, K. and Vanden Eede, M. (1979), "Inter-industry and intra-industry specialisation do occur in world trade" *Economics Letters*, 3, pp. 261-5.

Glejser, H., Goossens, K. and Vanden Eede, M. (1982), "Inter-industry versus intra-industry specialization in exports and imports (1959-1970-1973)" *Journal of International Economics* 12, pp. 353-69.

Greenaway, D. (1982), "Identifying the gains from pure intra-industry exchange" *Journal of Economic Studies* 9, pp. 40-56.

Greenaway, D. (ed) (1985), *Current Issues in International Trade: Theory and Policy* (London: Macmillan).

Greenaway, D. and Milner, C. R. (1981), "Trade imbalance effects and the measurement of intra-industry trade" *Weltwirtschaftliches Archiv*, 117, pp. 756-62.

Greenaway, D. and Milner, C. R. (1983), "On the measurement of intra-industry trade" *Economic Journal* 93, pp. 900-8.

Greenaway, D. and Milner, C. R. (1986), *The Economics of Intra-Industry Trade* (Oxford: Basil Blackwell).

Greenaway, D. and Milner, C. R. (1987), "Intra-Industry Trade and Effective Protection" in *Journal of Economic Studies*, 14.

Greenaway, D. and Tharakan, P. K. M. (eds) (1986), *Imperfect Competition and International Trade: The Policy Aspects of Intra-Industry Trade* (Brighton: Wheatsheaf Press).

Grubel, H. G. and Lloyd, P. J. (1971), "The empirical measurement of intra-industry trade" *Economic Record*, 47, pp. 494-517.

Hager, W. (1982), "Protectionism and Autonomy: How to Preserve Free Trade in Europe" *International Affairs* vol. 58, pp. 413-28.

Havrylyshyn, O. and Civan, E. (1983), "Intra-industry trade and the stage of development: a regression analysis of industrial and developing countries", in *Tharakan* (1983).

Helleiner, G. K. (1981), *Intra-Firm Trade and Developing Countries* (London: Macmillan).

Helpman, E. (1981), "International trade in the presence of product differentiation, economies of scale and monopolistic competition" *Journal of International Economics* 11, pp. 305-40.

Hufbauer, G. C. and Chilas, J. G. (1974), "Specialization by industrial countries: extent and consequences" in Giersch (1974).

Kierzkowski, H. (ed.) (1984), *Monopolistic Competition and International Trade* (Oxford: Oxford University Press).

Krugman, P. (1984), "Import protection as export promotion: international competition in the presence of oligopoly and economies of scale", in Kierzkowski (1984).

Krugman, P. (1987), "Strategic Sectors and International Competition" in R. Stern (ed), *US Trade Policies in a Changing World Economy* (MIT Press).

Lancaster, K. (1980), "Intra-industry trade under perfect monopolistic competition" *Journal of International Economics* 10, pp. 151-76.

Markusen, J. R. (1983), "Factor movements and commodity trade as complements" *Journal of International Economics* 13, pp. 341-56.

Mayes, D. (1978), "The Effects of Economic Integration on Trade" *Journal of Common Market Studies* Vol. 17, pp. 1-25.

Mundell, R. A. (1957), "International trade and factor mobility" *American Economic Review* 47, pp. 321-35.

Pagoulatos, E. and Sorensen, R. (1975), "Two-way international trade: an econometric analysis" *Weltwirtschaftliches Archiv* 111, pp. 454-65.

Pomfret, R. (1986), "On the Division of Labour and Intra-Industry Trade", *Journal of Economic Studies* Vol. 13, pp. 56-63.

Rayment, P. B. (1976), "The homogeneity of manufacturing industries with respect to factor intensity: the case of the UK" *Oxford Bulletin of Economics and Statistics* 38, pp. 203-9.

Robinson, E. A. G. (1960), *Economic Consequences of the Size of Nations* (London: Macmillan).

Schwamm, H. (1980), "In connection with the UNCTAD Code of Conduct on Restrictive Business Practices" *Informations Internationales.*

Tharakan, P. K. M. (ed) (1983), Intra-industry Trade: *Empirical and Methodological Aspects* (Amsterdam: North Holland).

Van Den Bulcke (1985), "Intra-Firm Trade of Multi-National Enterprises", Paper presented to European International Business Association Conference Strathclyde University.

Venables, A. J. (1987), "Trade and Industrial Policy under Imperfect Competition: Some Simulations for EC Manufacturing" (mimeo, University of Sussex).

Verdoorn, P. J. (1960), "The intra-block trade of Benelux", in Robinson (1960).

Viner, J. (1950), *The Customs Union Issues* (New York: Carnegie Endowment).

Willmore, L. N. (1974), "The pattern of trade and specialisation in the Central American Common Market" *Journal of Economic Studies* 2, pp. 113-34.

Winters, L. Alan (1987), Britain in Europe: A Survey of Quantitative Trade Studies, *Discussion Paper No. 110*, London, Centre for Economic Policy Research. *Journal of Common Market Studies*, Vol. XXVI.

2. THE DO'S AND DON'TS OF INTERNATIONAL COUNTERTRADE

JOSEPH R. CARTER
Michigan State University
Joseph R. Carter is Assistant Professor of Purchasing Management at Michigan State University. Dr. Carter holds the B.S. and M.B.A. degrees from Northeastern University and the D.B.A. degree from Boston University. He is the author of several articles and book chapters.

JAMES GAGNE
Phillip Townsend Associates, Inc.
James Gagne is Manager of the Phillip Townsend Associates, Inc., European office. Mr. Gagne holds the M.A. degree in labor economics from the University of Massachusetts. He is the former managing and economics editor of CPI Purchasing.

The exchange of goods for other goods rather than for money is on the upswing, but many U.S. managers are unenthusiastic about this countertrade. The authors argue that mixing countertrade and offshore sourcing can lead to real strategic advantage. They offer materials managers practical advice about how to approach this often-misunderstood practice.

Saudi Arabia agreed to buy ten 747 jet aircraft from Boeing with payment in crude oil, discounted at 10 percent below posted world prices.[1] Levi Strauss & Company set up a factory for the production of jeans in Hungary and agreed to supply the plant with designs and materials, with the understanding that Hungary would manufacture and market the jeans.[2] General Electric won a contract for a $150-million electric generator project in Rumania by agreeing to market a corresponding $150-million worth of Rumanian products in markets to which Rumania would not normally have had easy access.[3] In 1986, the Venezuelan government negotiated a contract with Caterpillar Tractor Company's World Trading Corporation under which Venezuela would trade 350,000 tons of iron ore for heavy Caterpillar equipment. Caterpillar subsequently traded the iron ore to Rumania.[4] In 1986, Albania began offering items such as spring water, tomato juice, and chrome ore in exchange for a contract to build a $60-million fertilizer and methanol complex.[5]

Has the world gone crazy? Is cash no longer the preferred method of payment for goods and services? The answer to these questions is somewhat ambiguous. Money

Reprinted from "The Do's and Don'ts of International Countertrade" by Joseph R. Carter and James Gagne, *Sloan Management Review*, (Spring 1988), pp. 31–37, by permission of the publisher.

is still the preferred method of payment, but increasingly payments are being made in goods rather than in money. The word this year for the astute multinational materials manager is *countertrade.*

In simple terms, countertrade is a word used to refer to all international and domestic trade in which goods are exchanged for goods. The ancient business of trading a few sheep for a head of cattle has grown over the last twenty years into a sophisticated worldwide trading activity with a significant economic impact on the global market. Countertrade has grown from an estimated 2 percent of world trade in 1975 to a conservatively estimated 8 percent in 1985 and 10 percent in 1986. This 10 percent figure translates into more than $150 billion in today's international economy. Likewise, the number of countries that mandate some form of countertrade has grown from a mere fifteen in 1975 to more than eighty-eight in 1984.

In a 1985 survey of major U.S. multinational companies, the U.S. Association of Countertrading Corporations found that 85 percent of respondents had received countertrade demands; these demands came from sixty-five different countries. That same year, the U.S. International Trade Commission surveyed more than 500 major U.S. companies and found that $7.1-billion worth of American exports in 1984 were linked to countertrade deals; armaments accounted for more than 80 percent of the countertrade deals. Exports associated with nonmilitary countertrade quadrupled between 1980 and 1984; the monetary value jumped from $285 million to $1.4 billion in that period.

Forms of Countertrade

The modern concept of countertrade started with simple trading of goods and services for other goods and services, and evolved into a diverse set of activities that includes five distinct types of trading arrangements.[6]

Barter is the direct exchange of goods or services or both between two parties without a cash transaction. Although it is the simplest arrangement in theory, barter has become unpopular in practice. If goods are not exchanged simultaneously, one party ends up financing the other party for a period of time. Barter also risks sticking one party with goods it does not want and cannot use. For these and other reasons, barter is viewed by multinationals as the most restrictive countertrade arrangement, and is primarily used for one-time deals with trading partners who are not creditworthy or trustworthy.

Counterpurchase is reciprocal buying in the international marketplace. It occurs when a company agrees to buy a certain amount of materials from a country to which a sale is made. For example, U.S. Company X sells some of its products to foreign Country Y. In exchange, Company X agrees to spend some set percentage of the proceeds importing goods produced by Country Y. Both trading partners agree to pay for the majority of their purchases in cash and to fulfill their individual sales obligations within a specified time period, usually less than five years.

Offset is similar to counterpurchase in that the supplier is required to purchase goods or services with an agreed percentage of the original sale. The difference is that the supplier can fulfill this obligation with any company in the country to which the sale is being made. Offset arrangements happen most frequently in countries with centrally planned economies. For example, in 1982 McDonnell Douglas Corporation reportedly agreed to buy airframe components and other goods from Canadian companies in exchange for a $2.4-billion commitment from Canada to buy jet fighter planes over the next fifteen years.[7]

Compensation or *buy-back* occurs when a company builds a plant in a country, or supplies technology, equipment, training, or other services to the country, and agrees to take a certain percentage of the plant's output as partial payment for the contract. For example, Occidental Petroleum negotiated a $20-million deal with the U.S.S.R. under which Occidental would build several plants in the Soviet Union and receive ammonia over a twenty-year period as partial payment.

Switch trading refers to the use of a specialized, third-party trading house in a countertrade arrangement. The third-party trading house buys the selling company's counterpurchase credits and sells them to another company that can better use them. For example, Company X concludes a countertrade arrangement with a country in which it agrees to take some goods as partial payment. Company X cannot really use and does not want these goods; therefore, it sells the contract for these goods to a third-party trading house at a discount. The third-party trading house, in turn, finds another company that can use the goods and resells the contract at a profit. Switch traders frequently substitute trade credits, which can be spent later, for cash. Switch trading is often used by companies or countries to correct trade imbalances, as in the following illustration: Hungary sells chemicals to France at a certain value, and France credits Hungary's trade account for a certain number of trade credits, which Hungary can use in the future to buy some prespecified French goods. But Hungary does not want to buy French goods. Therefore, Hungary sells these credits to a third-party trading house at a discount. The third-party trading house then searches for a country or company that needs to buy French goods and sells the credits to this country or company at a small profit.

In 1983, the National Foreign Trade Council (NFTC) conducted a survey of 110 United States firms active in the international market to determine what forms of countertrade they were engaged in. Table 1 presents the results of this survey. The NFTC found that 55 percent were engaged in counterpurchase; 24 percent were engaged in offset arrangements; 9 percent practiced compensation; 8 percent used switch trading; and only 4 percent were involved in barter agreements.

In a 1986 survey of sixty-nine Fortune 500 companies performed by the authors, a somewhat different mix of countertrading activities emerged. Table 2 represents the results of this survey. Seventy-three percent of the respondents were practicing offset. The next most common arrangement was counterpurchase, followed by compensation, barter, and switch trading; these were practiced by 60 percent, 22 percent, 19 percent, and 3 percent of the respondents, respectively. Given the difference in surveys, methodology, and companies, it would be unwise to make too large a point of the difference between survey results. Still, several trends do seem apparent. First, the survey results suggest that countertrade activities have increased during the 1980s. This finding is consistent with the NFTC study that showed that the number of countries mandating countertrade grew from approximately fifteen to approximately eighty-eight

Table 1
COUNTERTRADE PRACTICES, 1983

Percentage of Responding Companies That Engaged in Each Countertrade Practice	
Counterpurchase	55%
Offset	24%
Compensation	9%
Switch Trading	8%
Barter	4%

Note: Survey was conducted by the National Foreign Trade Council.

Table 2
COUNTERTRADE PRACTICES, 1986

Percentage of Responding Companies That Engaged in Each Countertrade Practice	
Offset	73%
Counterpurchase	60%
Compensation	22%
Barter	19%
Switch Trading	3%

Note: Survey was conducted by the authors.

between 1975 and 1984. Second, companies are obviously practicing more than one form of countertrade simultaneously; apparently offsets and counterpurchases are the most common arrangements. Third, the much higher percentage of companies involved in barter (along with the drop in switch trading) indicates that companies are getting directly involved in countertrade activities, rather than relying on a third-party trading house to work out arrangements for them.

In the material that follows, we will first propose a general model for countertrade implementation, and then take a closer look at how the materials management function can integrate countertrade and offshore-sourcing arrangements.

A Countertrade Implementation Model

Implementing a countertrade strategy can be confusing at first, and the process is sufficiently delicate that it *must* be managed well to be successful.

Figure 1 illustrates a process flow of activities the multinational company might use to establish a countertrade practice. First, analyze the opportunity. Identification

Figure 1
COUNTERTRADE IMPLEMENTATION

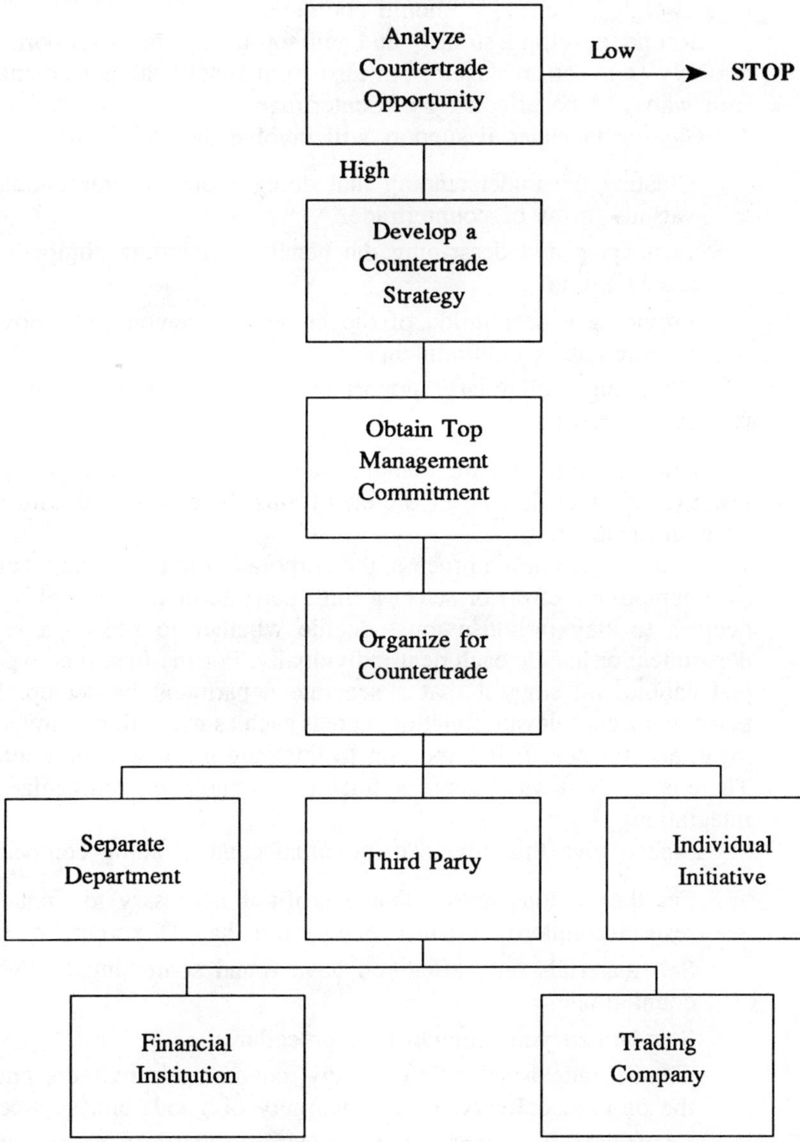

of an opportunity or of its perceived benefits may be driven by top-level executives, materials managers, or marketing and sales personnel. If the opportunity or benefit is perceived as low, then the process should end here. If the perceived benefits appear to outweigh the costs, it should continue.

Second, develop a strategy and gain top-management support. Support is necessary not only from top managers, but also from functional-level managers throughout the firm who will be affected by countertrade.

Gaining managerial support will involve the following:

- Creating the understanding that doing business internationally requires using various forms of countertrade.
- Identifying and describing the benefits, including competitive advantages, that would accrue.
- Providing a description of the broad requirements for moving into the countertrading environment.
- Obtaining preliminary support from foreign companies or countries interested in countertrading.

Third, organize for the countertrade effort.[8] Two organizing principles are as follows: (a) clear leadership of the effort must be established, and (b) the effort should be multifunctional.

At this phase in the process, the corporation must decide whether it should handle the countertrade effort or select a third party to manage the effort. The company that decides to stay in-house must decide whether to set up a separate countertrade department or handle each deal individually. For the firm that expects to do more than just dabble, we suggest that a separate department be set up. It should consist of personnel from relevant functional areas such as marketing, purchasing, manufacturing, legal, and finance. It is important to integrate the new department into the company. There is no "best way" to accomplish this, some firms reorganize themselves to foster integration.

Experts give this advice to potential countertrading companies.

- For the obvious reason that a profit is necessary to finance business growth, restrict countertrade sales to no more than 15 percent of gross revenues.
- Sell materials only after you have found something for which to countertrade.
- Standardize your countertrade procedures.
- Countertrade wisely. Few, if any, countertrade partners guarantee the quality, the on-time delivery, or the warranty of goods and services.
- Coordinate important countertrade functions such as purchasing, marketing, and financing.
- Use your imagination in making a countertrade deal. Remember, everything is negotiable.
- Temper your expectations. Few countertrade partners will barter goods or services they can sell for cash.[9]
- Report all income to the Internal Revenue Service. This is the law.

The company that chooses to use a third-party provider must decide whether to use a trading exchange, a financial institution like a bank, or both. For the multinational company embarking upon countertrade for the first time, we recommend that an experienced third party be hired.

Some general recommendations for firms that want to use a third-party trading-exchange include the following.

- Make sure the third-party exchange provides access to a variety of desirable goods and services.
- Interview some of the third party's former clients. Are they happy with the service provided? Would they use this trading exchange again?
- Verify the credit rating of both the barter exchange and its client members.
- Make certain that your countertraded products will not be dumped into your own markets to compete with your own sales.
- Make sure the third-party exchange covers an adequate geographical area to meet your company's needs.
- Find out if the third-party exchange has a good communication network. Is it one that will disclose all goods and services available for trade?
- Determine whether the third party keeps its system fluid by controlling the number of clients in any one product line; the most effective exchanges do.
- Find out if the countertrade exchange provides consulting services in addition to bartering and brokerage services.

Figure 2 compares using a third-party trading company with performing the tasks in-house. The right third party brings the company a great deal of countertrade

Figure 2
PROS AND CONS OF USING A THIRD-PARTY TRADING COMPANY

	Advantages	Disadvantages
In-House	Lower Cost Control Flexibility Direct Contact	Close Department Coordination Education and Training Manpower Needed
Third Party	Countertrade Expertise Contacts Network in Place Legal Acumen	Impersonal Self-Interested Lack of Confidentiality Commission

experience, international contacts, an existing network, and legal and political international acumen. On the other hand, using a third party creates the potential for impersonal service, self-interested advice, lack of security and confidentiality, and a large commission fee.

Managing countertrade in-house provides the company with lower costs, greater control, increased flexibility in deal making, and direct contact with the partner. The in-house route has disadvantages, as well: It requires closely coordinating several functional departments, training inexperienced personnel, and using scarce managerial resources.

Role of Materials Management

Corporate responsibility for countertrade often falls to the international materials management department. That department is usually responsible for offshore sourcing as well. (The increase in countertrade activities over the past few years has been matched or exceeded by the increase in offshore sourcing.)

Countertrade arrangements and offshore sourcing can be integrated if viewed as important parts of a multinational's overall strategic plan for obtaining resources. Good opportunities for sourcing through countertrade can be found in countries just beginning to impose countertrade requirements, where competition for sources of supply is also just beginning. One problem, which gets worse in a strong economy, is that suppliers of popular products become increasingly reluctant to countertrade. In such situations, a company may have to settle for dealing with a number two or number three choice of supplier, rather than with its number one choice.

Perhaps the primary reason multinational companies shift a share of their purchases to offshore sources is to satisfy countertrade obligations in customer countries. Many multinationals view countertrade as a catalyst that generates future sales opportunities. Forging strong supplier links before exploiting sales opportunities in a foreign country requiring countertrade can avoid problems resulting from unreasonable customer demands.

On the other side of the partnership, countries that impose countertrade requirements understand the following: (a) the benefits of developing long-term relationships with multinational corporations, which include using the multinational as a marketer of their products; (b) the importance of technology transfer from industrialized nations; (c) the need for improving manufacturing techniques in order to become globally competitive; and (d) the resulting increased employment and economic development. These less developed countries see countertrade as the best way available to obtain a position in the multinational corporation's global materials network.

It is clear that a corporation that chooses to engage in countertrade needs to have a global materials management strategy. Having a strategy encourages longer-term partnerships, as well as the transfer of technology, quality controls, and manufacturing skills from industrial countries to less developed nations. In the final analysis, a materials management strategy fosters an environment where a premium is placed upon efficient materials sourcing.

Strategic Sourcing

With multinational corporations fast becoming global trading companies, the purchasing department has become an integral part of a firm's global materials sourcing strategy. It is being asked to expand its traditional role in material procurement and to perform a wide variety of tasks, not all of which are related to its traditional function. For example, 11 percent of the Fortune 500 companies responding to our survey reported that the purchasing department was involved in selling goods from countertrade deals for which the company could find no internal use. More important, 27 percent of these same companies stated that the purchasing department initiated contacts with prospective trading partners. In these cases, purchasing first identified potential sources of supply in countries with mandatory countertrade laws, and only then involved the marketing function; this is a clear reversal of conventional countertrade roles. Historically, marketing would locate a potential market for the goods manufactured by the multinational and consummate a countertrade arrangement in order to complete the sale. Purchasing would subsequently become responsible for disposing of the goods taken in countertrade.

For example, one multinational company developed a practice called "reverse countertrade." Company representatives began by presenting foreign trading partners with their current and future sourcing requirements. Only after they had established the availability of these goods and the feasibility of purchasing them did the company representatives get around to the multinational's main objective—selling its own goods abroad.

The purchasing department is also involved in many traditional activities related to countertrade arrangements. For instance, many multinational corporations make use of purchasing's expertise in negotiations when pounding out countertrade arrangements with foreign trading partners. In our survey, 54 percent of the respondents reported that the purchasing department negotiated countertrade contracts; 49 percent reported that purchasing set the monetary value of goods accepted in countertrade; 46 percent reported that purchasing found internal uses for countertrade materials; 43 percent reported that purchasing determined the quality of goods accepted in countertrade; and 41 percent reported that purchasing conducted on-site visits of potential countertrade partners' foreign production facilities. Table 3 summarizes the roles played by the purchasing function in international countertrade.

Table 3
INTERNATIONAL COUNTERTRADE AND THE PURCHASING DEPARTMENT

With Which Areas is Your Purchasing Department Involved?	
Negotiating	54%
Setting Values	49%
Finding Uses	46%
Assuring Quality	43%
Visiting Sites	41%

Purchasing's involvement with countertrade arrangements has for the most part favorably affected international sourcing. When involved early in the process, purchasing has discovered that countertrade can lead to low-cost sources of supply. It is not uncommon for a countertrade arrangement to result in a beneficial relationship that lasts long after the countertrade arrangement is completed. In our survey, 53 percent of the companies surveyed said that they continued to source from suppliers after the countertrade was completed. Not surprisingly, these same firms were, for the most part, the ones in which purchasing played a prominent countertrade role. Purchasing personnel, by training, tend to look beyond the one-time buy and to assess sourcing relationships for their long-term potential. And, as we mentioned earlier, foreign trading partners are for the most part quite willing to foster long-term relationships with multinational corporations by giving favorable countertrade terms and conditions.

A major role played by purchasing is to assure the quality of goods and services purchased from vendors, regardless of whether the vendors are foreign or domestic. In many instances, purchasing works closely with domestic suppliers to maintain or improve the quality of incoming materials. This quality-check relationship does not seem to exist to the same extent with foreign countertrade partners. In our survey, 30 percent of the respondents said that purchasing worked with countertrade partners while setting initial product specifications, but only 5 percent said that purchasing worked with these partners to maintain or improve the quality of goods after the arrangement went into effect.

Involve Materials Management Early

Some multinational corporations' countertrade arrangements have failed because the materials management department was not involved until it was too late. For example, one multinational corporation concluded, without the assistance of materials management, a $90-million countertrade arrangement with a foreign trading partner. Subsequently the multinational asked its materials management department to dispose of the goods taken in the arrangement. Materials management quickly realized that the goods were of inferior quality, could not be used internally, and would have to be sold at a loss.

This example highlights the qualities that materials management can bring to countertrade arrangements. While the marketing function may agree to almost anything to consummate a sale, materials management professionals are far more inclined to keep the traditional criteria of price, quality, delivery, and service in mind when evaluating and negotiating countertrade arrangements. Many companies are adopting a policy that no countertrade arrangements can be made without the involvement and final approval of the materials management department.

Should materials management take a more active role in countertrade negotiations? We believe the answer is "yes," for several reasons. First, cost reduction has become a major corporate goal, and countertrade can be a major source of low-cost materials and services. Second, multinationals that find and develop foreign sources of quality materials will have a strategic advantage over their slower competitors, who may be stuck with what is left. Third, countertrade is here to stay, so developing long-term partnerships makes good sense—and the materials management department is best equipped to foster those relationships.

Discussion

Tables 1 and 2 demonstrate a trend in countertrade arrangements that has serious implications for the multinational corporation. In the authors' 1986 survey, the most common type of countertrade arrangement was offsets, practiced by 73 percent of the companies. The increase in offset trading, along with the decrease in switch trading, may indicate that multinational corporations are getting directly involved in countertrade arrangements and that this involvement is apt to be long term. More fundamentally, the trend in countertrade seems to be away from one-time, short-term arrangements and toward long-term partnerships. Multinationals are looking for permanent foreign sources that can be developed into a part of their global sourcing strategy.

This trend is not unexpected. As we mentioned, many countries view countertrade as an internal economic development strategy. With the advent of the debt crisis in third-world countries, money from public sources is difficult to obtain. Private investment by multinational corporations through countertrade mechanisms has become the most viable way for third-word countries to obtain investment capital.

Multinational corporations also view a longer-term relationship with third-world countries as beneficial. First, these countries can be a prime source of low-cost labor and materials. Second, these same countries have relatively untapped markets for many goods marketed by multinational firms.

The switch from short-term arrangements (where manufactured goods are traded for commodities and cash) to longer-term supplier investment strategies has significant implications for the multinational corporation. It must now view countertrade partners as an important part of overall corporate strategy, rather than as a source of goods whose usefulness is questionable.

What, then, should be the strategic objective of countertrade? Should a multinational corporation merely view countertrade as a necessary evil of marketing products abroad? Insightful multinational companies are beginning to view countertrade as another competitive weapon in their strategic sourcing arsenal. They are moving beyond the reactionary practice of finding uses for goods no one really wants and probably cannot use. These multinationals have reversed the traditional process and are first looking for market opportunities, and then identifying potential countertrade partners who can best help them exploit these opportunities.

References

1. J. D. Honigberg. "New Trading System Encourages Global Procurement." *Countertrade and Barter Quarterly*, Winter 1985, pp. 45-50.
2. H. Sender. "The Booming World of Countertrade." *Dun's Business Month*, January 1984, pp. 76-78.
3. D. B. Yoffie. "Profiting from Countertrade." *Harvard Business Review*, May-June 1984, pp. 8-16.
4. J. Mann. "Venezuela to Barter Iron Ore with Caterpillar." *Wall Street Journal*, 29 April 1986.
5. J. Gagne. "Countertrade: Tactics for International Chemical Procurement. *CPI Purchasing*, April 1987, pp. 38-43.
6. W. E. Norquist. "Countertrade: A New Horizon for Purchasing." *Journal of Purchasing and Materials Management*, Summer 1987, pp. 2-6.
7. P. Maher. "The Countertrade Boom: A Crummy Way to Do Business...But Here's How to Do It." *Business Marketing*, January 1984, pp. 50-56.
8. At this juncture it is also necessary to decide whether the multinational firm wants to countertrade domestically or internationally or both. Unknown to many multinational firms, nonmonetary trade is very popular domestically. The opportunity for countertrade may, for any specific company, be just as great in the U.S. as it is internationally.
9. There are exceptions to this principle. If a sale involves two currencies that are fluctuating or expected to fluctuate in the future, countertrade is sometimes used as a hedge mechanism to protect each party from financial risk.

II THE GLOBAL FLOW OF TECHNOLOGY

3. CULTURAL CONSTRAINTS ON TRANSFER OF TECHNOLOGY ACROSS NATIONS: IMPLICATIONS FOR RESEARCH IN INTERNATIONAL AND COMPARATIVE MANAGEMENT

BEN L. KEDIA
Louisiana State University

Ben L. Kedia (Ph.D., Case Western Reserve University) is a Professor of International Management and Chairman of the Department of Management at Louisiana State University in Baton Rouge. Correspondence regarding this article can be sent to him at the Department of Management, College of Business Administration, Louisiana State University, Baton Rouge, LA 70803-6312.

RABI S. BHAGAT
University of Texas, Dallas

Rabi S. Bhagat (Ph.D., University of Illinois) is a Professor of Organizational Behavior and International Management in the School of Management at the University of Texas at Dallas.

Cultural variations across nations and organizational culture-based differences between organizations that are involved in the transfer of various kinds of technologies are considered two major factors that influence the success of transfer. Relevant contributions from cross-cultural studies on management and organizations are integrated into the literature on organizational culture and diffusion of innovations, and a conceptual model is developed. Implications for research in international and comparative management are discussed.

In the field of international management, issues concerning effective transfer of technology have been regarded as central to the field's mission. A great deal of emphasis has been placed on economic factors that affect transfer of technology (Contractor & Sagafi-Nejad, 1981; Marton, 1986; Pugel, 1978). But there have been almost no theoretical or empirical analyses on the constraining influences of the cultural factors involved in such transactions. Because such transfers generally involve two organizations located in two distinct cultures for a fairly long period of time, it is surprising to note the absence of emphasis on the role of cultural constraints on such transfers. In this paper, we (a) present a conceptual model of technology transfer across

Reprinted from the *Academy of Management Review* Vol.13, No. 4 (October 1988) by permission of the publisher.

nations that explicitly takes into account the roles of two kinds of cultural factors and receptivity to technological change on the part of the recipient country, (b) advance some research propositions that explain the various links of the model, and (c) examine the relevance these propositions have for future research in international and comparative management.

Before we delineate the conceptual model, we present an analysis of the trends in research in this area. First, there are studies that describe how technology gets transferred, what types of technology are likely to get higher levels of commitment on the part of the managers of the recipient organization, and the nature and the duration of the relationships as a function of the negotiations between the two enterprises (Balasubramanyam, 1973; Marton, 1986; Mason, 1980).

The second group of studies focuses on the absorptive capacity of the recipient organizations and the level of technological development of the host country (Baranson, 1970; Driscoll & Wallender, 1981; Dunning, 1981). Finally, there are case studies that examine the ingredients of the effectiveness of the technology transfer as a function of maturity of the industry, abilities of both the supplier and the recipient organizations, and the life-cycle stage of the technology involved in the transaction (e.g., Baranson & Harrington, 1977; Behrman & Wallender, 1976; Evenson, 1976; Marton, 1986).

Although these studies are helpful to the policy makers of a nation that seeks to lower the economic cost of imported technology by providing industry-specific lessons and negotiating guidance, they offer little in terms of our theoretical understanding of the constraining influences of the cultural factors involved in such transactions. Culture of the recipient organization, strategic management issues, and, perhaps more important, the cultural differences between the two nations involved, play significant roles in determining the efficacy of such transactions.

Many examples show what carefully reasoned economic analyses fail to explain: the failures of those technological transactions that should, indeed, succeed and the successes of those that ought to fail. If we are to better understand the effectiveness of technology transfers across nations, we need a conceptual framework that enhances the role of cultural variations across nations. A scheme depicting the relative importance of cultural variations across nations, organizational culture, and strategic management processes at the level of the enterprise as determinants of the efficacy of technology transfer between nations is presented (Table 1). It shows that the effectiveness of transfer of technology is most affected by variations in societal cultures of the two nations when one of them is an advanced industrialized nation (e.g., West Germany or Japan) and the recipient is a developing country (e.g., India or Brazil). Organizational culture-based differences and related strategic management processes play limited roles in such transfers. In contrast, the transfer of technology from one industrialized country to another industrialized country is most influenced by strategic management-related considerations at the level of the two enterprises involved.

For example, transfer of high technology from IBM of U.S.A. to Siemens of West Germany is likely to be viewed as a strategic issue by both of the transacting organizations. Strategic considerations play greater roles than either the societal culture or the organizational culture-based variations in determining the success of such transfers because of international competitiveness, relative position in the global marketplace, and the critical nature of the technology. On the other hand, transfer of

Table 1
AN EXAMINATION OF THE RELATIVE IMPORTANCE OF CULTURAL VARIATION AND STRATEGIC MANAGEMENT PROCESSES AS DETERMINANTS OF THE SUCCESSFUL TRANSFER OF TECHNOLOGY ACROSS NATIONS

	From Industrialized to other Industrialized Nations (e.g., U.S. to West Germany)	From Industrialized to Moderately Industrialized Nations (e.g., U.S. to South Korea)	From Industrialized to Developing Nations (e.g., West Germany to India)
Societal Culture	Least important	Moderately important	Most important
Organizational Culture	Moderately important	Moderately important	Moderately important
Strategic Management Processes	Most important	Moderately important	Least important

technology from an advanced industrialized to a moderately industrialized nation (e.g., between the United States or West Germany and South Korea or Taiwan) is influenced by all three of the factors, although only moderately. With this framework in mind, we developed a conceptual model (Figure 1) that depicts the role of cultural constraints and other important factors as determinants of efficacy of technology transfers across nations. The model has two causal antecedents (organizational culture-based differences and specific characteristics of the technology involved) and two moderating factors.

A Conceptual Model

The model suggests that the effectiveness of technology transfer is moderated by variations in societal culture-based differences and receptivity to technological change in terms of the absorptive capacity of the recipient organization. First, we consider the specific character of the technology involved.

Type of Technology

Essentially, the process of technology transfer is composed of the transfer of a systematically developed set of organized information, skills, rights, and services from a supplier organization located in a developed country (typically in the West) to a recipient organization located in a developing country (typically, but not always, in one of the third-world nations). In the case of process-embodied technology transfers, concern is with the transfer of blueprints or patent rights of the actual scientific processes and engineering details from the supplier country to a recipient country.

Figure 1
A CONCEPTUAL MODEL FOR UNDERSTANDING CULTURAL CONSTRAINTS ON TECHNOLOGY TRANSFERS ACROSS NATIONS

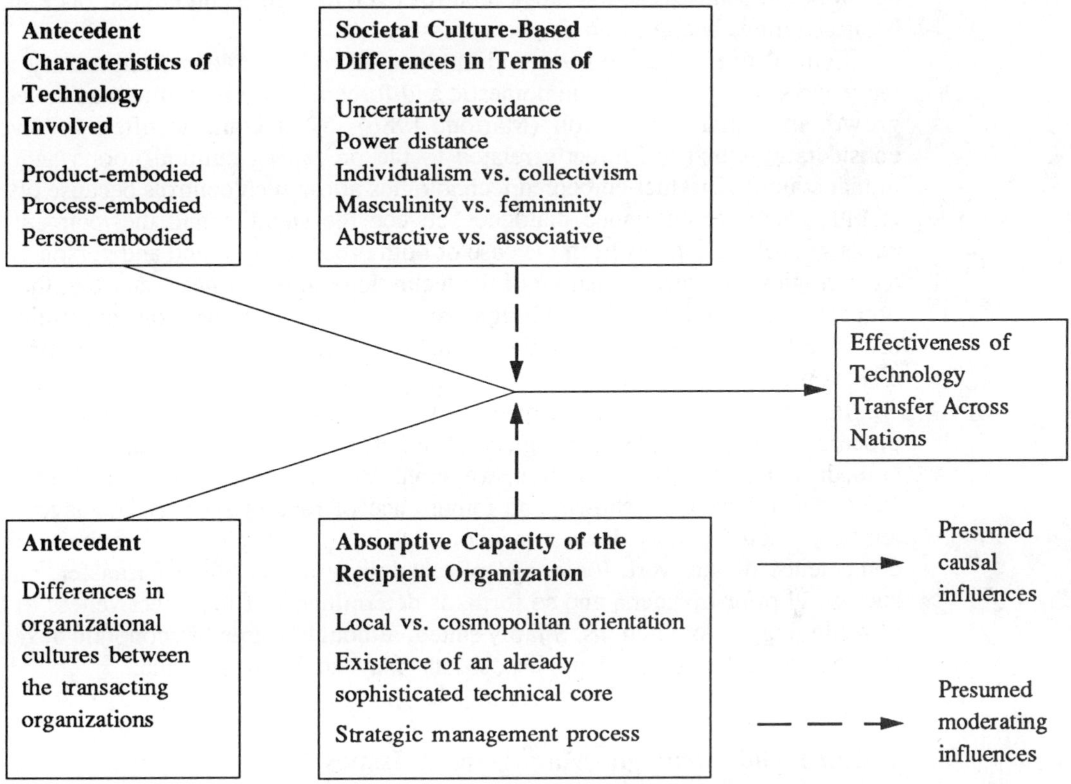

Examples include transfer of chemical technology for the manufacture of synthetic fabrics and off-shore petroleum exploration technology. In the case of product-embodied technology transfers, one transfers the physical product itself. Examples would be heavy earth-tilling machinery and sophisticated computer components. Finally, in the case of person-embodied technology transfers, the transfer depends on the efficacy of a mission undertaken by the supplier organization in developing a sophisticated local technical core to implement and diffuse the imported technology.

Hall and Johnson (1970), who recommended the use of this scheme for the classification of technology, clearly recognized that the process of technology transfer in the domain of international commerce is in no way similar to the transfer of a commodity. They imply that the marginal cost of reproducing a technical capability in another foreign location due to transfer is only a small fraction of the original cost of the technology itself. Effectiveness of transfer depends to a large extent on the type of characteristics of the technology involved (i.e., whether it is process-embodied, product-embodied, or person-embodied). We argue that compared to product-embodied technologies, process-embodied and person-embodied technologies are considerably more difficult to transfer across nations because cultural and strategic management factors play larger roles in such transfers and diffusions. The acquisition and generation of industrial technology have become critical aspects of economic planning in the developing countries, and strategic control over foreign technologies, once they have been acquired, becomes an important issue.

Control over dissemination and application of technology is necessary to retain the technological advantage in domestic and foreign markets, and to manage economic growth in a planned fashion (Marton, 1986). Such controls often involve many considerations that are directly related to the prevailing cultural norms and patterns in that country. Product-embodied technologies allow such controls because often there is little room for continued dialogue between the supplier and the recipient organizations involved. However, in the case of both process-embodied and person-embodied technologies, the intrinsic nature of the technology makes it necessary that the supplier organization exercise control through various means, ranging from constraints in the use of technology in the subsidiaries, affiliates, and licensees, to restrictions in the diffusion and utilization of such technologies.

In recent years, almost all types of technology transfers have involved products, processes, and people, even though some are clearly more process-embodied or people-embodied than others. In addition, we should recognize (as Davidson & McFetridge, 1985, and others have shown) the importance of factors such as language, common ancestry, shared history, level of economic development, physical proximity, technical competence of the work force, age of technology at the time of transfer, number of successful prior transfers, and so forth, as determinants of the effectiveness of transfer of technology across nations. Simply stated, although degree of economic development is a major factor, cultural predispositions play an important role.

Culture and Strategic Management Issues

At one point in the history of technology transfer, such transfers took place primarily among western nations (i.e., transfer of technology from Western Europe to the United States and vice versa). However, this is not the case today. In fact, transfers of technology from the United States to ASEAN (Association of South East Asian Nations) countries and other nations in South America have become important issues in the 1980s (Marton, 1986; McMillan, 1984). Although the technology transfers among developed nations rely greatly on strategic orientations of transacting organizations, the transfers to developing countries depend on the compatibility of the cultures of the nations involved in such transactions. The practice of adopting and implementing Western technologies of the process and person-embodied types in the context of some of the moderately developing countries has not been a simple case of "borrowing" or imitating, as has been suggested in many popular business periodicals. Indeed, a realistic appraisal of technological diffusion strategy should focus on the structure of preferences that exist in the recipient country at the time of transfer. In addition, such appraisals also should carefully examine the unique strengths and weaknesses of variations in the societal culture, organizational culture, and strategic management practices between the transacting organizations in two different nations. The primary unit of analysis is at the level of the organization located in the context of its own societal culture. The unrecognized roles that cultural variations (societal and organizational) play on the transfer of process- and person-embodied technologies form the basis of our first proposition.

Proposition 1: Process- and person-embodied technologies are more difficult than product-embodied technologies to transfer and diffuse across nations because cultural differences at the organizational, as well as the societal, level play greater roles in such transfers.

Once the importance of cultural variations on process- and person-embodied technologies is recognized, as emphasized in Proposition 1, it should be noted that technology transfers across national boundaries are predominantly orchestrated and managed by organizations seeking economies of scale and other strategic business advantages. Careful attention should be given to the compatibility of cultures of the organizations involved and compatibility of the societal culture. First, we delineate the moderating role of societal cultural-based differences and compatibility between the transacting organizations.

Compatibility of Societal Cultures

Even though the influences of cultural variations have been recognized (Marton, 1986; McMillan, 1984), we did not discover in our review any specific theoretical analysis or empirical studies that rigorously underscore the importance of cultural variations across nations. What exists in the literature is an implicit recognition of the importance of the societal culture of the developing country as a major determinant of the effectiveness of technology transfers (e.g., Koizumi, 1982). Needless to say, the culture of the society to which technology is being exported makes a significant difference. But so does the culture from which the technology is being imported—a point that has remained surprisingly unrecognized in the literature. In the conceptual model, we have incorporated the work of Hofstede (1980) and Glenn and Glenn (1981) in order to advance research propositions that enable us to better understand the process of technology transfers in the context of cultural differences between the transacting organizations and nations involved. Although there are other relevant dimensions of cultural variations, such as McClelland and Winter's (1969) analysis, that might be potentially useful, we find the four dimensions of Hofstede and the one dimension of Glenn and Glenn to be particularly suited for developing our present analysis and for suggesting the propositions on effectiveness of technology transfer across nations. Such effectiveness depends on cultural compatibility between the two nations. According to Hofstede (1980), national cultures can be mapped according to their fit into a four-dimensional framework of (a) weak versus strong uncertainty avoidance, (b) individualism versus collectivism, (c) small versus large power distance, and (d) masculinity versus femininity.

With uncertainty avoidance, we are concerned with the extent to which people in a society feel the need to avoid ambiguous situations and the extent to which they try to manage these situations by providing explicit and formal rules and regulations, by rejecting novel ideas, and by accepting the existence of absolute truths and superordinate goals in the context of work organizations. In Hofstede's (1980) study, the highest scores on uncertainty avoidance were obtained for countries such as Greece, Japan, and most of the Catholic countries in Latin America, whereas low scores were obtained for Hong Kong, Singapore, and the Scandinavian countries. With individualism versus collectivism, we are concerned with the relationships between individuals and organizations in a society. At the individualistic end of this dimension, ties between individuals are, indeed, very loose, and people are supposed to look after their own self-interests in the domains of both work and nonwork. At the collectivist end, we find societies in which social ties or bonds between individuals are very tight, and people learn to distinguish between their own ingroups (e.g., immediate relatives, clans, and members of one's organization) and out-groups (e.g., members from a different community or a foreign country or people with whom one has less frequent contact). In individualistic countries, people are inner-directed, whereas in collectivist countries, individuals are more traditional and other-directed. Examples of individualistic countries are the United States, Great Britain, Australia, Canada, and the Netherlands. Colombia, Venezuela, Taiwan, Singapore, Greece, and Mexico are largely collectivistic in their orientation.

With the dimension of power distance, we are concerned with the extent to which less powerful members of a society accept the unequal distribution of power and rewards as normal features of their society. Hofstede (1980, 1983) has shown that different cultures possess different distributions of power in their organizational and social hierarchies and that the power distance norm can be used as a criterion for characterizing societal cultures. Tannenbaum, Kavcic, Rosher, Viahello, and Weiser (1974), in their analysis of hierarchy in work organizations in five countries, also found that differences in power are associated with significant differences in rewards, privileges, and opportunities among various levels of managements. Large power-distance countries include the Philippines, Mexico, France, Peru, Turkey, Brazil, and India. Small power-distance countries include Austria, Denmark, Sweden, and Israel.

With the fourth dimension, masculinity versus femininity, we are concerned with the extent to which the dominant values in a society emphasize assertiveness, acquisition of money and status, achievement of visible and symbolic organizational rewards (as opposed to an emphasis on quality of life and other less tangible outcomes). In masculine cultures there are sharp distinctions between assertive roles that men perform and service roles that women are expected to fulfill. Hofstede (1983) noted that in a masculine society, the public hero is a successful achiever, an aggressive entrepreneur, and that "big is beautiful" (p. 85). In contrast, feminine societies emphasize quality of life, preservation of the environment, helping others, and putting relationships before money and achievement. The emphasis is on "small is beautiful" (p. 85). Japan is the most masculine country in the world. Also masculine are the German-speaking countries: West Germany, Austria, and Switzerland. Moderately masculine are a number of Latin countries such as Venezuela, Mexico, and Italy. Some former colonies of Anglo countries also are moderately masculine in character, for example, India and the Philippines. The feminine countries are the four Nordic nations, the Netherlands, and some Mediterranean countries like Yugoslavia.

The following four propositions are advanced to reflect the importance of these four distinct cultural variations.

Proposition 2: Transfer of technology is easier between two organizations that are similar in terms of their societal/national culture-based tendencies to either avoid or embrace uncertainty generated in their organizational context due to such transfers.

Proposition 3: Technologies that might introduce significant changes in the distributions of power, status (real and symbolic), and rewards in the recipient organization of the developing country that emphasizes power distance are least likely to be effectively transferred.

Knowledge disavowal (Zaltman, 1983) would be fairly common in the organizations of these high power-distance countries despite the fact that the long-term economic implications of such transfers are positive. Knowledge disavowal reflects the tendency to selectively ignore information that might cause important structural as well as programmatic changes in the recipient organization. In India, for example, despite the existence of a rather sophisticated system of technical core and educated personnel, the ownership structure of Indian industry strongly influences the absorption of technology. The impact of regulatory policies and stringent laws on the acquisition and absorption of foreign technology by both public- and private-sector companies makes it difficult to introduce technologies that might affect traditional management and control-related processes (Palhan, 1985).

Individualistic countries generally are more effective in importing technologies than collectivistic countries. However, a closer examination makes this process somewhat less clear. Although there are numerous examples of failures in technology transfers that involve individualistic countries like the United States, Germany, and the United Kingdom, and some collectivistic countries like Venezuela (Marton, 1986), there are successful examples of technological diffusion in countries that are strongly collectivistic. Japan, Singapore, Hong Kong, and Taiwan are four of the five dragons of economic development in the Asian context. Their ability to absorb Western technology is remarkable, and we cannot cite many parallel examples of modern industrialization in Asia. However, these countries are high in masculinity. One of the consequences of masculinity is that economic growth is seen as more important than social welfare (which is not the case in Scandinavian countries) (Hofstede, 1980). Large-scale enterprises, projects, and performance-driven organizational systems are more popular. This orientation, coupled with collectivism, is, perhaps, responsible for successful transfers of technology to these nations. Otherwise, individualistic cultures are better able both to generate and to import technological advances.

Proposition 4a: Organizations located in individualistic cultures are more successful than organizations located in collectivistic cultures in their propensity to absorb and diffuse imported technology.

Proposition 4b: However, collectivistic cultures that are fairly masculine also are effective in such matters.

Collectivism, which sometimes dampens innovation in organizations, is, perhaps, held in check or counterbalanced by an emphasis on masculinity (Triandis, 1987). This tendency of masculine countries to emphasize economic growth and to foster performance-driven criteria in international trade and technology-related transactions leads us to advance our fifth proposition.

Proposition 5: Masculine cultures are more effective than feminine cultures in absorbing and diffusing imported technology in organizational contexts.

The growth of technology-related advances in these countries, as we have noted earlier, is phenomenal and without parallel in the history of world industrialization. Japan illustrates this pattern remarkably well. In the immediate post-war period, Japanese productivity compared to that of the United States was rather low: 5 percent in coal mining and chemicals, 10 percent in rubber, and 20 percent in rayon. Within a span of less than 40 years, Japan has rivaled the United States in integrated circuits and mainframe computers, and it leads both Europe and the United States in high technology trade to other developing countries (McMillan, 1984). How have Japan and its neighboring countries, such as South Korea (as pointed out my Naisbitt, 1981) and Hong Kong, which arc strongly masculine, been able to make these leaps in technology, especially in contrast to countries like the Netherlands, Sweden, and Finland, which are strongly feminine and were left relatively undamaged during World War II? The answers are complex and, perhaps, rooted in economic, historical, and cultural factors. But when we note that these Scandinavian countries are primarily feminine in orientation (Hofstede, 1983, p. 315), a clearer picture emerges. Masculine countries, more driven to compete, are more dynamic and action oriented. To compete successfully in the global economy, one has to rapidly learn strategies for successful implementation of imported technologies. One important caveat is in order. Even though we have illustrated the effectiveness of transfer in terms of Hofstede's dimensions, it should be noted that the idea emphasized here is one of compatibility between nations and receptivity to technological innovation. In future analyses, if more reliable and empirically anchored measures of such dimensions are available, one could use them also in addressing this issue of effectiveness of transfer.

With the final dimension of cultural variation that plays a role in determining the efficacy of technology transfers, we are concerned with the abstractive versus associative tendencies in a given culture (Glenn & Glenn, 1981). In associative cultures, people utilize associations among events that may not have much logical basis, whereas in abstractive cultures, cause-effect relationships or rational Judeo-Christian types of thinking are dominant. Glenn and Glenn (1981), who pioneered this inquiry in differentiating among cultures, clearly stated that associative thinking is not necessarily inferior to abstractive thinking; it is just different. Cognition and behavior in associative cultures often are diffuse. Communication is characterized by face-to-face contact, and it takes place among individuals who share a large body of information based on both historical and contextual modes (Hall, 1976). In contrast, a vast amount of communication in abstractive cultures tends to be conveyed through mass media and related technological mechanisms that are rather dissimilar compared to face-to-face types of communication.

In associative cultures, context is very important (Hall, 1976). The effectiveness of communication and innovation depends on the specific character of the context in which it takes place. Managers of work organizations from associative cultures also tend to be field-dependent (Gruenfeld & MacEachron, 1975)—a tendency to view the world in a somewhat undifferentiated and global fashion. Economic development and technological change foster field independence and abstractive thinking, the dominant mode in the majority of Western countries (Triandis, 1987). Technological changes for the sake of progress per se often are suspect in associative cultures, and smooth transfers, therefore, are bound to be more difficult to manage. The major reason for this is that effective transfer of technology implies that members of a culture are rather sophisticated in terms of their ability to absorb and utilize context-free information. This tendency is difficult to develop in cultures that function primarily by emphasizing context-dependent sources of information (Hall, 1976).

Proposition 6: Abstractive cultures are more effective than associative cultures in their ability to absorb and diffuse imported technology.

India and some countries in Latin America (e.g., Peru, Colombia, Venezuela) are more associative than European countries in general (Glenn & Glenn, 1981), and a closer examination of the recent literature on technology transfers also reveals that they are less effective in absorbing imported technologies in their organizational contexts (Marton, 1986: Sachs, 1986).

Potential Interaction

Although the above six propositions imply that the five cultural dimensions are distinct, it should be noted that they interact significantly. Theoretically speaking, we could generate additional propositions to reflect the complexity of these interactions. For example, we could suggest that transfer of process- and person-embodied technologies are considerably more difficult from organizations located in cultures that are high in individualism, moderate in masculinity and uncertainty avoidance, low in power distance, and are abstractive (such as the United States) compared with organizations located in cultures that are low in individualism, high in masculinity, uncertainty avoidance, power distance, and are associative (such as Venezuela). However, such propositions are beyond the scope of this paper. Our current research efforts are best directed at testing both the validity and the generalizability of the above-mentioned six propositions. When empirical results on these dimensions become available, research efforts could be redirected toward second or higher-order interactions among these five dimensions. In addition, it must be noted that even though we have utilized specific scores from Hofstede's (1980) data to develop the focused arguments in the propositions, the essential idea is one of compatibility between the cultures involved in the transference of a specific technology in a given situation. This is discussed in the concluding section.

Differences in Organizational Cultures

When examining receptivity of countries to technological change, we adopted the concept of negotiated order (Fine, 1984; Strauss, 1982; Strauss, Schatzman, Ehrlich, Bucher, & Sabshin, 1963) in order to understand the role of organizational culture-based differences in technology transfers across nations. Strauss and his colleagues argued that, basically, social order is negotiated, and that organized activity is not possible without some form of continued negotiations. Negotiations are contingent on the structural conditions of the organization, and they reflect patterned, not random, lines of communication in the context of the organization. Negotiations also have temporal constraints, and the structural changes (i.e., the adoption of technological innovations, etc.) might require a revision of the negotiated order. Although formal rules may refer to the transcending features of the organization, the concept of negotiated order focuses on (a) the number of negotiators, their experience, and whom they represent; (b) the sequence and frequency of negotiations; (c) the relative balance of power among the concerned parties; (d) the stakes and visibility of the outcome of negotiations; (e) the complexity of the issues; and (f) the alternatives to avoiding or discontinuing negotiations. We propose that if the negotiated orders in the cultures of the two transacting organizations are significantly different in terms of the above six dimensions, then transfer of technology between them would be a difficult process, and it might be unproductive for both parties. Such differences are conceptualized as one of two major antecedents in the model (Table 1).

Proposition 7: Differences in the negotiated orders of the cultures of the organizations involved in the transfer and diffusion of technology across nations adversely affect the effectiveness of such transfers.

Potential Interactions

Note that these six dimensions of negotiated order interact with each other much like the societal cultural dimensions. For example, it is likely that the sequence and frequency of negotiations will change the relative balance of power among the parties and the complexity and visibility of the outcomes. Similarity between the two organizations, regarding the six cultural dimensions would facilitate the recipient organization's receptivity of the technological diffusion.

Absorptive Capacity

With the final moderating link in the model along with societal culture-based differences we are concerned with (a) local versus cosmopolitan orientation, (b) the existence of a sophisticated technical core in the recipient organization, and (c) the differences in strategic management between the transacting organizations. Some organizations are more innovative despite their small sizes and other resource-related constraints (Kimberly, 1981). An organization's implementation of technical progress by adopting innovative production techniques and changes in design that accommodate these techniques (Child & Kieser, 1981) are dependent on the degree of cosmopolitanism that is inherent in the organization (Merton, 1968). The evolutionary strategies of diffusion of technology are based on the premise that no matter how impressive the performance characteristics of an innovative technology may be (either process- or person-embodied), its adoption and implementation are greatly dependent on the mix of the array of preexisting priorities and conflicting alliances present in the recipient organization.

In a cosmopolitan organization, such conflicts are managed more systematically and routinely, thus ensuring the success of the innovative effort, whereas in local organizations, the array of priorities often succumbs to immediate sociopolitical concerns, thus making it difficult for even or orderly diffusion (Rodgers & Shoemaker, 1971). In a related vein, the lack of a sophisticated technical core makes it harder for the innovation to occur in the first place—a point that, although well recognized, deserves reemphasis. Kiggundu, Jorgensen, and Hafsi (1983) documented and underscored this issue in their examination of the implementation-related issues in developing countries. There could, indeed, be a great deal of interest in utilizing imported technologies in an organization. The cultural factors of the organization and the societal culture-based context of these factors also might be appropriately matched. But the organization must have a sophisticated technical core and a strategic orientation to make this possibility a reality. Developing countries often are caught in situations of rapid change. Often, in such countries more emphasis is put on managing of multiple goals than on developing local talent to monitor the implementation stage of the imported technology (Marton, 1986; Neghandi, 1971). In short, various aspects of strategic management are important in determining the effectiveness of technology transfer.

Proposition 8: Cosmopolitan organizations in societies that also have a sophisticated technical and an appropriate strategic management orientation are more effective than local organizations in systematically managing technological transfers.

Implications

These eight propositions have implications for research in international and comparative management. The following guidelines are offered to stimulate research in this area.

Guide 1. Researchers should explicitly consider the interactions among technology and cultural variations in both societal and organizational contexts.

Our analysis suggests the need to consider the variations in each of these in order to explain the successes of transfers that, in purely economic terms, ought to fail and the failures of those that ought to succeed. The range of situations to which our ideas apply is depicted in Table 1. More specifically, our analysis is most appropriate in explaining transfer of technology from advanced industrialized countries to recently developing ones (e.g., from, say, West Germany to Brazil or Mexico). We used Japan as an example to illustrate the relevance of our theoretical analysis; however, Japan is no longer a developing country, even though it is clearly culturally dissimilar to many countries from which it imported technologies during the 1950s and 1960s. Therefore, variations in strategic management processes and in organizational cultures are superior predictors of efficacy of transfers than the differences in societal culture when we reconsider the Japanese case today. Cultural differences begin to exert much stronger influences when the importing organization is located in a developing country.

Also, researchers should be more explicit regarding the respective cultural profiles of the importing and exporting organizations as well as their respective societal culture-based differences. Empirical findings on propositions reflecting interactions among the Hofstede and Glenn dimensions can aid in extending the significance of their dimensions to other situations.

Guide 2. Researchers should explicitly recognize the absorptive capacity and related organizational context-based variables when considering the transfer of technology. We need to know much more about the dynamics of the absorptive capacity and the negotiated order that exist in the organization importing the technology. Where do ideas for technological innovations come from? How are they developed? How do potential parties remain informed about the new developments that might affect their well being and that of various coalitions?

The processes of absorption and diffusion of technological innovation are by no means linear, and there is evidence that potential adopter enthusiasm would dampen considerably if the parties in key brokerage roles are threatened (Kimberly, 1981). There are examples of innovations that are warmly received by the boundary-spanners of both the organizations in two societies, but when it comes to actual implementation, the idea may either lie dormant for years or get sidetracked by policy vacuums (Louis & Corwin, 1982). The point is that in developing future research designs on technology transfers, researchers should be sensitive to the differences between rhetoric and reality that often accompany some transactions.

Guide 3. Researchers should place greater emphasis on interdisciplinary frameworks. Future research strategies on the effectiveness of various types of technology transfers should not be based only on economic factors. The need for interdisciplinary frameworks to explain the entire process is urgent at this point in theory development. In the past, we have grappled only in a minor way with the complexity of technology transfers across nations. Developing countries have many concerns besides economic growth and development. Technologies that do not match the needs of their socio-political and cultural contexts are likely to be greeted with more vague rhetoric. Not all countries need to share the individualistic biases that underlie most of our theories of diffusion of technology (Chesanow, 1985; Triandis, 1987, in press). Hofstede (1980) observed that in an eagerness to assist other developing countries to adopt Western methods and techniques, we often forget our ethnocentric biases. Adler (1986) echoed this concern. It would be more effective if significant advances in the field of cross-cultural studies of management and organization were incorporated in future theories and research on technology transfers. Both developed countries and developing countries would benefit from such an interdisciplinary orientation. The ideas presented in this paper are offered to stimulate further research and thinking in this growing and important area in the field of international and comparative management.

References

Alder, N. J. (1986) *International dimensions of organizational behavior.* Boston: Kent.

Balasubramanyam, V. (1973) *International transfer of technology to India.* New York: Praeger Scientific Press.

Baranson, J. (1970, May) Technology transfer through the international firm. *American Economic Review*, Papers and Proceedings, 435-440.

Baranson, J., & Harrington, A. (1977) *Industrial transfers of technology by U.S. firms under licensing arrangements: Policies, practices and conditioning factors.* Washington, DC: Developing World Industry and Technology, Inc.

Behrman, J., & Wallender, H. (1976) *Transfer of manufacturing technology within multinational enterprises.* Cambridge, MA: Ballinger.

Child, J., & Kieser, A. (1981) Development of organizations over time. In P. C. Nystrom & W. H. Starbuck (Eds.), *Handbook of organizational design* (Vol. 1, pp. 28-64). New York: Oxford University Press.

Chesanow, N. (1985) *The world class executive.* New York: Rawson Associates.

Contractor, F. J., & Sagafi-Nejad, T. (1981) International technology transfer: Major issues and policy responses. *Journal of International Business Studies,* 12(2), 113-135.

Davidson, W. H., & McFetridge, D. G. (1985) Key characteristics in choice of international technology transfer mode. *Journal of International Business Studies,* 6(2), 5-21.

Driscoll, R., & Wallender, H. (1981) Control and incentives for technology transfer: A multinational perspective. In R. W. Moxon & H. V. Perlmutter (Eds.), *Controlling international technology transfer: Issues, perspectives and implications* (pp. 273-286). New York: Pergamon Press.

Dunning, J. H. (1981) Alternative channels and modes of international resource transmission. In R. W. Moxon & H. V. Perlmutter (Eds.), *Controlling international technology transfer: Issues, perspectives and implications* (pp. 3-27). New York: Pergamon Press.

Evenson, R. (1976) International transmission of technology in production of sugar cane. *Journal of Development Studies,* 1, 1-13.

Fine, G. A. (1984) Negotiated orders and organizational cultures. *Annual Review of Sociology*, 10, 239-262.

Glenn, E. S., & Glenn, C. G. (1981) *Man and mankind: Conflict and communication between cultures*. Norwood, NJ: Ablex.

Gruenfeld, L. W., & MacEachron, A. E. (1975) A cross-national study of cognitive style among managers and technicians. *International Journal of Psychology*, 10, 27-55.

Hall, E. T. (1976) *Beyond culture*. Garden City, NY: Anchor/Doubleday.

Hall, G., & Johnson, R. (1970) Transfer of United States aerospace technology to Japan. In R. Vernon (Ed.), The technology factor in international trade (pp. 305-358). New York: Columbia.

Hofstede, G. (1980) *Culture's consequences: International differences in work-related values*. Beverly Hills, CA: Sage.

Hofstede, G. (1983) The cultural relativity of organizational practices and theories. *Journal of International Business Studies*, 14(2), 75-89.

Kiggundu, M. N., Jorgensen, J. J., & Hafsi, T. (1983) Administrative theory and practice in developing countries: A synthesis. *Administrative Science Quarterly*, 28, 66-85.

Kimberly, J. R. (1981) Managerial innovation. In P. C. Nystrom & W. H. Starbuck (Eds.), Handbook of organizational design (Vol. 1, pp. 84-104). New York: Oxford University Press.

Koizumi, T. (1982) Absorption and adaptation: Japanese inventiveness in technological development. In S. B. Lundstedt & E. W. Colglazier, Jr. (Eds.), Managing innovation: The social dimensions of creativity, invention and technology (pp. 190-206). New York: Pergamon Press.

Louis, K. S., & Corwin, R. G. (1982) Organizational barriers to utilization of research. *Administrative Science Quarterly*, 27, 4, 623-640.

Marton, K. (1986) *Multinationals, technology, and industrialization*. Lexington, MA: Heath.

Mason, R. H. (1980, January-February) A comment of Professor Kojma's Japanese type vs. American type of technology transfer. *Hototsubashi Journal of Economics*.

McClelland, D. C., & Winter, D. G. (1969) Motivating economic achievement. New York: Free Press.

McMillan, C. J. (1984) The Japanese industrial system. New York: Water de Gruyter.

Merton, R. K. (1968) *Social theory and social structure*. New York: Free Press.

Neghandi, A. R. (1971) American management abroad: A comparative study of management practices of American subsidiaries and local firms in developing countries. *Management International Review*, 11(4-5), 97-107.

Naisbitt, J. (1981) *Megatrends*. New York: Warner.

Palhan, S. K. (1985) *Technology policy and India's experience in technology transfer*. New Delhi: Government of India. Ministry of Industry.

Pugel. T. (1978) *International technology transfer and neo-classical trade theory: A survey*. Working paper, New York University.

Rodgers, E., & Shoemaker, F. (1971) *Communication of innovations: A cross-cultural approach*. New York: Free Press.

Sachs, J. (1986, February 22) A tale of Asian winners and Latin losers. *Economist*, pp. 63-64.

Strauss, A. (1982) Interorganizational negotiations. *Urban Life*, 11, 350-367.

Strauss, A., Schatzman, L., Ehrlich, D., Bucher, R., & Sabshin, M. (1963) The hospital and its negotiated order. In E. Friedson (Ed.), *The hospital in modern society* (pp. 147-169). New York: Free Press.

Tannenbaum, A. S., Kavcic, B., Rosher, M., Viahello, M., & Wieser, G. (1974) *Hierarchy in organizations*. San Francisco: Jossey-Bass.

Triandis, H. C. (1987) *Collectivism and development*. Paper presented at International Union of Psychological Sciences, Hong Kong.

Triandis, H. C. (in press) Cross-cultural industrial and organizational psychology. In M. D. Dunnette (Ed.), *Handbook of industrial and organizational psychology*. Chicago: Rand McNally.

Zaltman, G. (1983) Knowledge disavowal in organizations. In R. Kilman, K. Thomas, D. Slevin, R. Nath, & S. Jarrell (Eds.), *Producing useful knowledge for organizations* (pp. 173-187). New York: Praeger.

4. TECHNOLOGY TRANSFER TO DEVELOPING COUNTRIES VIA MULTINATIONALS

KATHERIN MARTON

Professor of Economics at the Graduate School of Business Administration, Fordham University, New York, since 1977; previously Professor of Economics at the City University of New York (1972-77); author of MULTINATIONALS, TECHNOLOGY AND INDUSTRIALIZATION (1986).

In the last two decades, there has been a very rapid increase in technology-transfer agreements between firms in different countries, largely through the activities of multinational enterprises. Industrial technology has increasingly become a marketable commodity, both within the operations of multinational enterprises and through various contractual arrangements for the provision of technology and services to unaffiliated companies. The commercialisation of technology, mostly in the form of lump-sum fees and royalties for technical know-how and services, has increased considerably. Receipts from the export of technology in the case of five developed countries, namely the United States, Britain, France, the Federal Republic of Germany and Japan, increased from $1.93 billion in 1965 to around $11 billion in 1983.[1] The highest receipts, which amounted to $7.91 billion in 1983 as against $1.53 billion in 1965, were obtained by American-based companies.[2] This rapid increase in the commercialisation of technology has been influenced by several major factors, including the fast pace of technological innovation, the growing use of technology licensing and other contractual arrangements and the higher importance accorded to technological development in the national policies of both industrialised and developing countries.

Although most technology transactions have taken place between firms in industrialised countries, payments for technology by developing countries have also increased significantly in recent years. By the early 1980s, annual payments for technology and services from these countries rose to around $2 billion, from $230 million in 1965.[3] By the early 1990s such payments, it is estimated, could exceed $6 billion.[4] The increase in aggregate technology flows to developing countries has been accompanied by major changes in the pattern of transfer, in terms of the sectoral coverage of the technologies transferred and in their country-wise distribution. More importantly, however, the conditions under which technology transactions have taken place have undergone major changes. Technology-transfer arrangements between private parties have increasingly become subject to fairly well-defined regulatory norms and measures pursued by developing-country governments. Consequently, technology transfer to developing countries has taken place under very different conditions from those prevailing among companies in developed countries, where the terms of transfer are wholly determined by the parties concerned. These differences stem not only from the very different techno-economic characteristics of industrialised and developing countries but, more particularly, from the role which governments in developing countries have exercised over these transactions.

Reprinted from *The World Economy*, 9:4, 1986, pp. 409–426 by permission of the publisher.

Regulatory approaches towards the acquisition of foreign technology have varied among those countries which adopted such measures and they have also changed over time. The expanding scope of governmental regulation of the process for the acquisition of foreign technology during the 1970s has increasingly given way to more liberalised measures and guidelines in the 1980s. These relaxations have nevertheless taken place in certain countries within the framework of regulatory norms. The current environment in several developing countries is characterised by the adoption of different approaches towards foreign technology, largely depending on the need for, and complexity of, specific technology and know-how. This trend has emerged partly because of expanding national priorities and the technological needs for international competitiveness and partly because of greater indigenous capability in several industrial sectors.

The focus of this article is on recent developments in the technology-transfer policies and experience of developing countries. In order to place current developments in perspective, the pattern of technology transfer during the 1960s and 1970s is briefly reviewed. Although the major factors and elements which shaped technology transfer during these decades continue to operate in the 1980s, new trends have emerged in several fields which will have a more pronounced impact in the current decade. Technology-transfer arrangements have undoubtedly become among the most important relationships between enterprises in developed and developing countries. Even though technology flows are continuing to take place in an environment where several factors encourage their rapid growth, there are also factors that militate against a faster pace of technology transfer to developing countries and industries.

Concept of Technology Transfer

The transfer of industrial technology implies the transfer of specialised production and management know-how between different parties which are generally industrial enterprises. In several industries, technological knowledge is embodied in machinery and equipment; and information on machinery operations provides operational technology. In international business activities, however, the transfer of technology is viewed in more specific terms and is usually conceived as the transfer of specialised know-how, which may be either patented or non-patented, from one enterprise to another. Transmission of such knowledge enables the recipient enterprise to manufacture a particular product or provide a specific service. As distinct from the sale of machinery and equipment which embodies technology, the transfer of technology, in most cases, calls for a sustained relationship between two enterprises over a period of time, so that the receiving enterprise can reproduce the product with the desired level of quality standards and cost efficiency.[5]

The nature of foreign-technology transfer generally differs in scope and magnitude between licensee enterprises in industrialised countries and those in developing economies. In the case of the former, the need for technology is primarily for patented or proprietary know-how. The advanced technological capabilities of licensees and their on-going production and research activities enable these companies to absorb and adapt licensed technology once the technical specifications and the rights to use patented or proprietary information are required. Often they improve on the licensed technology and introduce adaptations and innovations. Moreover, licensors and licensee companies are operating in a similar technological environment; and local suppliers and subcontractors can manufacture required inputs once technical information is provided. The requirements of a qualified and skilled labour force seldom pose major problems. Furthermore, because of similarities in the application of technologies and of final products in the countries of the licensor and the licensee, major process and product adaptations may not be necessary in most instances.

In the case of industrial-technology transfer to companies in developing countries, however, the need of these enterprises is not only for product design and production know-how but for a much broader range of technological functions. Because of the limited availability of intermediate materials and inputs, the technological requirements in most cases extend considerably beyond the acquisition of patented or proprietary designs or production know-how. The licensee company usually needs technical assistance in the preparation of feasibility and market studies, project planning, the specification of inputs and machinery, production know-how, supervision of project implementation and start-up and initial operations. Quality-control requirements for locally-purchased inputs and foreign sources of intermediates frequently have to be defined by the licensor. The production know-how required may often be non-proprietary and may even be widely diffused in industrialised countries in the specific industrial sector. The effective utilisation of foreign technology in developing countries may consequently require a much larger package of industry-specific technology and know-how. The assimilation of foreign technology and its adjustment to different factor endowments and conditions are also a far greater task for enterprises in these countries than in the case of licensees in industrialised economies. Apart from project implementation and production technology, much greater support is required in managerial and marketing operations. Thus the technological needs of enterprises in developing countries tend to be of a composite nature and cover various stages of project preparation, implementation and operations.

Channels of Technology Transfer

Traditionally, the most important channel of technology transfer has been through foreign direct investment by multinational enterprises based in developed countries. The growth of corporate multinationalisation has been accompanied by technology flows from parent companies to their foreign subsidiaries and affiliates. The close relationship between investment and technology flows is indicated by the high share of technology receipts from affiliated companies out of total payments received for technology and technical services. In 1983, for example, in the case of American corporations, 78 per cent of receipts from technology was from affiliated companies and this share showed relatively little variation throughout the 1970s.[6] For British corporations, 55 per cent of technology receipts was from affiliated companies during the late 1970s, indicating the greater propensity of British companies to license their technology to unaffiliated companies.[7]

Due to the close relationship between the transfer of industrial technology and foreign investments by multinational enterprises, the flow and stock of foreign investments in developing countries serve as indicators of the magnitude and rate of growth of foreign-technology inflow. The flow of foreign direct investment from developed market economies to all receiving countries increased from $4.1 billion in 1960 to $12.1 billion in 1970 and to $41.8 billion in 1980. Investments in developing countries accounted for $1.8 billion in 1970 and $7.6 billion in 1980, at current prices[8]—that is, approximately 30 per cent of total foreign investments during the last two decades. More than half of such investments have been from the United States. The share of foreign investments in developing countries from Japan and the Federal Republic of Germany, however, has tended to grow more rapidly in recent years than from the United States.

Foreign investments in developing countries increased by about 15 per cent annually during the 1970s.[9] The distribution among various countries, however, was very uneven and most of these investments were concentrated in a few countries. These last included the larger developing countries, particularly in Latin America, and those which were rich in natural resources. These enabled multinational enterprises to have access to large internal markets or scarce raw materials. Since the early 1970s, foreign direct investment also increased in countries which have been utilised as export platforms because of cheaper labour and lower transport costs. All the same, the flow of foreign direct investment has remained very limited to the least developed economies where local demand has been considered, by multinational enterprises, to be inadequate and factor advantages were not significant. Thus, during the 1970s, out of a total investment flow of $7.9 billion to developing countries, 57 per cent or $4.9 billion was invested in Latin America, mostly in Brazil and Mexico.[10] In the same period, multinational enterprises invested $2.4 billion in South and East Asia, mostly in Hong Kong, Singapore and Malaysia. At the same time, investments by multinational enterprises in the manufacturing sector were very limited in most African developing countries, in the Caribbean and in smaller Latin American countries. Foreign investments in North Africa, for example, accounted for only 2 per cent of the total flow of investments to developing countries.[11]

Foreign investment flows from industrialised to developing countries have traditionally taken place in the extractive and primary goods sectors (accounting for almost half of the total until the late 1960s), particularly petroleum, non-fuel minerals and plantation industries. In the 1970s, however, especially in the latter half, investments in the manufacturing sector increased fairly rapidly. Apart from such light industries as textiles, cement and durable consumer goods, foreign direct investment has also grown rapidly in the intermediate and capital goods sectors, such as chemicals, petrochemicals and the production of a wide range of engineering goods, especially in countries with large internal markets or those with special factor advantages. These investments have been accompanied by the inflow of more complex and advanced technologies. Investments in manufacturing by multinational enterprises based in the

United States, Britain and Japan constituted an important share of total investments in the manufacturing sector during the 1970s, ranging from 70 per cent in Nigeria to nearly 50 per cent in Brazil, Ghana, Malaysia and Peru, 25-30 per cent in Argentina, Mexico and Singapore and 5-10 per cent in the Republic of Korea, Indian and Thailand.[12]

Joint Ventures

Although technology transfer in conjunction with foreign direct investment has remained the most important channel in most developing countries, the ownership structure of foreign operations has changed to a large extent in several countries in the last decade. In these countries, as a result of regulatory measures on foreign investments, joint ventures have become an important form of multinational enterprise participation and, in many cases, production operations which would formerly have been undertaken through wholly foreign-owned subsidiaries have increasingly been implemented through joint ventures between foreign and domestically-owned companies. Alternatively, multinational enterprises have established affiliates with varying levels of local shareholding. Joint-venture requirements have primarily aimed to increase domestic participation and control on the part of local industry. These measures, however, have also exercised an important effect on the control of technology by parent companies and on local diffusion of technology. Regulatory control, which has sought to channel flows of foreign direct investment into priority sectors and restricted the extent of foreign ownership in various fields, has also directed the sectoral distribution of foreign-technology flows.

With the increased regulation of foreign investments in several countries during the 1960s and 1970s, joint ventures have become a fairly common form of operation for multinational enterprises. In Mexico, for example, since 1973, after promulgation of the Law for the Promotion of Mexican Investments and Regulation of Foreign Investments, out of the 1,724 proposals submitted for foreign direct investments until 1980, majority foreign ownership was only permitted in 44 cases.[13] Similarly in India, during the period from 1969 to 1980, when guidelines on foreign technology were published (December 1969) and the Foreign Exchange Regulation Act was passed (1973), the number of majority foreign-owned subsidiaries decreased from 198 in 1973 to 111 in 1980[14] as a result of divestment of foreign holdings while majority foreign holdings were not permitted in the case of new investments, except where production was wholly export-oriented.

Despite the growing number of developing countries which require multinational enterprises to operate mainly through joint ventures in future, foreign investments in most developing countries continue to be mainly through wholly foreign-owned or majority foreign-owned subsidiaries. Even in the early 1980s, for multinational enterprises based in the United States, for example, the share of investments in wholly-owned or majority-owned subsidiaries has continued to be very high. It was 78 percent in Ghana, 81 per cent in Hong Kong, 76 per cent in the Philippines, 68 per cent in Singapore, 52 per cent in Thailand, 80 per cent in Argentina, 90 per cent in Brazil,

83 per cent in Chile, 66 per cent in Mexico, 84 per cent in Panama and 79 per cent in Trinidad and Tobago.[15]

In certain developing countries where foreign investments are regulated and screened, multinational enterprises have only obtained exemptions from joint-venture requirements if they provided specialised technology in priority sectors or assumed significant export commitments. This has, in several instances, brought about a gradual shift to the production of more technologically complex products, or those having considerable export potential, by subsidiaries and affiliates in these countries. In Malaysia, for example, about half of the approved foreign investments in 1981 were in the form of wholly-owned subsidiaries of multinational enterprises, but the share was much higher in machine-building industries.[16] Also, in the Republic of Korea, while the proportion of foreign investment through wholly or majority foreign-owned subsidiaries remained over 70 per cent during 1968-80, the ownership composition in several sectors changed significantly. In textiles, for example, the share of minority foreign-owned companies decreased from 34 to 13 per cent, in petroleum from 65 to 14 per cent and in the hotel sector from 86 to 19 per cent. At the same time, the share of minority foreign holdings in metal processing and machinery rose from 26 to 35 per cent.[17]

Licensing to Unaffiliated Companies

While subsidiaries, affiliates and joint ventures of multinational enterprises have constituted the dominant channels for technology transfer to developing countries during the 1970s, licensing activities between multinational enterprises and unaffiliated companies in developing countries have also grown rapidly. This trend has been influenced by the industrial policies of governments in several developing countries as well as increased production and technological capabilities of domestically-owned public and private-sector companies. These developments have crated a large and growing demand for foreign technology in most industrial sectors. At the same time, the regulation of foreign investment, which has restricted foreign equity participation in several industrial sectors, has increased the willingness of multinational enterprises and foreign companies possessing proprietary technology to transfer technology through licensing agreements. Given the importance of this new trend, the nature of foreign-technology acquisition and licensing by state-owned, public-sector enterprises and by private-sector companies in developing countries needs to be considered separately.

Public-sector Companies

In several developing countries, resource-based industries have either been nationalised or state participation in them has been increased substantially. Apart from the petroleum sector, where state-owned companies have been established in several developing countries, state-owned or public sector enterprises have become dominant in several countries of Latin America, Africa and Asia in various mineral-processing industries, petro-chemicals, fertilizers, agro-processing and certain manufacturing sectors, including capital goods production. Technology transfer in these fields is increasingly taking place through technology-supply arrangements and service contracts with foreign engineering companies and technology licensors in a number of fields. In petro-chemicals, for example, public-sector enterprises in Algeria, Saudi Arabia, Kuwait, Indonesia, Mexico and other oil-producing countries, together with state-owned corporations such as Petrobras in Brazil, the Indian Petrochemical Corporation in India and state-owned companies in Pakistan, Thailand and other oil-importing countries, are playing an increasingly significant role, with most of their technological needs being met through licensing and contractual arrangements.

In a number of developing countries, apart from utilities, communications and such basic industries as iron and steel, public-sector enterprises have played an important role in the production of fertilisers, chemicals and the manufacture of machinery and equipment. Fertiliser manufacture, for example, has been undertaken through state-owned corporations in India, Indonesia and the Middle East. In Brazil, for example, public-sector companies have a virtual monopoly in petroleum refining and have a major role in the mining sector and in the manufacture of steel and petro-chemicals. These enterprises include the largest companies in the country. In 1982, of the 200 largest companies in Brazil ranked by sales, 46 were owned by the government.[18] In the early 1980s, public-sector companies accounted for over one quarter of all technology agreements.[19] Similarly in India, where production by the public sector includes steel, heavy mechanical and electrical equipment, pharmaceuticals and petroleum exploration and development, most state-owned companies have developed an extensive network of licensing agreements with multinational enterprises based in developed countries.[20] The acquisition of foreign technology by public-sector enterprises has been facilitated by the government which often allocated foreign exchange for this purpose on a preferential basis.

Private-sector Companies

During the 1970s, in several countries, including Brazil, India, the Republic of Korea and Mexico, domestically-owned private-sector industrial groups were able to diversify their production extensively and to establish capacities for the manufacture of a wide range of technologically-advanced products, including various categories of machinery and equipment. The expansion of local private-sector production in these countries has relied heavily on foreign sources of technology, which has mostly been acquired through non-affiliate licensing agreements with multinational enterprises or, in certain cases, through joint ventures. During this period, in several of these countries, medium-size companies have also played an increasing role in the local manufacture of a wide range of consumer products and engineering goods which have also been based mainly on foreign technology. Since most of such production activities required standardised technologies which were available from various alternative sources, foreign technology suppliers have been willing to transfer such technologies without foreign equity participation. With the various restrictions which several governments imposed on foreign direct investments, such licensing arrangements provided the only means to derive revenues from these markets.

Transfer of technology by multinational enterprises and foreign licensors through licensing agreements to unaffiliated companies, however, has largely been concentrated in a few countries, including Brazil, Mexico and Argentina in Latin America, India, the Republic of Korea and some of the South-east Asian countries. In the Republic of Korea, for example, locally-owned firms accounted for 74 per cent of all licensing agreements with foreign companies by 1980.[21] In India, out of 2.833 cases of foreign technical collaboration in the period from 1969 to 1979, 2,418 cases related to technology licensing to non-affiliated local companies and only 15 per cent of the cases had foreign equity participation, usually with minority holdings of up to 40 per cent.[22] But in most African countries, and in the smaller Latin American and Caribbean countries, there have been relatively few cases of technology licensing to non-affiliated companies.

While licensing of foreign technology to unaffiliated companies in developing countries has increased in the last two decades, this constituted a very small share of global technology transfer, measured in terms of payments. In the case of American companies, for example, out of total receipts of $7.9 billion in fees and royalties in 1983, payments by developing countries came to $1.27 billion.[23] From this amount, approximately 15 per cent came from unaffiliated companies in developing countries which accounted for only about 2 per cent of the global licensing revenues of the United States.

Trends in Technology Regulation

Until the early 1970s, in most developing countries with the exception of India, foreign technology was imported by local industrial enterprises, including subsidiaries and affiliates of multinational enterprises, without any restrictions. In many instances, there were no formal technology agreements between parent companies and their affiliates, although certain royalties and lump-sum payments were made by the latter towards centralised research and development and the supply of technological assistance as required. The remittance of payments for royalties and technology fees, however, was generally subject to foreign-exchange control, either by the central bank or the finance ministry.

The regulation of foreign investments in several developing countries in the 1960s and 1970s created a broader framework for technology flows. Not only did such regulation have a major impact on the channels used to transfer technology but it also affected the sectoral orientation of technology flows which would otherwise have accompanied foreign investments. At the same time, such regulation also pointed to the need to review the nature and pattern of foreign-technology inflow. The regulation of foreign technology was initially undertaken in Japan from the 1950s. There a highly effective combination of regulatory and promotional policies for foreign technology was implemented.

In developing countries, technology regulation was initially adopted in India, primarily with a view to conserve foreign exchange. The 1969 guidelines issued by the Indian Government were among the earliest policy announcements relating to foreign-technology acquisition in developing countries. During the 1970s, several countries in Latin America introduced legal and regulatory measures to screen and review the inflow of foreign technology. The Andean Group countries (Bolivia, Colombia, Chile, Ecuador and Peru and subsequently Venezuela, while Chile withdrew from the Group) formulated Decision 24 for regional regulations of foreign investments and Decisions 84 and 85 for foreign-technology acquisition. Argentina adopted Law N19231 in 1971 with modifications in 1974 and 1981. Brazil's Normative Act 015-INPI and Mexico's Law on Registration and Transfer of Technology which was promulgated in 1972 and amended in 1982 established the regulatory provisions for foreign-technology acquisition. During the 1970s, regulatory measures were also introduced in several other developing countries, particularly in South-east Asia, including the Republic of Korea, Malaysia and the Philippines, and in some countries of Africa, particularly Nigeria. In some countries, such policies have been linked with those on foreign direct investments while, in others, the policies have been more closely related to indigenous technological development.

Despite the differences in the form of regulation, such as by legal enactment, as in Mexico and Brazil, or by administrative guidelines, as in Indian and the Republic of Korea, the intent of regulation has been similar. In earlier phases, regulation aimed to reduce the costs of foreign technology and permissible maximum-payment levels were established, apart from assessment of the costs of equipment and maintenance inputs required to be imported as part of foreign-technology usage. Subsequently, measurement of costs has also included various indirect costs arising out of restrictive provisions imposed by technology licensors. Consequently, considerable attention was given to the terms and conditions incorporated in technology agreements and norms and guidelines were prescribed by regulatory agencies in countries where such regulation was introduced. These guidelines prohibited the inclusion of unduly onerous or restrictive provisions by licensors, including tie-in clauses for the supply of inputs, restrictions on exports and the like. By the mid-1970s, greater scrutiny was also made of legal aspects, such as the governing law, the settlement of disputes and the like, and various technological issues. Furthermore, in some countries, as in India, foreign-technology inflow in certain non-essential sectors was prohibited, while in other countries, for example in Brazil, certain types of technology transactions, such as the transfer of know-how without patent rights, were strongly discouraged and approved only exceptionally. Varying degrees of flexibility were provided in different countries, principally by way of exceptions to the regulatory norms or guidelines.

By the late 1970s, in those developing countries where technology-regulation measures were adopted, governmental control over foreign-technology inflow became fairly extensive and involved the analysis and evaluation of proposed foreign-technology agreements from a legal, economic and technological viewpoint. Through a decade of experience in these countries, administration of the laws and guidelines has improved substantially; and a considerable degree of flexibility and pragmatism is now a common feature in most of these countries. The regulatory pressure has also eased, with increased capability on the part of domestic companies to negotiate effectively with foreign technology suppliers.

In spite of the adoption of technology regulation in several developing countries, technology flows increased throughout the 1970s. In Brazil, for example, where technology contracts have been subject to fairly rigorous scrutiny, the number of technology contracts increased from 1,117 in 1972 to 1,761 in 1980.[24] Agreements for the supply of specialised technical services to Brazil numbered 2,839 during 1979-81.[25] Similarly, in Mexico, subsequent to the introduction of regulatory measures, technology payments increased significantly, from $173 million in 1975 to approximately $300 million in 1980.[26]

Trends Towards Liberalisation

In several countries where governments adopted technology-regulation measures in the 1970s, these measures were significantly modified in the latter half of the 1970s and early 1980s. Although fairly strict control over the process for technology acquisition has continued in certain countries, as in Brazil, regulatory measures have been relaxed in other countries, as in the Republic of Korea and India. In some countries, the inflow of foreign technology has been promoted by various incentives. Several factors have accounted for these changes in policies. With growing industrialisation, development plans have increasingly involved diversification and production in more technologically-advanced fields, where the availability of technology is limited to a few foreign companies. In such cases, owners of technology, which are mostly multinational enterprises, have not always been willing to transfer their technology under the rigorous terms of technology regulation, particularly if this is accompanied by controls over foreign investments. Technology payments required for new and complex technologies may have to be significantly higher than the maximum rates prescribed in national guidelines for the manufacturing sector as a whole. The effective absorption of more complex and advanced technologies may also require a longer period, which often exceeds the duration prescribed in guidelines. The broader impact of the slowdown in economic growth in recent years, particularly in countries facing critical debt situations, has also slowed the pace of technology inflow in these countries and has necessitated promotional measures and relaxations in regulatory guidelines.

The trend towards liberalisation in technology regulation has been accompanied by differentiated policies for different kinds of industrial technology. While regulatory controls continue to be applied for relatively mature and standardised technologies, the acquisition of the latest techniques in high-technology areas and sectors of special priority is increasingly being encouraged and promoted through various incentives, including exemptions from regulatory norms and guidelines. In several instances, the inflow of advanced technologies has been promoted by relaxations in regulations relating to foreign investments and the extent of foreign capital ownership. Thus in countries where joint ventures are generally the only permissible means for capital participation by multinational enterprises, governments have permitted the entry of wholly foreign-owned subsidiaries if the inflow of complex and sophisticated technologies has been involved.

The liberalisation of foreign-technology acquisition has taken different forms. In some countries, as in the Republic of Korea, the regulatory provisions and guidelines were substantially changed, reflecting the new liberalised policy during 1979-81. In others, for example in Mexico, Brazil and India, the new approach has been implemented within existing legislation and guidelines. In most of these countries, the regulations have already provided for exceptions to the norms for technologies which were considered to be in the national interest. Under this provision, since the early 1980s, the regulatory agencies have broadened the scope of exceptions far beyond previous levels.

One country which has effected major liberalisation in its foreign-technology regulations in the Republic of Korea. A short review of these new measures follows, together with a review of the effects of liberalisation on foreign-technology flows and other implications of liberalisation.

Experience of the Republic of Korea

Since the early 1960s, the Korean authorities had regulated the acquisition of foreign technology within the framework of the Capital Inducement Act. The Act had only prescribed general provisions for foreign-technology acquisition and more specific directions in this regard were provided by periodically issued guidelines which stipulated well-defined norms for permissible contractual terms (3 per cent royalties and, generally, contract duration of up to three years). In the 1960s, the number of foreign-technology agreements was rather limited; and during the 1962-72 period, only about 320 agreements were entered into, with payments during this period of about $10 million.[27] In the 1970s, however, with the implementation of the Third and Fourth Development Plans, local companies turned increasingly to foreign technology suppliers and there has been rapid growth in the number of technology agreements. In 1978 alone, 297 agreements were approved and payments rose rapidly, from $11.5 million in 1973 to $85 million in 1978.[28]

In the late 1970s, with the formulation of the Fifth Development Plan (period up to 1986), which aimed at the rapid development of the machine-building and other high-technology sectors, it was considered that the existing foreign-technology regulations would constitute a major constraint on the implementation of the plan. Consequently, in the late 1970s, the Korean government adopted a series of liberalisation measures related to technology acquisition. The new policies were introduced in 1978, but their scope and coverage expanded considerably in 1979. Within the framework of these measures, the government approval system for technology agreements was greatly simplified and lager latitude was given to the parties to define the terms and conditions of the contract. In 1979, in order to streamline the approval system, which had caused administrative delays in processing agreements, an automatic approval system was introduced. According to the guidelines issued by the Economic Planning Board, such automatic approval meant that technology agreements would be evaluated, approved and registered by the ministry dealing with the usage of the proposed technology, which would make the approval and registration most technology agreements a *'one stop'* process.

In 1979, the first stage of the automatic approval system was implemented for agreements in heavy industries (except atomic power, computer manufacture and defence) and for contracts with a duration of less than three years, initial payments of less than $30,000 and royalties of less than 3 per cent. The same procedure was also applicable to agreements involving payment of fixed sums below $100,000. In 1980, all agreements (except those in atomic energy and defence industries), which did not exceed a duration of ten years or royalty payments above 10 per cent and down-payments of $500,000 or, in the case of outright purchase of technologies, exceeding $1 million, were approved automatically. Agreements exceeding the above duration and payments were required to obtain the approval of the Economic Planning Board.

Following the introduction of these measures, the number of technology agreements between Korean and foreign companies has increased rapidly. While during the 1962-77 period, 842 agreements were entered into, this number rose to 222 in 1980 and 432 in 1984.[29] Technology payments have also grown sharply from $58 million in 1978 to $107 million in 1980.[30] This increase was partly due to the larger number of agreements entered into in the years following liberalisation and partly because of the nature of technologies which have increasingly included more advanced and sophisticated techniques and processes. While the new liberalised measures have facilitated the acquisition of a wide range of foreign technologies, certain negative effects have also become manifest. An analysis of the agreements entered into during the 1979-82 period, for example, showed that repetitive acquisition of foreign technologies had increased significantly over previous years and, within the automatic approval system, less consideration was given to the technical evaluation of agreements which often resulted in the acquisition of outdated technologies, particularly by companies in the medium-scale sector. The liberalisation also resulted in higher royalty rates for fairly standardised technologies and also in lump-sum payments. A larger proportion of agreements also contained more unfavourable terms and conditions for Korean licensees than in the period prior to the adoption of liberalisation measures. Provisions have often been included in recent agreements which avoid licensor's responsibilities for the performance of the licensed technology and in the case of infringement of third-party industrial property rights.[31]

While the liberalisation of foreign-technology regulation has been the most comprehensive and far reaching in the Republic of Korea, increased encouragement of foreign-technology inflow has also taken place in some other countries, particularly India. During the 1969-79 period, the Foreign Investment Board, the regulatory authority in India, approved 2,833 agreements.[32] In the early 1980s, with greater liberalisation of foreign-technology inflow, the number of technology agreements entered into between domestic and foreign companies increased rapidly and reached 526 in 1980 and 673 in 1983.[33] By 1984-84, technology payments were about $400 million, from about $150 million in 1980-81.[34]

Global Trends

Since the early 1970s, the introduction of technology regulation in several developing countries has had a significant impact on the nature and terms of foreign-technology acquisition in countries which adopted such measures. Extensive regulation of foreign-technology flows, however, has taken place in relatively few developing countries. In the majority of countries, governments have exercised rather limited influence.

Trends in Regulation

It is possible to classify developing countries into three broad groups on the basis of their approach towards the regulation of foreign technology.

First, there is the large majority of countries where there is no regulations of foreign technology and no restrictions are exercised on remittances of fees and royalties for technology. These include certain countries in East Asia, such as Hong Kong, Singapore, Taiwan and Thailand, which have registered a rapid rate of industrial growth, besides most countries in Africa and some countries in Latin America and the Caribbean. In some countries, as in Sri Lanka, Chile and Egypt, major policy changes took place during the 1970s which led to a more open-door approach towards foreign investment and technology. A similar policy has been followed in several countries of Africa, including most countries in North Africa.

A second group of countries comprises those where a certain degree of selectivity is exercised regarding the entry and operations of foreign companies, but without the adoption of explicit regulatory measures towards foreign technology. This includes Bangladesh, Indonesia, Pakistan, Kenya, Ghana and other countries where foreign-investment proposals require the approval of governmental agencies, but no specific approval is necessary for contracts relating to foreign technology and services.

The third group of countries comprises those where foreign-technology agreements are reviewed by a governmental agency, which administers the relevant laws or administrative guidelines. The countries which fall into this category include the Andean Pact countries, Brazil, India, Malaysia, Mexico, Nigeria, the Philippines and the Republic of Korea. As discussed above, the regulatory approaches have varied among these countries and also over a period of time. Brazil, for example, has followed a policy of encouraging foreign investments without restrictions on ownership, but has fairly rigid regulatory measures for foreign-technology and service agreements. India, on the other hand, has been restrictive in allowing foreign investments, particularly majority holdings, but has recently adopted a more flexible approach towards technology agreements, especially in high-technology areas. In the Republic of Korea, foreign investments were initially encouraged in the 1960s, but are much less so at present, while in recent years the acquisition of foreign technology has been greatly facilitated. In Mexico, since 1973, restrictions have been imposed on majority foreign holdings in most cases and fairly comprehensive legislation was also enacted on foreign-technology agreements, but implementation of the latter has been fairly flexible.

By the early 1980s, two major trends have become manifest in developing countries. First, in countries where the acquisition of foreign technology has not been regulated by the government or where its scope has been very limited, governments are paying increasing attention to foreign technology and the conditions of acquisition. While at present no specific regulatory measures may have been adopted, varying degrees of scrutiny are being exercised regarding the terms of technology transfer in the evaluation of foreign-investment proposals. A second important trend is visible in countries which have experience of over a decade with regard to foreign-technology regulation. In these countries, where fairly rigorous regulatory norms were introduced in the 1970s, there is increasing relaxation and liberalisation for the acquisition of more advanced technologies. This orientation in government outlook, which as been referred to as the 'new pragmatism', reflects the realisation that the adoption of strict measures may be counter-productive for the acquisition of advanced technologies. Thus, in several countries which were among the first to regulate the activities of multinational enterprises, both as investors and technology suppliers, policies have become differentiated. The sectors in which continuing control is exercised, or in which inflows of foreign investments and technology are encouraged and promoted, are bound to change over time, with changes in priorities and in capabilities of local industry. A dual approach, however, is expected to continue during this decade in most developing countries where a significant level of industrialisation has been reached.

Trends in Technology Flows

Foreign technology will undoubtedly continue to play a critical role in programmes of industrialisation if the objectives of industrialisation are to be achieved within targeted periods in different countries. Since, in most developing countries, the predominant proportion of foreign-technology inflow takes place through foreign direct investments, such investments by multinational enterprises will largely influence the nature and pattern of future flows of foreign technologies. Even though host-country governments can influence and promote technology inflow to a certain extent, the major determinants for foreign investors will continue to be the size of the domestic market, access to raw materials and advantages for export-oriented production, together with political and economic stability. Thus, apart from resource-rich developing countries, foreign direct investment flows will continue to be directed to large relatively advanced markets, such as Argentina, Brazil, Mexico, India and China, and to South-east Asian countries, including for export-oriented production.

The extent to which the trend of foreign direct investment flows which prevailed in the 1970s will continue depends on several factors. Two important issues stand out in the regard.

First, the debt problem of developing countries seems particularly severe in several of the traditionally largest receivers of foreign direct investments, such as Argentina, Mexico, Brazil, Venezuela and the Republic of Korea. The various restrictions which these governments are imposing or may impose on foreign-exchange outflows and the effects of austerity measures on local demand may act as disincentives for any significant increase in the inflow of foreign direct investments and, with it, of foreign technology.

Secondly, future growth of foreign direct investment flows for export-oriented production may also be hampered by certain emerging trends. An increase in protectionist measures in the United States and West European countries for traditional imports from export-oriented developing countries would strongly reduce the flow of such investments to these countries for offshore production of multinational enterprises. Apart from growing protectionism, certain technological developments may also further lower the attractiveness of these countries for offshore sourcing by multinational enterprises. With the increasing application of micro-electronics in production, automation of production processes in several sectors will reduce the labour component in final production. By reducing the labour-cost component through such processes, the low-wage factor advantage of traditionally labour-intensive export countries will decrease. Furthermore, the increased adoption of just-in-time inventory systems in the United States and Western Europe would mitigate against growth in the foreign sourcing of production and foreign direct investment flows which such production would require.

These trends indicate that the downturn in the rate of growth of foreign direct investment flows to developing countries, which started in the early 1980s, may continue through most of the current decade. At the same time, technology flows through alternative arrangements such as joint ventures and licensing agreements with unaffiliated companies are bound to increase in several countries. As pointed out earlier, the growing public-sector and private-sector domestically-owned companies in several of the countries would undoubtedly need and acquire a wide range of foreign technology. With advances in industrialisation, particularly in the newly industrialising countries, the need for foreign technology is growing rapidly and domestic companies are increasingly able to acquire and use foreign technology through licensing arrangements.

Taking account of the factors which influence foreign investment flows, such flows to the least developed countries are bound to remain limited. In several industrial sectors, particularly in those which use more sophisticated technologies, the limited local demand will not provide adequate returns for major investments by multinational enterprises. It is also in these countries that, because of low capital mobilisation and limited technological absorptive capacity of domestic companies, foreign technology cannot usually be acquired and utilised through licensing arrangements alone. Consequently, in the current decade, the uneven distribution of foreign-technology flows among the more advanced and the least developed countries of the Third World is likely to continue and may become even more accentuated.

References

1. For the United States, *Survey of Current Business*, United States Department of Commerce, Washington; for Japan, *Balance of Payments Monthly*, Bank of Japan, Tokyo; for the United Kingdom, *Business Monitor: Overseas Transactions*, Department of Trade and Industry, London; for France, *Statistiques et Etudes Financieres*, Ministry of the Economy, Finance and the Budget, Paris; and for the Federal Republic of Germany, *Monatsbericht der Deutsche Bundesbank*, Bundesbank, Frankfurt.
2. *Survey of Current Business*, various issues.
3. Rana K.D.N. Singh, 'Long-term Needs and Expectations of Developing Countries in Technology Licensing', paper prepared for the annual meeting of the Licensing Executives Society, Atlanta, Georgia, September 1981.
4. *Ibid.* Projections are based on figures of the Centre on Transnational Corporations, United Nations (UNCTC), New York.
5. Such a definition is presented in Jack Baranson, *International Transfer of Industrial Technology by US Firms and their Implications for the US Economy* (Washington: United States Department of Labor, 1976).
6. 'Fees and Royalty Payments of US Affiliates and US Parents', *Survey of Current Business*, various issues.
7. 'Overseas Royalties and Similar Transactions in 1977', *Trade and Industry*, Department of Trade and Industry, London, 1980.
8. *Transnational Corporations in World Development*, Third Survey (New York: United Nations, 1983).
9. *Salient Features and Trends in Foreign Direct Investment* (New York: Centre on Transnational Corporations, 1983) p. 15.
10. *Ibid.* Table 21.
11. *Ibid.* Table 21.
12. For foreign ownership in the manufacturing sector of several developing countries, see Katherin Marton. *Multinationals, Technology and Industrialization* (Lexington, Massachusetts: Lexington Books, 1986) ch. 2.
13. *Investment, Licensing and Trading: Korea*, Business International Corporation. New York, 1984, p. 4.
14. *Investment, Licensing and Trading: India*, Business International Corporation. New York, 1985, p. 3.
15. A survey of the current literature on the ownership of multinational enterprises in selected developing countries is presented in Marton, *op. cit.*, ch. 2.
16. Tan Siew-Ze and M. Kulansingnam, *New Forms of Foreign Investment in Malaysia: a Preliminary Survey* (Paris: OECD Development Centre, 1981).
17. Koo Bohn-Young, *Status and Changing Forms of Foreign Investment in Korea* (Paris: OECD Development Centre, 1982) Tables 27 and 28.
18. *Investment, Licensing and Trading: Brazil*, Business International Corporation, New York, 1985, p. 6.

19. Relatorio, Instituto Nacional de Propriedade Industrial, Rio de Janeiro, 1981, p. 8.
20. The process of technology acquisition by public-sector companies is demonstrated by the case analysis of Hindustan Machine Tools by R.S. Mascarenhas, *Technology Transfer and Development: India's Hindustan Machine Tool Company* (Boulder: Westview Press, 1982).
21. *The Comparative Studies of National Experience in Technology Policies: the Case of the Republic of Korea* (Seoul: Technology Transfer Centre, Korean Institute of Science and Technology, 1981).
22. *Foreign Investment Policy in India* (New Delhi: Indian Investment Centre, 1980) p. 6.
23. 'Fees and Royalty Payments of US Affiliates and US Parents', *Survey of Current Business*, August 1984.
24. For 1982, see S.K. Fung and J.E. Cassiolato, *The International Transfer of Technology to Brazil through Technology Agreements* (Cambridge, Massachusetts: MIT Press, 1976); and for 1981, see *Relatorio*, 1981.
25. *Relatorio*, 1981, p. 8.
26. *Anuario Estadistico: Inversiones Extranjeras y Transferencia de Tecnologia* (Mexico City: Direccion General de Inversiones Extranjeras y Transferencia de Tecnologia, 1981).
27. *The Comparative Studies of National Experience in Technology Policies: the Case of the Republic of Korea, op. cit.*, Appendix, Table 5.
28. *Ibid.*, Appendix, Table 4.
29. L. Young-Hoi, Korea's *Experience on Technology Transfer* (Seoul: Economic Cooperation Bureau, Ministry of Finance, 1985) p. 3.
30. *Costs and Conditions of Technology Transfer through Transnational Corporations* (Bangkok: ESCAP-UNCTC Unit, 1984) p. 70.
31. *Ibid.*, Pt 2, Sec. D.
32. *Investment, Licensing and Trading: India*, 1985, Table 2, p. 17.
33. *Ibid.*, p. 4.
34. S.K. Palhan, *Technology Policy and India's Experience in Technology Transfer* (New Delhi: Ministry of Industry, 1985), Annex, Fig. 7.

III THE GLOBAL FLOW OF CAPITAL

5. CULTURAL INFLUENCES ON INTERNATIONAL CAPITAL STRUCTURE

WILLIAM S. SEKELY
University of Dayton
William S. Sekely is Associate Professor and Chairman of the Department of Marketing at the University of Dayton. His recent publications include those on export management, multinational capital structure, and international product-communication strategies.

J. MARKHAM COLLINS
University of Tulsa
J. Markham Collins is Associate Professor of Finance and Director of Graduate Business Programs at the University of Tulsa. He has published papers in the areas of multinational financial structure, international cash management, and master limited partnerships.

Many studies have been conducted on the impact of various factors on international capital structure. The literature still reveals disagreement on the significance of the industry and country effects in determining capital structure, and the basis of country differences. This paper presents the results of a study of the debt structure of 677 firms in 9 industries headquartered in 23 countries. The results of this study tend to agree with the hypothesis that cultural differences are correlated with the significant country and minimal industry influences which are found. Further, there appear to be some inter-country influences caused by underlying cultural patterns among groups of countries.

Probably no topic in financial management has received more interest than that of capital structure. Indeed, if an optimal capital structure exists, management need only finance the firm using these optimal proportions and the objective of maximization of the value of the firm is assured. In fact, any movement toward that optimal capital structure reduces the cost of capital and increases the value of the firm.

The topic becomes more complex when one moves from consideration of domestic to multinational firms. Here one must consider the capital structure of foreign subsidiaries as well as that of the consolidated parent organization. Does one establish a target capital structure at the parent level and require subsidiaries to employ that structure? or does one find an optimal capital structure for each subsidiary, letting the consolidated parent's structure reflect the sum of the parts? Multinational managers would be better armed to make such choices if they understood why capital structure differs internationally.

Reprinted from the *Journal of International Business Studies,* 19:1 (Spring 1988), pp. 87–100 by permission of the publisher.

A number of studies on international capital structure have been published, many addressing various factors which might be determinants of it. In a review article in this journal, Stanley cited 102 references (Stanley, 1981). The two variables most often examined as capital structure determinants are industry and country. However, the literature reveals disagreement on the significance of the industry and country effects in determining capital structure.

One of the earliest examinations of the impact of industry and country found no significant industry effect for firms that are in the same industry but headquartered in different countries (Stonehill and Stitzel 1969). Other studies (notably Remmers, et al. 1974, Toy et al. 1974, Aggarwal 1981, and Errunza 1979) have found both industry and country effects to be significant, although not in every case examined.

In a more recent and comprehensive study, Collins and Sekely examined 411 companies in 9 countries and 9 industries (Collins and Sekely 1983). They found significant differences in the capital structures for firms headquartered in different countries, but less evidence was found for the impact of industry.

For the most part, the studies cited above found country influence to be significant. However, none explains the reason(s) behind the country effect. Stonehill and Stitzel suggested country-specific economic variables and cultural variables. Collins and Sekely examined several economic variables (size, tax rate, inflation) but found no significant relationships to capital structure. These authors suggested cultural factors influenced the capital structure decision, but did not attempt to measure or document the cultural influence.

Most other disciplines acknowledge cultural factors as playing a significant role in multinational business; however, finance tends to minimize the significance of cultural differences. This may be a serious mistake, for as Ball and McCulloch point out, "the study of foreign cultures is of primary importance to those in international business because cultural differences exert a pervasive influence on all of the business functions" (Ball and McCulloch 1982).

The authors of this paper recognize capital structure differences result from firm-specific policy decisions. They also recognize these decisions are based, in part, on the firm's managerial perceptions of the risk relative to the benefit of using fixed-cost debt financing. Prior studies support the contention that firms within an industry have more similar capital structures than firms across industries (Scott 1973) and firms headquartered in the same country have more similar capital structures than those firms headquartered across countries (Collins and Sekely 1983). Thus, firm-specific decisions may result in different capital structures for firms in the same industry and/or country, but these differences are less than the differences one finds across all industries or all countries.

Given that no prior study has established a significant relationship between an economic variable and international differences in capital structure, and given the conclusions of some earlier works that cultural factors must play a role, this research attempts to discover whether cultural factors are important determinants of capital structure. If some underlying relationship among countries can be shown to influence capital structure, future research should include more variables than simply economic ones in attempting to explain capital structure differences.

One of the major difficulties in this analysis is determining what is meant by cultural variables. Cultural factors cover a wide spectrum and include the whole set of social norms and responses that condition a population's behavior. It is these that make one social environment different from another and give each a shape of its own. While there is a great deal of discussion and debate over exactly what constitutes culture, most definitions include the following elements: social institutions, belief systems, aesthetics, language, and material culture. It is this last element, which includes a society's economic structure and technological capabilities, that probably is most closely related to the capital structure tendencies of a society. Specific areas most likely to influence capital structure include the different legal and tax systems, which give rise to differences in property rights across cultures. However, the potential impact on capital structure is not limited to the material portion of culture. There are a number of other aspects of a society's culture which also could impact on the financial structure of a firm.

It is not the purpose of this paper to determine which cultural elements play the most critical role in influencing multinational capital structure. This paper is limited in its purpose to determining if some broad cultural influence on capital structure can be found, beyond the more traditional industry and country influences. If this cultural influence exists, it should be reflected in the similarities of capital structure in organizations situated in countries having similar cultural backgrounds. If such similarities are found, it suggests further research on international capital structure can be enhanced by including variables such as the social and legal structures of countries in addition to the more traditional economic variables.

Scope of the Study

This present study extends the existing literature dealing with capital structure of firms headquartered in different countries in two ways:

1. More comprehensive conclusions are drawn from the analyses that were conducted. This is because the database was expanded significantly from that used in previous studies, both in terms of numbers of countries and also in terms of geographic coverage.

2. An analysis is conducted that goes beyond the statistical analysis of differences in debt ratios between companies. By disclosure of specific industry-country patterns of these ratios, it allows more direct evaluation of the impact of culture on capital structure.

In order to test the various aspects of the preceding two objectives, extensive examinations were made of the differences in capital structure between multinational companies in different industries and headquartered in various countries. Aspects of this have been the primary questions of a number of previous studies. After discussion of the differences mentioned above, two formal hypotheses were developed to test differences between and within various cultural groupings of countries. These have not been addressed directly in previous literature.

Methodology

This study employs data for 677 firms in 9 industries headquartered in 23 countries. These are the same industries and countries examined by Stonehill & Stitzel and Collins & Sekely plus firms from 14 other countries. Following these previous studies, the 10 firms in each industry/country cell with the highest level of sales were selected for the sample, with all firms included when less than ten. Data were obtained from *Moody's Industrial Manual* for the United States and *Moody's International Manual* for all foreign firms. By using a single source, the problem of inconsistent accounting treatments should be reduced, although not eliminated.

One-way and two-way analyses of variance were used in earlier studies to examine the impact that industries and countries have on the capital structure of the multinational firms being studied. However, several recent studies have shown that the distribution of debt ratios have not met the necessary conditions for use of parametric procedures. In the most recent of these, Martin and Henderson found that both major conditions for use of parametric procedures in the analysis of capital structure, normality of distribution of ratios within industries and equal variances across industries, did not occur[Martin and Henderson 1984].

The nonparametric analysis discussed below used the same data from 1979-1980 as the previously cited Collins and Sekely study and included data from the same time period for the additional countries. The debt ratio was defined as total debt to total assets at book value and calculated as one minus the rate of stockholders' equity to total assets.

The analysis utilized the Kruskal-Wallis test[1] to examine the 165 industry/country aggregate cells for consistency of country rankings among industries and industry rankings among countries.[2] To the extent that patterns can be found in these analyses, conclusions can be made as to the consistency of capital structure approaches taken by corporations in various countries, industries, or cultural groupings.

Results of Study

Debt ratios were calculated for all 677 companies in 9 industries and 23 countries. Averages for the 165 industry/country cells were than computed. Table 1 shows the results of these computations. These figures were then used as the basis of further analysis.

Given the significant interaction between the industry and country factors found in most previous studies, separate analyses for each factor were indicated (holding the other factor constant). Due to the differences in size of the 165 industry/country cells and the uncertainty of the underlying distributions which has been previously mentioned, a nonparametric test was used to examine the individual differences. The Kruskal-Wallis test for differences of ranks between multiple samples was used for the test. It uses the median ranks of the various country and industry debt ratios to test for differences between the samples.

Table 1
DEBT RATIOS FOR SELECTED INDUSTRIES AND COUNTRIES (ARRANGED IN ORDER OF INCREASING USE OF DEBT)

	Alcoholic Beverages	Auto-mobiles	Chemicals	Electrical	Foods	Iron & Steel	Nonferrous Metals	Paper	Textiles	Country Mean
Singapore		.22		.57	.28	.28	.38			.34
Malaysia	.20	.60	.41		.30	.38	.30	.77	.69	.37
Argentina		.42		.44	.35	.32				.38
Australia	.29	.50	.52	.51	.45	.53	.34	.48	.54	.46
Chile			.33	.28	.70	.48	.50	.47		.46
Mexico	.18		.47	.57	.59	.53	.47	.47		.47
South Africa	.59	.50	.51		.46	.53	.32	.42	.69	.50
Brazil		.66	.48	.53	.57	.61		.37		.54
United Kingdom	.45	.73	.50	.60	.55	.51	.57	.56	.52	.55
United States	.51	.58	.55	.54	.56	.54	.58	.58	.50	.55
Benelux	.41	.62	.60	.51	.64	.61	.49	.65	.54	.56
Canada	.55		.45	.52		.69	.61	.68		.58
India	.08	.75	.55			.49	.69	.74	.48	.60
Switzerland				.63	.54	.64				.60
West Germany		.57	.56	.66	.49	.60	.70	.70	.65	.62
Denmark	.66		.47	.74	.69	.52	.61	.74		.63
Spain		.59	.64	.45	.66	.82	.70	.85	.43	.64
Sweden	.79	.75	.67	.67	.63	.67	.64	.61	.60	.68
France	.56	.67	.72	.72	.78	.73	.67	.74	.74	.71
Finland	.40	.82	.71	.73	.77	.73	.72	.76	.82	.72
Pakistan		.87	.87				.71	.66	.70	.72
Norway			.76	.67	.79	.62		.82	.75	.74
Italy		.49	.65	.79	.85	.87	.86	.77	.83	.76
Industry Mean	.49	.58	.56	.59	.62	.61	.58	.63	.70	

Differences between Industries

The median ranks for the nine industries were computed. All the industries except alcoholic beverages had median ranks in the middle third of the total sample (i.e., median ranks between 56 and 110). Table 2 shows the ranks of all the industries among the test countries and the median rank for each industry. The Kruskal-Wallis test was conducted on the industry data. As might have been expected from observation, the differences in median rank were not found to be significant, even at the 0.1 significance level. Table 3 shows the results of this test. Thus, the influence of industry grouping appears to be minimal in the extended data set used in this study.

Differences in Countries

The same analysis was performed on the 23 countries among the various industries. Unlike the industry analysis, the country results showed clear groupings of differences. Seven countries had overall median rankings in the bottom third of all 165 country-industry cell rankings, 10 countries had overall median rankings in the middle third of all rankings, and 6 countries had overall median rankings in the top third of all rankings. There was a fairly strong pattern of economic development and the degree of debt used in the various countries. All the countries using little debt, with the exception of Australia and to a lesser degree South Africa, were less developed nations. All the countries using a great deal of debt, except Pakistan, were industrialized nations. The Kruskal-Wallis test was conducted on the country differences. It was found to be significant at greater than the 0.001 level. Thus, there appears to be a very definite relationship between country and use of debt in the extended data set that was examined. This influence is at least somewhat related to the economic development level of the country. Table 4 shows the results of the analysis.

Influence of Culture

The aspects just examined were very similar to a number of earlier studies. The following analyses are different in that they are looking for groups of countries with similar cultural attributes to help explain some of the differences in capital structure between multinational companies headquartered in different parts of the world. The first step in accomplishing this was to determine the appropriate groupings of countries.

One frequently used methodology for classification is the use of simple but meaningful groups of countries known as "cultural realms." These are groupings that have "fundamental unity of composition, arrangement, and integration of significant traits which distinguish them from other realms" (Broek and Webb 1973). Broek, James, and several others have developed cultural models for dividing the world into homogeneous groupings (Broek and Webb 1973; James 1976). While the specific terminology differs from model to model, the basic groupings are very similar. The model used in the present study utilizes the relevant parts of the Broek and James models. Seven cultural realms were identified for the 23 countries used in the study.

Table 2
DEBT-RATIO RANKS FOR SELECTED INDUSTRIES AND COUNTRIES (ARRANGED IN ORDER OF INCREASING USE OF DEBT)

	Alcoholic Beverages	Auto-mobiles	Chemicals	Electrical	Foods	Iron & Steel	Nonferrous Metals	Paper	Textiles	Country Median Mean
Singapore		6.0		77.0	6.0	6.0	17.5			6.00
Malaysia	3.0	88.0	20.5		9.5	17.5	9.5		120.0	17.50
Argentina		22.5		25.0	15.0	11.5				18.75
Mexico	2.0		33.0	77.0	84.0	59.5	33.0	33.0		33.00
Chile			13.0	6.0	25.5	37.5	46.0	33.0		35.25
Australia	8.0	46.0	55.5	51.0	27.5	59.5	14.0	37.5	64.0	46.00
South Africa	84.0	46.0	51.0		30.0	59.5	11.5	22.5	120.0	48.50
Brazil		109.0	37.5	59.5	77.0	93.0		17.0		68.25
United Kingdom	27.5	135.0	46.0	88.0	68.5	51.0	77.0	72.5	55.5	68.50
United States	51.0	81.0	68.5	64.0	72.5	64.0	81.0	81.0	46.0	68.50
Canada	68.5		27.5	55.5		120.0	93.0	117.0		80.75
Benelux	20.5	96.5	88.0	51.0	101.5	93.0	41.5	104.0	64.0	88.00
India	1.0	143.5	68.5	125.5		41.5	120.0	139.0	37.5	94.25
West Germany		77.0	72.5	109.0	41.5	88.0	125.5	125.5	104.0	96.00
Switzerland				98.5	64.0	101.5				98.50
Spain		84.0	101.5	27.5	109.0	156.5	125.5	160.5	24.0	102.75
Denmark	109.0		33.0	139.0	120.0	55.5	93.0	139.0		109.00
Sweden	153.0	143.5	113.0	149.0	98.5	113.0	101.5	93.0	88.0	113.00
Pakistan		164.0	164.0				129.5	109.0	125.5	129.50
France	72.5	113.0	131.0	131.0	151.0	143.5	113.0	139.0	139.0	131.00
Finland	19.0	156.5	129.5	135.0	149.0	135.0	131.0	146.5	156.5	135.00
Norway			146.5	113.0	153.0	96.5		156.5	143.5	145.00
Italy		41.5	104.0	153.0	160.5	164.0	162.0	149.0	159.0	156.00
Industry Median Rank	27.5	88.0	68.5	82.5	80.5	61.8	81.0	109.0	104.0	

Table 3
RESULTS OF KRUSKAL-WALLIS TEST DIFFERENCES BETWEEN INDUSTRIES

Industry	$\sum_{i=1}^{K} \frac{[R-(1/2)n^*(N+1)]}{n}$
Alcoholic Beverages	16276.9
Automobiles	1186.1
Chemicals	1216.8
Electrical	277.5
Foods	.4
Iron & Steel	158.2
Nonferrous Metals	142.3
Paper	4658.2
Textiles	2706.8
Total	26623.2

Kruskal-Wallis Test Statistic = 11.66
Level of Significance — Not significant at the .1 level

The realms and countries grouped in each one are:

Anglo-American:	Australia, Canada, South Africa, United Kingdom, and United States
Latin American:	Argentina, Brazil, Chile, and Mexico
West Central Europe:	Benelux, Switzerland, and West Germany
Mediterranean Europe:	France, Italy, and Spain
Scandinavia:	Denmark, Finland, Norway, and Sweden
Indian Peninsula:	India and Pakistan
Southeast Asia:	Malaysia and Singapore

Table 5 shows the groupings that were established. Also shown are the median ranks for the industries, countries, and cultural groups examined.

Analyses were conducted on the country industry cells in these groupings to determine if there were patterns of differences that could be determined. More specifically, the hypotheses tested in this study can be formally summarized as follows:

(1) $H^1{}_0$: Multinational companies located in different cultural realms have the same financial structures.

$H^1{}_1$: Multinational companies located in different cultural realms have significantly different financial structures.

Table 4
RESULTS OF KRUSKAI-WALLIS TEST DIFFERENCES BETWEEN COUNTRIES

Country	$\sum_{i=1}^{K} \frac{[R - (1/2) n^* (N+1)]}{n}$
Argentina	16641
Australia	16384
Benelux	841
Brazil	1837.5
Canada	45.4
Chile	9361.5
Denmark	1650.9
Finland	18769
France	16555.1
India	19.5
Italy	23005.1
Malaysia	13995.6
Mexico	9620.0
Norway	16120.2
Pakistan	15345.8
Singapore	18301.2
South Africa	7170.0
Spain	1937.5
Sweden	10370.0
Switzerland	75
United Kingdom	1764
United States	2116
West Germany	780.1
Total	202705.4

Kruskal-Wallis Test Statistic = 88.81
Level of Significance — Significant at the .001 level

(2) H^2_0: Multinational companies located in the same cultural realms, but possibly different countries, have the same financial structures.

H^2_0: Multinational companies located in the same cultural realms, but possibly different countries, have significantly different financial structures.

Table 5
DEBT-EQUITY RANKS FOR SELECTED CULTURAL GROUPINGS AND INDUSTRIES

Cultural Group	Alcoholic Beverages	Auto-mobiles	Chemicals	Electrical	Foods	Iron & Steel	Nonferrous Metals	Paper	Textiles	Country Median Rank	Group Median Rank
Anglo-American											59.5
Australia	8.0	46.0	55.5	51.0	27.5	59.5	14.0	37.5	64.0	46.00	
Canada	68.5		27.5	55.5		120.0	93.0	117.0		80.75	
South Africa	84.0	46.0	51.0		30.0	59.5	11.5	22.5	120.0	48.50	
United Kingdom	27.5	135.0	46.0	88.0	68.5	51.0	77.0	72.5	55.5	68.50	
United States	51.0	81.0	68.5	64.0	72.5	64.0	81.0	81.0	46.0	68.50	
Latin-American											33.0
Argentina		22.5		25.0	15.0	11.5				11.75	
Brazil		109.0	37.5	59.5	77.0	93.0		17.0		68.25	
Chile			13.0	6.0	125.5	37.5	46.0	33.0		33.25	
Mexico	2.0		33.0	77.0	84.0	59.5	33.0	33.0		33.00	
Mediterranean Europe											130.5
France	72.5	113.0	131.0	131.0	151.0	143.5	113.0	139.0	139.0	131.00	
Italy		41.5	104.0	153.0	160.5	164.0	162.0	149.0	159.0	156.00	
Spain		84.0	101.5	27.5	109.0	156.5	125.5	160.5	24.0	102.75	
Central Europe											90.0
Benelux	20.5	96.5	88.0	51.0	101.5	93.0	41.5	104.0	64.0	88.00	
Switzerland				98.5	64.0	101.5				98.50	
West Germany		77.0	72.5	109.5	41.5	88.0	125.5	125.5	104.0	96.00	
Scandinavia											131.0
Denmark	109.0		33.0	139.0	120.0	55.5	93.0	139.0		109.00	
Finland	19.0	156.5	129.5	135.0	149.0	135.0	131.0	146.5	156.5	135.00	
Norway			146.0	113.0	153.0	96.5		156.5	143.0	145.00	
Sweden	153.0	143.5	113.0	149.0	98.5	113.0	101.5	93.0	88.0	113.00	
Indian Peninsula											125.5
India	1.0	143.5	68.5	125.5		41.5	120.0	139.0	37.5	94.25	
Pakistan		164.0	164.0				129.5	109.0	125.5	129.50	
Southeast Asia											13.5
Malaysia	3.0	88.0	20.5		9.5	17.5	9.5		120.0	17.50	
Singapore		6.0		77.0	6.0	6.0	17.5			6.00	
Industry Median Rank	27.5	88.0	68.5	82.5	80.5	61.8	81.0	109.0	104.0		

Differences between Cultural Groupings

Table 5 shows the median ranks that were computed for the various cultural groups previously described. Using these divisions, the Kruskal-Wallis test for differences of rank was run on the median ranks of the various cultural groups. The results of the test indicate differences between the groups that are significant beyond the .001 level. Thus, the null hypothesis of no significant differences between the cultural groups must be rejected. Table 6 shows the calculations for this test. Table 6 also shows that the variance between cultural groups is very widespread. That is, the significant results come about because of wide variation between expected values and those found in four of the six cultural groups, not just a large deviation between one group and all the rest.

Low debt ratios are found in the Southeast Asian group, the Latin American group, and the Anglo-American group of countries. High debt ratios are found in the Scandinavian countries. Mediterranean countries, and the Indian Peninsula. The West Central European countries appear in the middle of the rankings. Thus, while there is a relationship between level of economic development and use of debt, it is not a very strong relationship. The Anglo-American group, with some of the most developed and industrialized countries in the world, are only very moderate user of debt compared to the average. The Indian Peninsula countries, on the other hand, with very low levels od development and industrialization, are very heavy users of debt. Also, while proximity is surely a contributing factor in similarities of country capital structure patterns, it is by no means sufficient, as the differences between Mediterranean Europe, West Central Europe, and Scandinavia show.

Table 6
RESULTS OF KRUSKAL-WALLIS TEST DIFFERENCES BETWEEN CULTURAL GROUPS

Cultural Group	$\sum_{i=1}^{K} \frac{[R - (1/2)n^* (N+1)]}{n}$
Anglo-American	19932.1
Latin-American	32119.1
Mediterranean Europe	35306.4
Central Europe	2.4
Scandinavia	31275.9
Indian Peninsula	6446.9
Southeast Asia	31570.0
Total	156652.8

Kruskal-Wallis Test Statistic = 68.63
Level of Significance — Significant at the .001 level

Differences within Cultural Groupings

In addition to testing for significant differences of debt ratios between the cultural groupings, each cultural group was tested for differences between the median ranks of the specific country-industry cells that made up the group. The null hypothesis of no differences in ranks could not be rejected at the 0.05 level for nay of the cultural groupings. There were differences at the .1 level for three of the cultural groupings, the Anglo-American group, the Mediterranean group, and the Scandinavian group. In the case of the Anglo-American group, most of the variation comes from the rankings in the Australian cells. In the case of the Mediterranean European group, most of the variation comes from the Italian cells, and in the Scandinavian group, the variation occurs between the more southern countries, Denmark and Sweden and the northern ones, Norway and Finland. Thus, while some variations exist within the cultural groupings, they are not very significant and usually the result of the differences in one country. Table 7 shows the results of the Kruskal-Wallis test for differences with the cultural groups.

Table 7
RESULTS OF KRUSKAL-WALLIS TEST DIFFERENCES WITHIN CULTURAL GROUPS

Cultural Group	Kruskal-Wallis Test Statistic	Level of Significance
Anglo-American	8.51	.1
Latin-American	5.93	N. S.
Mediterranean Europe	4.84	.1
West Central Europe	2.14	N. S.
Scandinavia	6.25	.1
Indian Peninsula	2.59	N. S.
Southeast Asia	.80	N. S.

Conclusions

The results of this study tend to confirm and strengthen the conclusion that cultural differences contribute to the significant country and minimal industry influences found in Stonehill and Stitzel (1969) and Collins and Sekely (1983). The study shows the original results are reasonably stable since 14 countries and 214 companies were added to those examined by Collins and Sekely with consistent results.

Further, examination of the ranks of the debt ratios shows distinct groups of countries with respect to the country median rank. While these groupings do not conclusively prove the cultural impact on financial structure, they do give clear indication of the influence in that direction. The results also imply that cultural analysis may be of significant value in financial planning by multinational corporations.

The present study found little industry impact on the debt ratios, which appears to contradict some of earlier works. However, there are several reasons that might reconcile the current results with previous studies.

First, a partial explanation for the reduction of industry influence comes from an overall reduction of industry distinctions. The number of large, multinational companies that are engaged in activities in only one industry has continued to diminish over the past several decades. Thus, as Bowen points out, "there is potential conglomeration effect which would tend to favor the null hypothesis of no industry influence" (Bowen, Daley, and Huber 1982).

Second, a significant increase in overall use of debt was found between the Stonehill and Stitzel study, using 1964 data, and the more recent studies that use 1980 data. However, the increase was not uniform across industries. The three industries that had the highest debt ratios in the earlier study increased by an average of 7.1%, while the three industries with the lowest ratios in the earlier study increased by 12.0%. This tended to diminish the industry influence on the debt ratio.

A third reason, especially concerning the differences between the Errunza results and those this study, were expressed in his summary. Errunza states that, "The assumptions of perfect and complete capital markets that underlie the modern theory of capital markets frequently do not hold in countries outside the U.S., especially in developing countries" (Errunza 1979). Thus, one may find differences in capital structure between different industries occurring, not because of the industry influence, but because of the "desire to conform to local financial norms" (Errunza 1979).

The results of this research once again support the argument that there are country effects on capital structure and that these result, in part, from cultural differences. Further, there appear to be some inter-country influences caused by underlying cultural patterns among groups of countries. Such cultural patterns may influence the development of financial institutions, attitudes toward risk, and/or attitudes toward debt. The influence of culture strongly suggests that future research examine the effects of social and legal arrangements on capital structure. Whatever the link between culture and decisionmaking, these differences do cause capital structure to differ between countries, and must be considered by financial managers in the global environment.

Notes

1. The Kruskal-Wallis test is a nonparametric procedure used in the experimental situation where K random samples have been obtained, one from each of K possibly different populations, and we want to test the null hypothesis that all of the populations are identical against the alternatives that some of the populations tend to furnish greater observed values than other populations (Conover 1971). The test statistic T is defined as:

$$T = \frac{12}{N(N+1)} \sum_{i+1}^{K} \frac{\left[R - (1/2)\, n^{*} (N+1)\right]}{n}$$

Where: T = Kruskal-Wallis test statistic

n = size of i random sample

$$N = \sum_{i+1}^{K} n$$

R = sum of the ranks assigned to sample i

2. Theoretically, 207 cells should have been developed. However, several countries did not have large companies in some of the industries.

References

Aggarwal, Raj. 1981. International differences in capital structure norms: An empirical study of large European companies. *Management International Review:* 75-88.

Bowen, Robert M., Lane A. Daley & Charles C. Huber. 1982. Evidence on the existence and determinants of inter-industry differences in leverage. *Financial Management,* Winter: 10-20.

Broek, Jan O. M. and J. W. Webb. 1973. *A geography of mankind.* New York: McGraw-Hill.

Conover, W. J. 1971. *Practical nonparametric statistics.* New York: John Wiley and Sons.

Child, John & Monir Tayeb. 1983. Theoretical perspectives in cross-national organizational research. *International Studies of Management and Organizations,* Winter: 23-70.

Collins, J. Markham & William S. Sekely. 1983. The relationship of headquarters, country and industry classification to financial structure. *Financial Management,* Autumn: 45-51.

Errunza, Vihang R. 1979. Determinants of financial structure in the central American common market. *Financial Management,* Autumn: 72-77.

James, Preston E. 1976. World view of major culture regions. In Fred E. Dohis and Lawrence M. Sommers, ed., *World Regional Geography: A Problem Approach.* New York: West Publishing Co.

Martin, Linda J. & Glenn V. Henderson. 1984. Industry influence on financial structure: A matter of interpretation. *Review of Business and Economic Research,* 19(2): 57-67.

Moody's industrial manual. 1981. New York, Moody's Investor Service, Inc.

Moody's international manual 1981. New York, Moody's Investor Service, Inc.

Remmers, Lee, Arthur Stonehill, Richard Wright & Theo Beekhuisen. 1974. Industry and size as debt ratio determinants in manufacturing internationally. *Financial Management,* Summer: 23-32.

Scott, David. 1972. Evidence on the importance of financial structure. *Financial Management,* Summer: 45-50.

—— & John D. Martin. 1975. Industry influence on financial structure. *Financial Management,* Spring: 67-73.

Stonehill, Arthur & Thomas Stitzel. 1969. Financial structure and multinational corporations. *California Management Review,* Fall: 91-96.

——, Theo Beekhuisen, Richard Wright, Lee Remmers, Norman Toy, Antonio Pares, Alan Shapiro, Douglas Egan & Thomas Bates. 1975. Financial goals and debt ratio determinants: A survey of practice in five countries. *Financial Management,* Autumn: 27-41.

Toy, Norman, Arthur Stonehill, Lee Remmers, Richard Wright & Theo Beekhuisen. 1974. A comparative international study of growth, profitability, and risk as determinants of corporate debt ratios in the manufacturing sector. *Journal of Financial and Quantitative Analysis*, November: 875-886.

6. NEW FORMS OF INVESTMENT IN DEVELOPING COUNTRIES BY US COMPANIES: A FIVE INDUSTRY COMPARISON

LAWRENCE G. FRANKO

Lawrence G. Franko is Professor of Finance and Strategy at the College of Management, University of Massachusetts at Boston.

This article examines the use of NFI's in DC's by 70 U.S. corporations in five industries. More specifically, it explores: (1) the extent of use of reduced and non equity forms of involvement by U.S. firms in DC's in the mid-1980s; (2) the motives and patterns of rejection or acceptance by U.S. firms of NFI's; and (3) the interaction of patterns of acceptance or rejection with host-country development polices.

This study surveys the use of "new forms of investment" (NFI's) in developing countries (DC's) by the 70 leading, internationally active U.S. corporations in five industries: automobiles, motor vehicle parts, food processing, pharmaceuticals and computers. The sample includes four U.S. auto producers, the 10 leading auto parts producers, the 29 largest food processors, 12 leading pharmaceutical firms and the 15 top computer industries. Developing countries were defined as all countries outside of the OECD and the Soviet bloc, plus Turkey.

The aims of the study were, first, to determine the extent that NFI's are used in DC's, and second, to examine motives and patterns of U.S. corporate behavior with respect to acceptance or avoidance of such NFI's. "NFI's" were defined as minority and 50-50 equity participation, as well as licensing agreements between U.S. and host-country firms.

A third aim was to derive judgements and hypotheses linking the NFI practices of U.S. firms to host DC development policies. In the absence of comprehensive data on the nature, activities and motives of the host-country partners or collaborators in NFI's, and careful consideration of the macro and microeconomic policy environment in particular host countries, definitive judgements on the virtues or evils of NFI's from the host-country point of view are not possible. However, the patterns of corporate practice examined here do interact with the host-country development strategies and policies. These interactions will be commented upon when appropriate.

The author would like to gratefully acknowledge the support of the OECD Development Center for sponsoring the original research, the research assistance of Jeanne Gibson and Ms. Laureen Morrow, and the Faculty Editor, Ellen Auster, for her insights, suggestions and editorial preparation.

Reprinted from the *Columbia Journal of World Business* Vol.22, No. 2 (Summer, 1987) by permission of the publisher.

The findings indicate that the use of NFI's by U.S. firms was primarily a function of the interaction of competitive behavior in oligopolistic industries and the ownership and trade-protection policies of a number of DC governments. NFI's were generally avoided by companies who were industry leaders and accepted by second rank, or "outsider" firms attempting to match the geographical spread of their larger brethren. The minority of these NFI's were found in only a few DC's which pursued aggressive ownership policies, import substitution, and protected market "development" policies. NFI's were considerably less common in the export promoting DC's not known as "newly industrialized countries," or NIC's, who are viewed as having pursued the most effective development strategies of the past two decades.

Automobiles and Automobile Components

The use of NFI's by U.S. automobile manufacturers in developing countries is limited in scope and importance.

By 1984, Ford and Chrysler had 100% ownership of essentially all of their manufacturing and assembly operations in both developed and less developed countries. Although General Motors had nine minority and 50-50 owned joint ventures in DC's, only one of these operations, (that in Korea), could be considered a full-scale auto manufacturing undertaking. At least three operations were producing components for local wholly-owned GM assembly facilities (Table 1). The comparatively tiny American Motors (AMC), only bringing in 3.3 billion dollars in sales while GM was bringing in 74.6 billion, was the only automobile manufacturer that had joint ventures, and joint ventures with licensing accords that appeared significant relative to the firm's total volume of business (Table 1).

This limited use of NFI's by American automobile manufacturers, and the somewhat more frequent use of minority and 50-50 ventures in DC's by the 10 leading U.S. motor vehicle component manufacturers (See Table 2 and the discussion below) can best be understood in the context of a world automotive industry that is constantly changing.

During the 50's and 60's, exports from U.S. auto producers increasingly gave way to local assembly, primarily as a result of tariff barriers. During the period 1953-1973 exports of completely built units and completely knocked down units decreased from 55% in 1953 to 31% in 1963 to 19% in 1973 (Gerald Bloomfield, *The World Automotive Industry,* 1978, p. 156).

The development of a motor vehicle industry within a new country typically evolves through the following stages: (1) completely built vehicles are imported by dealers; (2) completely knocked down vehicles imported from overseas are assembled locally; (3) more and more locally made constituent parts are used for assembly of completely knocked down vehicles; and finally (4) full local manufacture of motor vehicles (Bloomfield, p. 159). Most countries having partial local ownership are in the second or third phase, the assembly of completely knocked down vehicles. Virtually all such assembly (or assembly plus use of local components) has taken place as a

Table 1
US COMPANIES IN THE AUTOMOBILE INDUSTRY: MINORITY AND 50-50 JVS IN DEVELOPING COUNTRIES (1983)

Company (ranked by size)	Size $Bn 1983	No. of Foreign Operations	No. of DC Operations	No. of Minority & 50-50 JVs in DCs	% of DC Ops. which are minority or 50-50 JVs	% of all Foreign Ops. which are minority or 50-50 JVs in DCs	Location and % Ownership of Minority JVs in DCs with product line where known
General Motors	74.6	73	27	9	33%	12%	Tunisia (20%), Egypt (31%), Korea (50% with Daewoo Industries) auto & truck mnufacturer, Kenya (49%), Ecuador (36.95%) vehicle assembly, component manufacture, Eduador (22%) assembly, Mexico (40%) components, Mexico (40%) assembly of diesel engines, Venezuela (49%) assembly (radiators)
Ford	44.5	17	4	0	0	0	Plans to acquire 30% of a Turkish vehicle assembler
Chrysler	13.2	1	1	0	0	0	Various licensing and technical assistance contracts with assemblers of exported Chrysler CKD kits, some of which replace previous equity positions
AMC	3.3	5	5	5	100	100	Mexico (40%) auto assembly, Egypt (minority) assembly, Venezuela (minority) assembly, Indonesia (minority) assembly, P. R. China (31.35%), estab. 1983, jeep production
Total Industry		96	37	14	14.6%	38%	

Table 2
US AUTO COMPONENTS INDUSTRY: MINORITY JVS IN DCS (1983)

Company (ranked by size)	Size $Bn 1983	No. of Foreign Operations	No. of DC Operations	No. of Minority or 50-50 JVs in DCs	% of DC Ops. which are minority or 50-50 JVs	% of all Foreign Ops. which are minority or 50-50 JVs in DCs	Location and % Ownershiup of Minority JVs in DCs with product line where known	Main Product Line of Firm other than auto % non-auto related
Rockwell	8.1	38	7	1	14%	39%	Mexico (N. A.); auto components	Aerospace, electronics, energy, power tools (78%)
TRW	5.5	28	2	0	0	0		Electronics & space systems, industrial & energy equipment (68%)
Bendix (Acquired by Allied Corp. 1983)	4.4	22	12	3	25	14	Mexico (40% + 40%); Venequela (NA); auto components	Aerospace electronics, metal working equipment (53%)
Dana	2.8	20	8	7	88	35	Argentina, Brazil, Colombia, India, Mexico, S. Korea, Venezuela	Industrial power drive (22%)
Borg Warner	3.5	30	8	1	12.5	3	Mexico (49%); air conditioning	Air conditioning, chemical and plastics, industrial equipment (63%) Industrial power drive (22%)

Eaton	2.7	49	10	8	80	16	India (33%); axles Malaysia (40%); Mexico (40%); Mexico (25%) Phillipines (30%); Singapore (40%); Venezuela (49%) Zimbabwe (49%)	Industrial control components, special vehicles (53%)
Cummins	1.6	13	8	4	50	31	India (50%), engines Brazil (36%), Brazil (21%), Mexico (40% state co. ptr.), Licensing, agreements in China, S. Korea, Venezuela	
Paccar	1.4	10	1	1	100	10	Mexico (49%); diesel trucks	Railroad cars, mining & logging equipment (24%)
Timkin	0.9	7	2	0	0	0		Specialty steels (some for use in auto industry) (22%)
Champion	0.8	26	6	0	0	0		Coating equipment, specialty steels (30%)
		243	64	25				

result of host-country trade restrictions and local content requirements. Table 3 summarizes the nature of such requirements on four DC's where NFI are found. The full manufacture stage is less common in most developing countries largely because of the difficulties in achieving economics of scale in either assembly or parts production within their small DC market.

Almost all of the automobiles and automobile manufacturers in developing countries direct their products towards highly protected local markets. A reverse flow of exports from developing countries to developed markets of vehicles and components is just beginning, but will likely be slow in developing, despite strong government pressures to export (Bloomfield, p. 158). Although the "world car concept" was highly publicized, efforts to integrate production and component plants on a global basis have met with only moderate success (Harvard Business School, *Note on the World Auto Industry in Transition,* 1982, p. 23). This effort was impeded by pressure from local suppliers, the problem of excess capacity, and the heavy investment required to establish new "common" plants. Where it has met with some success, e.g., in Ford's export of engines from Brazil or Chrysler's exports from Mexico, it has taken place in a wholly or majority MNE-owned context.

Table 3
SELECTED AUTO POLICIES OF DEVELOPING COUNTRIES

Mexico	Local content requirement of 75%; imports of components must be offset by exports; import licenses required; tariff of 35%–100%; government ownership in some firms (e.g., DINA); Engines must be produced in Mexico.
Brazil	Local content requirement of 95%; tariffs of 185%–205%; imports of cars currently embargoed; tariffs on parts and equipment reduced in return for export commitments from manufacturers—VW committed to export $1.5 billion worth (1973–1983); AM committed to 1.0 billion (1976–1986); government GEIA agency coordinates industry development; limited government ownership (e.g., 45% of Fiat).
Nigeria	Local content of 30% required after three years production (scheduled to rise to 50% in 1983); tariffs range between 50% and 250%; imports of cars with engines of 2500cc and above prohibited; others require import licenses; government ownership.
Korea	Local content of 62%–94% except for Ford Granada (21%) and Peugot 604 (20%) which carry absolute requirements of five Korean cars exported for each CKD kit imported; 80% tariff; imports require license from Auto Trade Association (rarely granted); export targets negotiated by companies and government; government overseeing restructuring of industry.

Source: **Motor Vehicle Manufacturers Association** and **Auto Situation: 1980**, as cited in Harvard Business School, *Note on Auto Sector Policies*, 1982, Exhibit 5, p. 24

General Motors

General Motors has the most instances of minority or 50-50 ventures in DC's among American vehicle producers (Table 1). Nonetheless, its executives state that wholly-owned subsidiaries are preferred because they permit a "greater degree of action and total control within the system," (GM, questionnaire response, 1984). GM executives interviewed further explained that their use of minority or 50-50 forms is essentially limited to countries where joint ownership is required by law.

In spite of minority or 50-50 joint venture making up a significant proportion of the number of GM's DC subsidiaries (9 out of 27,) these ventures account for a very small amount of GM's business in DC's, and a tiny proportion of the activity of the total corporation. Moreover, only one of the nine (the 50-50 venture in Korea) can be said to be undertaking auto production, *per se*. The others either assemble GM vehicles from export CKD (completely knocked down) kits for highly protected local markets, or as in Mexico and Venezuela, produce components for supply to a 100% GM owned auto manufacturing subsidiary.

Limited in importance and isolated from GM's core activities by trade barriers as they may be, these NFI's are a relatively new form of activity for the world's largest vehicle manufacturer. Until the 70's, GM was a firm that regularly announced that it "never" departed from wholly-owned operations. Only when smaller, essentially non-American competitors' acceptance of such ventures, combined with host country preferences and pressures, began to threaten GM with exclusion from established DC markets, notably in Latin America, did ownership policy change. A recent example of this is the establishment of a joint venture between GM and Daewoo Precision Industries Ltd. of South Korea to produce starters, alternators, ignition distributors, and coils (*Business Week,* November 12, 1984). GM was attracted by the lower wage rates in South Korea, which would reduce the cost of sourcing components.[1]

Ford

Until 1983, Ford had no minority or 50-50 joint ventures in the DC's. This practice was directly linked to the firm's leading role in the world auto industry as a *'supra-national'* specializer and integrator of production across borders. Ford's practice of first producing components and sub-assemblies in factories in different nations, and then assembling them after cross-border shipment on a regional or even global basis, has its closest parallel in the integrated operations of IBM in the international computer industry. Both have structured their supply and logistics systems on a "product by (national) plant" basis, treating Europe or Latin America as "one factory" to the maximum extent possible. Ford also has some of the most highly harmonized or standardized brand name, image, style and other marketing policies across borders in the industry: a Ford product, wherever it is produced. Moreover, although Ford is not the largest auto producer, it does have the most lengthy experience in international manufacturing and assembly operations. It has historically led General Motors in absolute volume of business done outside the U.S. market. Thus, for most purposes, Ford sees itself as a global industry leader with less of a need or desire to enter into joint venture or co-production relationships.

Notwithstanding Ford's 100% or dominant majority ownership policy, the firm has begun to acquire a 30% stake in a Turkish vehicle assembler. This change in policy appears to be based on Ford's experience in having a minority position in Japan's Mazda and in having been able to maintain minimal competition between Ford products and that of its associate company. Given Ford's historic supranational integration and strong corporate marketing identity, however, there appears little probability of any major shift toward acceptance of minority and 50-50 ventures, or other co-production *'new forms'* on the part of the firm in DC's.

Chrysler

Chrysler's lack of minority or 50-50 joint ventures in DC's as of 1983/84 (Table 1), or indeed any equity ownership positions in DC's other than a 100% owned subsidiary in Mexico, represents a radical change in that firm's practice since the 60's and 70's. Chrysler was one of the few automobile companies based in any advanced country to accept minority positions during the 60's. Its purpose in doing so was to try to match the international scope of the dominant GM and Ford companies. Chrysler's behavior provided a textbook illustration of the "Wells effect;" the acceptance by a smaller, follower company in an oligopolistic industry of less than controlling ownership. This is a result of one or more factors including: (1) the desire to match the country an market risk profiles of large oligopolistic competitors, and to keep rough parity (or gain) in relative world market share, with constrained financial and managerial resources; (2) a lack of bargaining power compared to dominant competitors *vis-a-vis* host governments seeking to impose, or host firms seeking to obtain, foreign skills without ceding ownership control; and (3) the MNE firm's own relative inexperience or lack of knowledge of foreign operations (Stopford and Wells, 1972; Franko, 1971).

Chrysler's "catch-up" effort proved vain, as the combination of the firm's high-cost, low market share position, and its unintegrated, international joint venture network proved unable to withstand Japanese competitors and world recession in the late 70's. From 1970-1981, Chrysler went through a "demultinationalization" process: selling off or otherwise eliminating all but one equity position in each overseas activity. All but one of Chrysler's minority positions were sold, as were many 100% and majority ventures. The one minority company that was kept, in Mexico, was made into a 100% owned company and was very closely integrated with U.S. operations.

American Motors

American Motors, by far the smallest U.S. automobile vehicle producer, and one of the smallest vehicle producers worldwide, has all of its five equity ownership positions in DC operations in the form of minority joint ventures (Table 1). AMC also has licensing arrangements with firms in Bangladesh, India, Korea, Kenya, Morocco, Pakistan, Sri Lanka, the Philippines, Taiwan and Thailand, primarily for assembly of its Jeep vehicles from components and CKD kits exported from the U.S.A.

AMC has long presented a proto-typical example of a resource constrained firm in an oligopolistic industry, (with some remaining product strengths, e.g., the "Jeep" line), pursuing an oligopolistic "market matching," international "catch-up" strategy. As in other industries, and as in the early history of Chrysler, a competitively weak firm has offered host-countries what they perceive to be a better deal in the hope of gaining world market share by foreclosing or limiting local market access by industry *'majors'*.

AMC's propensity to undertake minority ventures in LDC's, which dates back to the 60's, has been reinforced by the French Renault's acquisition of a 40% shareholding in the firm in 1979. During the late 60's and early 70's Renault was one of the most aggressive "offerers of joint ventures" to Latin American, African, and Eastern European partners, in an effort to gain world market share at the expense of "100% holdouts" GM and Ford. Indeed, it is most doubtful that GM would have accepted the joint ventures it did in Ecuador, Venezuela, Tunisia and Egypt if the French company's effort to pry loose American companies' historical hammer locks on Latin American markets since the days of the Andean Common market (including in Allende's Chile), had not been so strong. Since the early 80's, Renault has had minority participation in vehicle assembly and components manufacturing in several Latin American countries, including Mexico, Colombia, Peru, and Argentina (Franko and Heptonstall, 1981).

The largest, most recent of AMC's "new forms" agreements has been its highly publicized minority-equity entry into the People's Republic of China:

> **AUTOMOTIVE JOINT VENTURE**
>
> China—The Beijing Jeep Corp, a joint venture established by American Motors Corp of the US and the Beijing Automobile Works, was officially inaugurated in mid-January. AMC, which holds a 31.3% equity share in the venture, contributed US$8 million in cash and the equivalent of US$8 million in advanced technology. The plant will produce a new four-wheel drive model, known as the BJ 212, which will require less material to construct than other models presently produced in China and also will consume less fuel . . . . Although the vehicles produced at the factory will be primarily for sale in the PRC, some products will be exported through AMC's sales outlets. The US firm hopes the Peking operation will serve eventually as a regional base from which it can more effectively compete in the Asian market. (*Business China*, Feb. 15, 1984).

It should be noted that according to the US Department of Commerce, the Chinese-made vehicles are not intended to be exported to the US. Also, according to the agreed schedule of operations, it will be some six to seven years before a fully AMC vehicle will be manufactured and only then could exports be envisaged. In the meantime AMC will be supplying components and intermediate products (*New York Times*, May 6, 1983; *Business China*, Volume IX, no. 11, p. 48).

Thus, as in so many other cases, a U.S. company's acceptance of a minority position is predicated on a "forward-integration link" aimed at marketing parent company exports and at isolating the ventures output from the firm's core business.

Auto and Vehicle Components

Minority and 50-50 ventures are more common among U.S. vehicle components manufacturers than they are in the four auto assembly companies. Twenty-five of the 64 (39%) of the subsidiaries and affiliates in DC's of the 10 leading U.S. components manufacturers are minority or 50-50 ventures (Table 2) and account for slightly more than 10% of all 243 foreign operations (by numbers) of these 10 component producers.

In general, minority and 50-50 ventures produce relatively low-technology items. They are also disproportionately located in countries with highly protected markets, such as Mexico and India, where government pressures for local majority ownership have been strong.

It is noteworthy that only three out of the ten U.S. parents, Eaton, Dana, and Cummins, account for 19 out of the 25 minority and 50-50 ventures. TRW, Timpkin, and Champion Sparkplugs have none at all. Most of these firms have been vigorously allocating their resources to activities other than auto parts and components: Rockwell to aerospace and factory automation, TRW to defense electronics, Borg Warner to chemicals, etc. The low-technology DC minority ventures are apparently aimed at capturing one last bit of returns from sectors in which companies are losing their firm specific advantages. From the U.S. corporate point of view they could be viewed as new forms of divestment.

Food Processing

The U.S. food processing industry can be described as a relatively stable oligopoly. The growth rate of the industry and the firms within it is low compared to other sectors, and companies jockey for what in other industries would be marginal changes of position.

With few exceptions (most notably Coca-Cola, CPC and the much smaller International Multifoods) U.S. food processors can be characterized more as "U.S. companies with foreign operations" rather than as widespread MNE's (see Table 4 column X3). Foreign sales rarely account for more than a third of total sales.

This domestic orientation of U.S. food processors appears to be due in part to the position held outside of North America by entrenched foreign competitors such as Nestle, Unilever, and Associated British Foods, who dominate not only European markets but also tend to have far more activity in Third World countries than the U.S. does. It is reinforced by the advertising intensive orientation of U.S. firms, whose vast domestic market lends itself to emphasizing brand differentiation, image and "customer pull" sales strategies.

In spite of this domestic orientation, the global competitive position of U.S. food processing firms is exceedingly strong. In 1983, 13 of the world's 20 largest food processing companies were U.S.-based, compared with 14 in 1970. The erosion in the world market share of U.S. firms in other industrial sectors such as steel, automobiles or consumer electronics sector. In 1960, U.S. food product company share was 65% of the total consolidated sales of the 12 largest food firms. It was still 65% in 1982 (see Table 5). Nestle's gains over these two decades took place at the expense of British and Canadian firms, not of U.S. companies.

Table 4
US FOOD PROCESSING COMPANIES: USE OF MINORITY AND 50-50 JOINT VENTURES IN DC'S (AS A % OF DC AND OF TOTAL FOREIGN OPERATIONS), COMPANY SIZE, ADVERTISING INTENSITY, AND % OF SALES FOREIGN

	% of DC operations which are 50-50 or minority JV's	% of total foreign operations 50-50 or minority JV's	Company size (sales, $bn 1983)	Advertising as a % of sales, 1983	Non-US as a % of total sales 1983
Observation	**Y1**	**Y2**	**X1**	**X2**	**X3**
R. J. Reynolds	5%	4%	13.5 ($bn)	4.6%	21%
Dart & Kraft	12	2	9.7	3.5	29
Beatrice	27	7	9.1	2.9	23
Gen Foods	25	10	8.6	5.1	25
Pepsico	0	0	7.9	6.1	20
CocaCola	0	0	6.8	6.7	43
Consolidated	7	1	6.6	6.6	22
Nabisco	19	6	6	3.8	33
Gen Mills	9	2	5.5	6.1	9
Ral-Purina	50	17	4.8	8	24
Borden	17	7	4.2	5.2	19
CPC Intl	0	0	4	4	65
Esmark	0	0	4	6	18
Heinz	30	4	3.7	6.8	36
Pillsbury	75	26	3.7	2.9	10
Carnation	42	17	3.4	1.9	32
Campbell	0	0	3.3	4.2	18
Quaker Oats	0	0	2.7	1.7	36
Kellogg	11	4	2.4	8.4	36
Intl Multfds	40	33	1.1	2.7	44
Gerber	50	33	.6	2.4	5

Sources: For Columns Y1, Y2 and X, see Table 5. Advertising/sales ratios and foreign sales % are from Annual Reports and Moodys.

Thus, at the industry or company level of aggregation, there is no trace of either a declining absolute competitive advantage or a skill-base erosion of U.S. firms. Furthermore, aside from some increased imports of Japanese noodles and other specialties, there seems to be little evidence of any shift in U.S. food processors' comparative advantage in international trade.

Table 5
US FOOD PROCESSING INDUSTRY: COMPANIES WITH MINORITY OR 50-50 JVS IN DCS (1983)

Company (ranked by size)	Size $Bn 1983	No. of Foreign Operations	No. of DC Operations	No. of Minority or 50-50 JVs in DCs	% of DC Ops. which are minority or 50-50 JVs	% of all Foreign Ops. which are minority or 50-50 JVs in DCs	Location and % Ownershiup of Minority JVs in DCs with product line where known	Main Product Line or Firm
R. J. Reynolds (Del Monte)	13.5	27	19	1	5%	4%	Guatemala (25%)	Tobacco, food processing (20%)
Dart & Kraft	9.7	79	17	2	12	2	Brazil (40%), batteries; Venezuela (20%)	Dairy products, margarines and oils, misc. consumer products
Beatrice	9.1	281	75	20	27	7	Mexico (5–24%, 2–49%, 27%, 48.99%); Trinidad (3–17.2%); Ecuador (49%); Malaysia (25%); Singapore (25%); Venezuela (48, 89.9%); China (50%); Hong Kong (24.5%, 44.4%)	Foods, dairy products
Gen. Foods	8.6	39	16	4	25	10	Brazil (45%, 50%)); Colombia (49%); Rep. of Korea (49%)	Coffee, wheat flour, cereal, pet foods
Consolidated	6.6	125	15	1	7	1	Indonesia (49%)	Vegetable proc., coffee
Nabisco	6.0	68	21	4	19	6	Mexico (49%, 30%); Venezuela (49%); India (38%)	Cookies & crackers, pkgd. food
Gen. Mills	5.5	43	11	1	9	2	Venezuela (16%)	Cereals
Ralston-Purina	4.8	6	2	1	50	17	Mexico (49%)	Animal feeds, pet foods, fisheries, cereals
Borden	4.2	68	30	5	17	7	Chile (50%); Mexico (50%); Colombia (2–50%); Hong Kong (50%)	Dairy products, animal food, pet foods

Heinz	3.7	28	3	1	30	4	Morocco (50%)	Vegetable processing, baby foods, fisheries
Pillsbury	3.7	23	8	6	75	26	Jamaica (38% flour mill, balance of shares publicly traded); Philipines (32% flour milling); Guatemala 25% flour milling, local partner is a family firm); El Salvador (10% flour mill); Mexico (49% pasta, flour mill); Hong Kong (50% soy sauce, Chinese food)	Wheat flours
Carnation	3.4	60	24	10	42	17	Dominican Republic (49%); Peru (3–41%); Jamaica (30%); Nigeria (40%); Phillipines (30%, 40%); Malaysia (25%); Singapore (30%)	Dairy products
Kellogg	2.4	25	9	1	11	4	Jamaica (48%)	Packaged cereals
IC Industries	2.2	34	4	2	50	6	Brazil (NA auto parts); Costa Rica (30%)	Canned milk, beverages, auto service
Hershey	1.7	5	3	2	67	40	Phillipines (30%); Brazil (22.5%)	Cocoa products
A. E. Stanley	1.7	8	1	1	100	13	Mexico (50% corn starch, oils, feeds)	Corn and soybean processing, food service, animal feeds
Int'l Multi-foods	1.1	6	5	2	40	33	Mexico (45%); Egypt (25%)	Wheat flours, corn milling
Gerber	0.6	3	2	1	50	33	Mexico (49%)	Vegetable processing, baby foods
		868	215	65				

Sources: Moody's Industrial Manual, 1984; The World Directory of Multinational Enterprises, 1983; Corporate Reports and Interviews.

Indeed, especially compared to British companies in the industry, one of the most salient characteristics of the U.S. food processing industry is its domestic agricultural base that was second to none, both in the scope of produce supplied and in economic productivity. British (and other European) firms had the mission of supplying the home country with "colonial produce" as a central part of their historical experience. During and after the time colonies became independent, firms like the U.K.'s Booker McConnell had to adapt to the new multi-dimensional reality in DC's in terms of increased local skills, availability to host countries of alternative sources of technical and marketing expertise and distribution channels, and host-country desires to own their own agricultural land and to supervise farming and plantation activities. NFI's became a largely defensive necessity for such supply seeking MNE's if they were to maintain any role in conducting business in and with the Third World (Cantwell and Dunning, 1984).

However famous, or infamous, one or two U.S. firms with a somewhat parallel experience in the sourcing end of the banana business have become,[2] the vast majority of U.S. food processing firms have had an entirely different history. The central theme in the development of U.S. food processing firms has been the development and application of new technologies of mass advertising, large scale distribution, and mass production to a fecund domestic source of agricultural supply.

The U.S. food processing industry has advertising and marketing as a prime strategic focus. Advertising expenditure levels in excess of 6% sales are hardly unusual in the industry (Table 4). It is also a remarkably capital intensive industry. Net fixed capital per employee in the top 15 U.S. companies averaged over $11,000 in 1975, compared, for example, to $8,500 in Aerospace, $6,800 in Electrical Equipment and $10,400 in Computers and Office Equipment. Corresponding figures for Pharmaceuticals and Chemicals were $13,400 and $22,900 respectively (Center for International Competitive Analysis Data Base).

The capital intensity of the U.S. firms plus their typically high level of advertising intensity yields a one-of-a-kind marketing mix that is peculiar to the U.S., Canada and to a new Northern European markets. This marketing mix uses mass media advertising to pull large volumes of produce through a large scale, capital intensive production system. It is not a strategy that appears either highly "appropriate" to DC factor proportions or to the DC's typically small fragmented markets, especially taking into consideration the limited development of mass advertising media in many Third World markets. Nor is the emphasis on proprietary brands and mass marketing congenial to "new forms" of foreign investment, especially if "new forms" is understood as shared equity ownership (Franko, 1971).

Thus, the typical U.S. food processor overseas operation is either a wholly-owned subsidiary or a majority joint venture. Eleven of the 29 leading U.S. food processing firms (including Pepsi Co., Coca-Cola, CPC International, United Brands, Archer Daniels Midland, Esmark, Campbell, Quaker Oats, Central Soya, Anderson Clayton, and Castle & Cook), have no minority or 50-50 joint ventures in developing countries. Only 65 (6%) of the 1074 foreign operations in which these 29 firms have held equity stakes have been minority or 50-50 joint ventures in DC's. Indeed, some of these firms (notably CPC) went to a good deal of trouble in the 60's to buy out or divest themselves of joint ventures, thus furnishing numerous observations for an early study on joint venture divorce in multinational corporate systems (Franko, 1971).

A number of patterns in U.S. corporate behavior can be statistically verified. It is clear for example, that the large U.S. firms have a lower proportion of their foreign and LDC operations as minority or 50-50 holdings than do the smaller companies in the industry (Table 5). Also, the more advertising intensive the parent company, the less likely it is that it will have many "new form" ventures relative to its total DC or international activity. (Multiple regression tests of the proportion of companies' foreign operations which were NFI with total company sales and expenditures on advertising as a percentage of sales. The regression coefficients were statistically significant of better than the 95% level of confidence.)

Moreover, it also appears that the more important foreign sales are to a U.S. food processing MNE, the less likely it is to have minority or 50-50 ventures constituting a significant proportion of its foreign operations. In this industry, as with most industries, joint ventures are sometimes used by essentially domestic companies "to test the water" of foreign operations.

An examination of the 65 minority and 50-50 joint ventures in the food industry that were included in our census reveals the following patterns:

- Joint ventures "imposed" by host governments and entered into by U.S. firms to retain access to the local market. In response to our questionnaire, General Foods cited the fact that it has four minority joint ventures in DC's (out of 16 subsidiaries in DC's, and 39 world-wide) partly because, "such ventures are the only means to legally operate in some countries."

- Minority positions in companies producing unrelated or distantly related diversified products, e.g., batteries by Dart and Kraft in Brazil; auto parts by IC industries in Brazil; soy sauce in Hong Kong by Pillsbury.

- Companies producing low technology, comparatively undifferentiated products whose low value-to-weight ratios (or local tariff protection) isolate them from "core" company activities elsewhere. Pillsbury has five ventures that fall into this category: four in Latin America and one in the Philippines. These operations produce mature, standardized products for Pillsbury (four mills and basic foodstuffs), and are also viewed by Pillsbury as a convenient method for expansion in certain markets. For example, in El Salvador Pillsbury owns 10% of one of the two principal four mills there. Pillsbury stresses the importance of this operation as establishing a "solid relationship for future expansion opportunities" while limiting current risk. In Mexico, Pillsbury's wholly-owned Mexican subsidiary recently (1981) merged with a Mexican pasta business to form a joint venture 51% owned by the Mexican company ORGOA, and 49% owned by Pillsbury. Due to local regulations, future expansion is now possible in Mexico for Pillsbury as a Mexican company, expansion which would not have been possible for a majority-owned foreign company. The patterns of Pillsbury's minority ventures are typical of those found in mature industries with standardized products that are not traded much across borders. As pointed out in extensive correspondence, in two out of five such ventures Pillsbury has the equivalent of total management control. The case of Gerber, the smallest company in our sample, illustrates the relatively rare use of minority and 50-50 ventures by U.S. companies in their Third World food processing activities. This company case also illuminates the usage of licensing linkages predominating where U.S. company position in international competition is relatively weak.

Gerber is a "follower" company world wide in the baby foods industry. Its principal competitor is the vastly larger, more powerful global Nestle of Switzerland. It is also a "U.S. centered" firm, with 95% of its sales being domestic. Gerber now has only two equity positions in the less developed world, following the sale of a wholly-owned subsidiary in Venezuela and a minority position in Brazil. One of these two remaining DC subsidiaries is a 49% venture in Mexico. This subsidiary was formerly 100% owned by Gerber. In 1982, 51% was sold to Grupo Coral, S.A. of Monterrey, Mexico. This arrangement is preferred because of "price control, unstable currency and government restrictions on the introduction of new product lines by foreign corporations."The Venezuelan operation, formerly a wholly-owned subsidiary for 25 years, was sold to a Venezuelan group in 1979-80, and Gerber now licenses technology to this group. The firm also has a license linkage in the Philippines and in a handful of developed countries. Gerber states that it is increasing its emphasis on licensing arrangements; "Licensing lessens the adverse effects of inflation, price controls and in some cases, the political climate, and frees investment capital for use in other areas" (Gerber Annual Report, 1983).

Gerber's use of "new forms" thus constitutes part of a defensive retreat from what was once deeper involvement in the Third World. It can tolerate this lessened control over its often former foreign operations because value to weight ratios are comparatively low, and national health and sanitary regulations, as well as local tastes, act as barriers to vigorous cross-border sourcing and coordination of the kind that underpins many companies' preference for 100% ownership.

In contrast to Gerber's use of licensing and minority joint ventures to "sweeten" a retreat from certain markets, firms that still feel in possession of strong proprietary technology or trade secrets (e.g., the formula for Coca-Cola) are reluctant to license food processing know-how. In spite of its experience with minority joint ventures discussed above, Pillsbury prefers not to license for two reasons:

- They want to remain involved in development of the business.
- They feel that by licensing they lose control over technology, which is one of Pillsbury's major resources.

Pillsbury has licensees only in Japan and Korea.

Cases of trademark licensing as well as licensing of bottles and cans in the beverage industry are also encountered. These rarely concern food processing *per se* and are usually undertaken by U.S. firms as a means of assuring markets for imported processed food goods by establishing vertical linkages. Analogous practices are often found in international fast food franchising, a form of trademark, and image and skill licensing, now spreading to parts of the Third World (especially Asia,) in which some U.S. food processors also participate via "restaurant" divisions.

Pharmaceuticals

Among pharmaceutical firms, the use of NFI's is extremely rare (Table 6). Propriety technology and trademarks are major determinants of success in the industry, and the strategy of these firms is to maintain close control over technology, as well as over marketing variables having to do with quality and reputation (especially among the medical profession) such as brand names, image, sales force recruitment, training, and relations with government health authorities.

Johnson & Johnson, an industry leader which has no minority or 50-50 ventures, argues that these relationships offer few business advantages. They are useful only when specific host country laws preclude 100% foreign ownership. Responding to our request for information J & J executives stated that:

> The type of operations is influenced by host country government policy. In those cases where we have joint ventures, the only reason for having a host country national or nationals as a joint venture partner is because of specific laws precluding a 100% foreign investment. While it has been argued that host country nationals as joint venture partners are advantageous from a business standpoint, this has not been our experience.
>
> We know of no advantage, competitive or otherwise of a joint venture as opposed to a wholly owned subsidiary.

Firms such as industry leaders Merck and Eli Lilly are known to have a similar view of non-controlled operations. Pfizer also pursues a policy oriented toward wholly-owned subsidiaries. Interviews with Pfizer executives have confirmed that they too see no advantage to NFI's in spite of their numerous operations in DC's. Indeed, none of the top six U.S. pharmaceutical firms appear to have had minority or 50-50 joint ventures in any DC as of 1983 (Table 6).

Among U.S. pharmaceutical firms, only the smaller companies have used minority or 50-50 joint ventures at all (Table 6). Even then, these smaller firms have used them only for a minuscule fraction of their international DC operations. Moreover, the country locations of the handful of extant minority or 50-50 ventures of U.S. pharmaceutical firms (e.g., predominately in Mexico, Korea, Nigeria and India), argue that the choice of such forms was primarily a response to legal restrictions and governmental pressures. The smaller firms, having less technological dominance and global spread than the major players in the industry, did not have the bargaining power to hold out for the 100% or majority positions gained by the industry leaders.

The overwhelming "non-use" of minority and 50-50 joint ventures by U.S. MNE's in the pharmaceutical industry at the current time continues the historical trend found by the Harvard Multinational Enterprise Project on U.S. drug companies' foreign investment behavior. At no time during any three year subdivision of the period 1951-1975 did the proportion of pharmaceutical subsidiaries established or acquired in DC's by U.S. MNE's as a minority or 50-50 venture excede 12% of all DC subsidiary establishment in pharmaceuticals (Curham, Davidson and Suri, 1977, pp. 320-360). Furthermore, even at this very low level, there was no discernible trend toward NFI's.

Table 6
US COMPANIES IN THE PHARMACEUTICALS INDUSTRY: MINORITY OR 50-50 JVS IN DCS (1983)

Company (ranked by size)	Size $Bn 1983	No. of Foreign Operations	No. of DC Operations	No. of Minority & 50-50 JVs in DCs	% of DC Ops. which are minority or 50-50 JVs	% of all Foreign Ops. which are minority or 50-50 JVs in DCs	Location and % Ownershiup of Minority JVs in DCs with product line where known	Main Product Line of Firm other than pharmaceuticals & % non-pharmaceuticals
Johnson & Johnson	6.0	118	36	0	0	0		First aid, hospital supplies, medical instruments (66%)
American Home Products	4.9	74	18	0	0	0		Household, food products, housewares (44%)
Bristol Meyers	3.9	109	39	0	0	0		Cosmetics, hair products, household products (37%)
Warner Lambert	3.1	93	37	0	0	0		Home health products, chewing gum (40%)
Pfizer	3.8	110	43	0	0	0		Consumer products, material science (17%)
Merck	3.2	83	14	0	0	0		Climate control equipment (23%)
Eli Lilly	3.0	105	19	3	16	3	Brazil (46%) Korea (50%) Ag. chem. Korea (50%) Pharmaceuticals	Cosmetics, agricultural chemicals, medical equipment (50%)

Abbott Labs	2.9	73	32	5	16	7	Thailand (49.9%) Nigeria (40%) India (40%) [Phillipines (40%) Real Estate] [Phillipines (29%) Real Estate]	Hospital & lab products, toiletries (50%)
Smith Kline	2.8	110	20	1	5	1	Mexico (49%)	Medical instruments (23%)
Upjohn	2.0	55	24	2	8	4	Korea (50%), Mexico (36.3%)	Chemicals, agricultural (35%)
Schering-Plough	1.8	128	42	1	2	1	Mexico (50%)	Consumer products (49%)
Sterling	1.9	9	2	1	50	11	India (less than 51%)	
Squibb	1.8	106	31	3	10	3	India (less than 51%) P. R. China (est. 1982, 50%) [Phillipines (less than 50%) Real Estate]	Medical supplies, toiletries (21%)
		1173	356	16				

Sources: **Moody's Industrial Manual, 1984. The World Directory of Multinational Enterprises.** Company reports and interviews, esp. Squibb (Exhibit 22, Form 10K, interviews), Johnson and Johnson, Pfizer and Bristol Meyers, **Scrip,** June 15, 1984.

Whether the number of minority and 50-50 ventures in the smaller pharmaceutical firms of our current sample is a harbinger of any significant change in U.S. company practice is doubtful. U.S. executive attitudes toward such arrangements in the pharmaceutical business appear far too negative to be amenable to change in the new future. Notwithstanding this general reluctance, however, individual firms may prove exceptions to the rule if they see opportunities to gain world market share by entering unconventional arrangements.

Squibb, despite its historic preference for 100% operations, is something of a current exception to the general rule. Squibb is a relatively small "catch-up firm" in the industry (Table 6) and joint ventures are being considered by management as one hoped-for means of gaining market share, especially in countries where 'old forms' of investments are prohibited and the industry 'majors' are reluctant to enter. For example, Squibb was the first pharmaceutical firm to enter China through a 50-50 joint venture with a local partner, the Shanghai Pharmaceutical Industrial Corp., (details are provided in Table 7). Overall, however, even at Squibb the use of NFI's is minuscule relative to the business it conducts through wholly-owned subsidiaries.

Host country laws, particularly in Latin America, have sometimes been aimed at influencing the pattern of foreign investment toward minority status. In the pharmaceutical industry, perhaps more than in others, results have not always measured up to the original intentions. The local laws which originally encouraged the formation of NFI's are in some cases becoming so stringent as to discourage foreign involvement altogether. For example, the 1983 Squibb 10K Report states that the company was in the process of discontinuing pharmaceutical operations in several Latin American countries, because of stringent host country regulations. These laws particularly affect price controls, the administration of which is sometimes more constraining on firms wholly- or partly-owned by foreign MNE's. Prices were so stringently controlled, states Squibb, that "price increases which, if and when granted, are inadequate to cover increases in wages and other costs." Mexico's recently released 'development program' for the pharmaceutical industry signals other problems for MNC's (Business Latin American, March 7, 1984, pp. 73, & 78-79). This new legislation strongly favors local firms that are majority Mexican-owned for public sector sales, financing and manufacture of raw materials. The reaction from some MNC's is anticipated to be a pullout, rather than acceptance of a minority ownership position.

Licensing

Information for determining the extent to which U.S. pharmaceutical firms engage in licensing arrangements with firms in less developed countries where they own no equity is limited and difficult to obtain. A study by Gary Gereffi noted that in 1977 ten MNE's had licensing arrangements with local firms in Indonesia, but he did not indicate whether the licensors were U.S. firms (Gereffi, 1983). Gereffi also noted that in Columbia and Mexico licensing arrangements are subject to governmental controls, but he did not reveal which firms are operating in those countries under such terms. He reported that over 90% of India's technological requirements in the pharmaceutical

Table 7
THE SQUIBB JOINT VENTURE IN CHINA: A PROFILE

Name:	Sino-American Shanghai Squibb Phamaceuticals Ltd.
Local Partner:	Shanghai Pharmaceutical Industrial Corp.
Product, capacity:	Over 20 kinds of prescription drugs of both Squibb and Chinese derivation; 6,000 sq. m. factory site.
Total investment:	US $8 million
Foreign equity:	50%; US $1 million cash, US $3 million loan.
Tax and incentives:	Separate agreement governs technology transfer; no royalty specified in JV.
Management:	10-member board, half from each side; PRC chairman, Squibb vice-chairman.
Duration:	15 years, renewable.
Labor:	N.A.
Marketing:	PRC partner to handle domestic distribution, no fixed esport set; either Squibb or JV label and trademark.
Operating status:	New plant under construction; targeted to start up in 1985.

Source: **Business China,** September 14, 1983, p. 132.

industry are acquired annually through external sources. Data on the identities of foreign licensors of Indian firms compiled by the Indian Ministry for Chemicals & Fertilizers shows that none of them are American. Italian firms, who operate without patent protection for pharmaceuticals in their home environment, predominate. Gereffi provides further support for the view that where licensing of non-equity affiliated firms occurs, the licensors are predominatly small and non-U.S. based. He stated that "some of the smaller TNC's (transnational corporations) in the advanced countries have started to demonstrate a strong interest in helping Third World nations industrialize particularly through the mechanism of technology transfer. Swedish firms appear to have taken the lead in the area" (Gereffi, p. 249) Unlike the Italian and Swedish firms, it appears that U.S. firms guard their technology more closely and do not liberally license. When instances of possible licensing by U.S. firms are discussed, the firms mentioned are characteristically smaller than U.S. MNE's. One example of this is in Peru where market demand for pharmaceuticals has been declining and MNE's are closing down and licensing their technologies. Upjohn, a U.S. firm with a relatively small market share, is currently considering this, (telephone discussion with Gary Gereffi, May 24, 1985).

The Computer Industry[3]

The market for computers is viewed as existing primarily in advanced industrialized countries. Computers, particularly large traditional main frame CPU (central processing units) or CPU-based systems, are extremely expensive and are generally associated with economizing on human labor; hardly a priority for labor-surplus DC's. Production sites for computers have also been established primarily in advanced countries. Final products typically met with low price elasticity of demand, and firms were not pushed to aggressively minimize cost by exploiting international differences in unit labor costs. Only advanced countries had work forces with the high skill levels and the technological knowledge necessary for the production of both computer hardware and for the software that allows the machines to function. Out of the 113 non-U.S. foreign production facilities of the 15 leading U.S. computer firms, 75 (66%) were located in developed country sites (Table 8).

Since the early 60's however, there has been a significant demand in the DC's for computers. Mainframes have been used for the particular exigencies of conducting censuses, compiling government budgets and statistics, central economic planning, accounting for large enterprises, and in some cases, military application. Since computers have always been more than just mainframes, computer firms discovered early that peripherals, ranging from card sorters to tape and then disc drives and other components, could be produced economically, at least as a quid-pro-quo for access to predominately government markets.

The evolution of the computer industry altered DC aspirations. The mini-computer was developed in the 70's, which was inexpensive compared to million dollar mainframe systems, and in the 80's there was the micro- or personal computer revolution. As the computer industry became more complex and specialized, DC demands and hopes mushroomed. Moreover, the technologies of these newer, smaller computers were seemingly more accessible to determined DC military, governmental and industrial elites. Governments of countries such as Brazil, Mexico and India have come to bargain with foreign computer firms over ownership and technology sharing as tenaciously (perhaps more tenaciously, given the direct military applicability of much of the technology) as they have in petroleum. As in most other industries, smaller outsider firms have obtained markets and licensing revenues sheltered from the otherwise omnipresent competition, in this case of the major firm, IBM.

The debt and foreign exchange crisis of the early 80's did not inhibit the efforts of local governments to build up a local "infant industry" behind trade barriers. Some DC's, notably Brazil and Mexico, continued to make even stronger efforts to oblige foreign firms to share either equity or technology, or both if they want local market access. Very few American firms will consider using partly locally owned foreign subsidiaries as important sourcing sites; they prefer to use the wholly owned DC facilities they already have so they can maintain complete control over quality, specifications and delivery schedules. The host rationale once again appears to be that of import substitution.

IBM is the leading firm in the industry with $42 billion in computer related sales. IBM has approximately 70% of the world mainframe market, 40% of the micro and PC market, and about 23% of the mini-computer market, establishing it as the market leader in all segments (derived from *Business Week*, February 18, 1985, *Value Line*, February, 1985). Not only has it captured about half of the industry's market but its sales are growing at a pace equal to the industry's growth rate. IBM's success is due to its extensive line of products, which add up to a "total systems approach," its lower costs of production (due to increased automation,) its extensive distribution system, its vast R&D expenditures and its reputation for quality, reliability and service. Moreover, company policy protects this reputation through tight control over its proprietary technology, marketing and production processes. Because of this, IBM perceives little advantage in accepting 50-50 or minority JV's in manufacturing. The risks of sharing its technology and jeopardizing the quality of its products and its reliable reputation from reduced control in foreign production facilities, are perceived as being greater than the benefits of possible lower cost production and access to new foreign markets. With a larger number of international manufacturing and distribution facilities, and its extensive experience, IBM dominates foreign markets, and as a policy does not enter into 50-50 or minority manufacturing JV's in foreign countries (Table 8). IBM holds to this policy even more so when licensing others. An exception to the rule was made in Japan during the 60's, however, IBM licensed its technology as a quid-pro-quo in order to maintain a 100% owned subsidiary of its own.

Although joint ventures are also perceived as undesirable by firms with lower market shares, these firms lack either the international marketing knowledge or the bargaining power of IBM.

"Second rank" or "outsider" firms were traditionally made up of the "Bunch:" Burroughs, Univac (a division of Sperry-Rand), NCR, Control Data Corporation and Honeywell, all of which compete primarily in the mainframe market. As the industry has grown in complexity to include much more than mainframes, outsiders now include the firms listed in Table 8 in the mini-computer, micro-computer and personal computer (PC) markets. These firms all have various disadvantages to some extent when competing with IBM, whether it be the lack of a total systems capability and limited product range, higher costs, or a poorer quality or service image. As a result, most have adopted a specialty or niche strategy by focusing on either particular products or particular customers in an attempt to capture or defend their market share.

Table 8 shows that many have also begun using new forms of investment to enter fast growing foreign markets in DC's, particularly in Brazil and Mexico. All of the firms listed, with the exception of Cray, have foreign subsidiaries for distribution, manufacturing or both. Table 8 breaks down the foreign manufacturing facilities of each company into the total number of DC operations and the total number of those which were undertaken as NFI's. IBM has many foreign manufacturing facilities, but only 17% of the are in DC's and all of these are wholly owned. In contrast, CDC, Hewlett-Packard, Honeywell and Apple have foreign manufacturing firms in DC's that are 50-50 or minority owned, and except for Honeywell, these constitute a large portion of their total DC operations (40-100%). Although establishing manufacturing facilities in DC's provides lower labor costs and access to new markets, the acceptance of 50-50 or minority ownership by these four outsider firms implies their need for immediate access to new markets. That they are willing to forego control over their technology, quality and management further indicates their relatively weak bargaining position. These firms are counting on these risks being outweighed by the benefits of increased

Table 8
US COMPUTER COMPANIES WITH MINORITY OR 50-50 JVS IN DCS (1984)

Company (ranked by size of comp. sales)	Size $Bn 1984		Foreign Sales as % of total Revenues	No. of all Foreign Manf'g. Operations	No. of all Foreign Manf'g. Ops. which are minority or 50-50	No. of DC Manf'g. Operations	No. of Minority or 50-50 JVs in DCs	% of DC Ops. which are minority or 50-50 JVs	% of all Foreign Ops. which are minority or 50-50 JVs in DCs	Location and % Ownership of minority JVs in DCs with product line where known. Licensing agreements with non affiliated DC firms in brackets
	Computer Sales	Total Revenues								
IBM	41.7	45.9	40%	23	0	4	0	0%	0%	
DEC	5.6	5.6	35	10	0	4	0	0	0	[Brazil, microcomputer]
CDC	3.9	5.0	24	7	7	6	6	100	86	Phillipines, (30%); Israel (9%), (33%); Romania (45%, peripherals); Iran (30%, computer terminals); Brazil (25%, mainframes)
Burroughs	3.9	4.9	40	13	4	3	0	0	0	
Hewlett-Packard	3.2	6.0	39	12	2	5	2	40	16	China (50%); Mexico (49%, personal computers)
Sperry	2.8	5.0	30	4	0	1	0	0	0	[Mexico, PCs; Brazil]
Tandy	a.	2.7	14	5	1	2	0	0	0	[Mexico, PCs]
NCR	2.4	4.0	46	14	2	2	0	0	0	
Wang	2.2	2.2	36	4	0	1	0	0%	0%	

Honeywell (HIS)	1.8	6.0	26	8	4	2	1	50	12.5	Malaysia (10%)
Apple	1.5	1.5	22	3	1	2	1	50	33	Mexico (49%, PCs)
D-G	1.2	1.2	30	5	1	4	0	0	0	[Brazil, minicomputers]
Amdahl	0.8	0.8	a.	3	0	1	0	0	0	
Prime	0.6	0.6	42	2	0	1	0	0	0	
Cray	0.2	0.2	a.	0	0	0	0	0	0	
				113		39	10			

Sources: 1983, 1984 Annual Reports; **Moody's Industrial Manual,** May, 1984; **Data Communications,** September 1984, pp. 64–66; **New York Times,** May 10, 1985; Financial Times, January 21, 1985.

a. not included.

market shares in those countries are areas. In particular, it is notable that most outsider firms that engage in new forms of investment are those who have small foreign sales as a percentage of total revenues. With the exception of Hewlett-Packard, those firms with 35% or less of their sales coming from foreign sales all are involved in NFI's. As mentioned, Apple has a minority-owned facility in Mexico, CDC has minority-owned facilities in Israel, Romania, Iran, Brazil and the Philippines, and Honeywell has one in Malaysia. Four other firms have entered into licensing agreements, all in Mexico and Brazil in which non-affiliated DC firms are contracted to manufacture computers by the U.S. firms. DEC, Data General and Sperry are contracting in Brazil, while Tandy and again Sperry are contracting in Mexico. The licensing agreements cover mini- and personal computer assembly whereas the joint ventures cover these and peripherals (printers, terminals, etc.).

Licensing agreements by U.S. computer firms in DC's are relatively recent, with four out of five in Table 8 occurring within one year alone, the most recent occurring in May 1985 by Tandy and Sperry in Mexico (*New York Times,* May 10, 1985). After a 1982 decree made it difficult to export computers to Mexico, or to set up 100%-owned manufacturing facilities for PC's there, both firms began accepting licensing arrangements.

Outsider firms, unlike IBM, also lack bargaining power. They are less likely to reject offers to joint-manufacture or license in DC's because they need more outlets for their products. IBM, on the other hand, pulled out of India in 1977 when it was faced with an ultimatum to accept or reject minority ownership. More recently, it bargained with the Mexican government during 1984 and the first half of 1985, and succeeded in becoming the exception to the 1982 decree. Because Mexico greatly needed the foreign exchange and increased exports which production of IBM PC's could bring, it yielded to IBM's inflexible policy and accepted a 100% IBM-owned PC facility (*The New York Times,* July 24, 1985, p. A1).

The remaining firms in Table 8, such as Burroughs, NCR, Wang and Prime, are not engaged in NFI's in DC's. Burroughs and NCR abandoned Brazil as a manufacturing location for mini-computers in 1978 because new regulations in the computer industry reserved the market for Brazilian mini-computer firms. These two firms have not responded with licenses, as did Sperry and DEC. One difference between these two outsider groups is the ratio each has of foreign sales to total sales. Companies like Burroughs and NCR with proportionately greater foreign sales appear less likely to enter into NFI's. Thus, greater access to foreign markets (and possibly greater foreign market share and experience) may preclude any perceived need to establish licensing arrangements or joint ventures which are generally held to be undesirable.

While outsider firms with a smaller proportion of foreign sales appear to accept a greater number of licensing arrangements and joint ventures, they still do not license or manufacture their most advanced technology. In Mexico for example, Apple is producing its Apple IIe and Hewlett-Packard is producing the HP 150 Computer, and neither of them are top of the line products. An exception to this is CDC, which in 1984 established a joint-venture in Brazil to manufacture a new mainframe. However, CDC only produces peripherals and terminals in other countries.

Outsider firms overall are more willing to undertake 50-50 or minority joint ventures and licensing agreements in rapidly growing foreign markets, especially where the market is closed to foreign firms through strict regulations, and the firms in questions have little international experience. These firms' small market share and consequent lack of bargaining power and experience leave them fewer options for survival in the computer industry.

Summary of Findings

As a general rule, this study confirms the fact that American firms taken as a group are reluctant to enter into minority or 50-50 joint ventures, and licensing arrangements in DC's. (for information on comparative U.S., European and Japanese corporate use of NFI's, especially minority and 50-50 joint ventures in DC's, see Dunning and Cantwell, 1984; Franko, *The European Multinationals*, 1976). Notwithstanding this general rule, there is a wide variation in American company practice in each of the industries surveyed: in all of them there is some use of NFI's.

Using minority and 50-50 ventures in DC's as an indicator of industry propensity to undertake NFI's (data on licensing were too fragmentary and anecdotal for comprehensive summarization,) U.S. auto parts producers had by far the highest average propensity to use NFI's among the five industries examined. Thirty-nine percent or 25 of the 64 DC manufacturing ventures of the ten leading U.S. auto parts producers were minority or 50-50 joint ventures (Table 9). Several licensing accords were also found. Fewer but still significant proportions of U.S. firms' ventures in DC's in food

Table 9
USE OF MINORITY AND 50-50 VENTURES IN MANUFACTURING BY AMERICAN FIRMS IN DC'S IN 1984

Industry	Numbers of US Firms Surveyed	Numbers of Manufacturing Operations in DC's	Numbers of Minority 50-50 Ventures in DC's	Percentages of all SDC Manufacturing Operations Minority and 50-50 JV's in DC's
Automobiles	4	37	14	14.6%
Auto Parts	10	64	25	39
Food Processing	29	297	65	22
Pharmaceuticals	12	356	16	4
Computers	15	38	10	26

Source: Derived from Tables 1, 4, 6, 8.

processing, automobiles and computers were minority or 50-50 joint ventures, and a number of licensing arrangements were found in each sector (Table 9). At the opposite end of the spectrum is the pharmaceuticals industry, with only 4% of fewer than 356 DC operations being undertaken as 50-50 or minority ventures. (U.S. licensing of non-equity affiliated firms in DC's also appears to be exceedingly rare in pharmaceuticals.)

"Americanness" is therefore not a satisfactory or complete explanation for U.S. company avoidance of NFI's relative to Japanese and European (or indeed other DC) parent firms. Industry specific, company strategy specific and host country specific factors appear to be much more powerful (and in the food processing industry statistically verifiable) determinants of U.S. company practice.

Four principal hypotheses have guided the course of this study, and are in turn illustrated and amplified by its results. These hypotheses relate parent corporate acceptance of avoidance of NFI's to:

Oligopolistic Competition

Avoidance of NFI's is linked to the reluctance of industry "insiders," "majors," or "market share leaders" to share or to relinquish decision making power or information that might impair their firm specific, low cost, market or technological differentiation competitive advantages. Conversely, "outsiders," market share laggards and newcomers are expected to be more willing to accept NFI's.

The reason for expecting such a behavioral distinction include resource and information constraints faced by smaller firms which are not faced by their larger, more internationally established brethren. Lagging firms bent on catching up with majors also are often moved to offer host-countries shared ownership or technology as a quid-pro-quo for preferred (or exclusive) market status as a seemingly low-cost means of defensively matching oligopoly leaders' geographical scope.

This distinction between "insider" and "newcomer" behavior with respect to sharing ownership and technology has been observed in the oil industry (Torrens, 1980; Franko, "Multinationals in the Middle East," 1976), as well as documented in an early study of the ownership policies of American manufacturing firms (Stopford and Wells, 1971). The predicted pattern is clearly observable in four of the five industries surveyed here. Its role in the fifth, vehicle parts, is rendered less clear by the multitude of products covered by that rubric, as well as by additional effects related to a second major hypothesis.

Shifts in the International Division of Labor

As products mature, become standardized, and face higher price elasticities of demand, and as technologies eventually diffuse to a circle of firms well beyond initial dominant oligopolists, even once dominant "majors" may find that it is in their interest to accept NFI's. If they do not, another firm from an industrialized country will, or a DC-based company may eventually succeed on its own without the skills, knowledge or technology of the advanced country company. Thus, for example, U.S. oil majors finally came to accept ownership and technology sharing with host producer companies after that path was charted by industry newcomers. Similarly, even General Motors, when faced with competition from offers by Renault or Fiat of NFI's to host countries, opted for a "if you can't beat them join them" strategy. Other U.S. parent companies pursued NFI's as a means for obtaining the last marginal returns for a technology whose control by the developed country company was waning, and then going on to something else. The adoption of such "portfolio re-alignment strategies" is especially made clear by U.S. firms in the auto components sector. There, cash generated from marginal returns from NFI's is being used in many cases to finance U.S. corporate diversification moves to newer, higher growth industries in the advanced countries. In effect, from the U.S. corporate point of view, such use of NFI's constitutes a new form of *divestment*.

The Role of Trade Protection

To the extent that weaker "outsider" firms in oligopolistic industries seek markets that are sheltered against competitors who have either lower costs or superior marketing and technology differentiation, and to the extent that outsider firms are prepared to offer NFI's in order to get such sheltering, there is an obvious link between host country trade and competition policies, and the willingness of outsider firms to enter into NFI's. When dominant firms attempt to parry such potential exclusion from particular DC markets by also accepting NFI's, there is a further link between NFI incidence and host trade and competition policy. Indeed, the case literature on multinational company host industry relations includes a number of specific instances of trade-offs of preferential or exclusive market access by countries in exchange for ownership or technology sharing (Franko, *The European Multinationals,* 1976).

If protection of a venture from external or domestic competition provides a "favorable" condition for NFI acceptance by foreign firms, isolation of such NFI's from competition with other parts of the investor's multinational enterprise system may provide the "necessary" condition for such acceptance, even by industry leaders. For example, small scale, high cost, highly protected minority vehicle assembly ventures in Ecuador, Tunisia and Egypt have little possibility of having a competitive impact on the rest of General Motors' multinational system. Consequently, GM accepts minority positions in such ventures and thus obtains exclusive or highly preferential access for its export-sales to those countries of its completely knocked down (CKD) vehicle kits and components.

Exactly what net welfare benefits host countries derive from such protectionist industrial policies, which simultaneously eliminate the possibility of host-country consumers doing comparison shopping for finished vehicles or components, create an "infant" company that requires permanent protection, and create a special interest group (managers, shareholders and employees) to lobby for permanent protection, remain extremely obscure to this author. These policies do, however, create propitious conditions for NFI's.

Aggressive Governments

If the necessary conditions for acceptance of NFI's by American firms have been created by oligopolistic competition, product maturity, protected markets, and "isolability" of ventures from multinational corporate systems, the sufficient condition has, in the great majority of cases, been host government ownership policy.

A summation of all of the NFI ownership and licensing arrangements identified among all 70 of the U.S. firms in this study broken down by host country location shows a very striking concentration of NFI ventures in a handful of countries. Table 10 ranks countries in order to the number of U.S. related NFI ventures found in the five industries surveyed. Mexico with 33 is far in the lead. Brazil, follows with 11, the Philippines with 9, Venezuela with 7 and India with 5. Indeed, 54% of all of the instances of NFI uncovered in our survey were located in these five countries, all of which were aggressively bargaining with foreign firms for local ownership of manufacturing enterprise.

Table 10
DISTRIBUTION BY HOST-COUNTRY OF "NEW FORMS" OF INVESTMENT BY 70 US CORPORATIONS IN FIVE INDUSTRIES: AUTOMOBILES, VEHICLE PARTS, FOOD PROCESSING, PHARMACEUTICALS AND COMPUTERS

Country	Number
Mexico	33
Brazil	11
Philipines	9
Venezuela	7
India	6
South Korea	5
Hong Kong	4
Malaysia	4
People's Republic of China	4
Colombia	3
Ecuador	3
Egypt	3
Jamaica	3
Peru	3
Singapore	3
Trinidad	3
Other	18
	122

Source: Compiled from Tables 1, 2, 3, 4, 5, 8; data from Dr. Lawrence G. Franko, International Competitive Analysis Project.

This pattern of the country distribution of NFI's constitutes *prima facie* evidence that any move or "trend" to the use of NFI's by American firms has first and foremost been in response to state interventions and requirements. Indeed, the historical record of American multinational investment summarized in the Harvard Multinational Enterprise data base, (a data base that provides a census of the foreign manufacturing and extractive activity of the 187 largest U.S. enterprises from the turn of the century to 1976,) shows that there was no "gradual trend" toward minority and 50-50 joint ventures on the part of American corporations during the past two decades. Rather, there was a quite disjointed shift to such NFI's during the 1973-75 period, a shift which was all but exclusively concentrated in Mexico, Brazil, Iran, India and the Philippines (Franko, 1987). With the exception of Iran, taken from the list by its post-revolutionary expropriations of almost all American-related enterprise, and the addition of Venezuela, the countries of concentration of U.S.-linked NFI's have been the same into the 1980's.

It is thought provoking to note that the DC's that have most aggressively bargained with U.S. enterprises for minority or 50-50 joint ventures, or for licenses for locally owned firms, are generally not to be found on current lists of "most successful" developing countries. To the extent that NFI's have been associated with import substituting industrialization economic policies, and to the extent that the indigenous owners of the majority equity in such ventures have come to have vested interests in permanent protection, this is hardly surprising.

Notes

1. In response to this, Chrysler, Ford and AMC are also currently exploring South Korea as a future source of components, and as a location of possible joint ventures for components production.
2. The evolving relationship between United Fruit, now United Brands, and the Central and Latin American Republics included some substitution of contract forming for owned plantations as early as the late 1950s. (Harvard Business School Case, United Fruit Company, Case Number No. ICH 2G39/2G40, 1958, p. 19). Politically, the move succeeded in lessening MNE/host country tensions. Economically, considerable climactic and soil risks were shifted onto small-holders who were dependent on a monopsonistic buyer.
3. Acknowledgement is due to Ms. Laureen Morrow for her assistance in the preparation of this survey.

References

Behrman, Jack, *The Roles of International Companies in Latin American Integration*, Lexington, MA: Lexington Books, 1972.

Bloomfield, Gerald, *The World Automotive Industry*, Newton Abbott; North Pomfret, VT: David and Charles, 1978.

Brandford, Sue, "Local Projects Beat the Multinationals", *Financial Times*, January 5, 1978.

Business China, various issues.

Business, Latin America, various issues.

Business Week, February 18, 1985.

Cantwell, John A., & Dunning, John G., "The 'New Forms' of International Involvement: British Firms in the Third World", Preliminary Draft, Meeting of Collaborating Researchers, OECD Development Centre, Paris, June 18-22, 1984.

Computerworld, February 27, 1984, p. 25.

Company Annual Reports, 1984.

Curhan, Joan P., Davidson, William, Suri, Rajan, *Tracing the Multinationals: A Sourcebook on U.S.-based Enterprises*, Cambridge, MA: Ballinger Publishing Co., 1977.

Data Communications, September, 1984, pp. 64-66.

Franko, Lawrence G., *The European Multinationals*, London: Harper & Row, Ltd., 1976.

Franko, Lawrence G., *Joint Venture Survival in Multinational Corporations*, New York: Praeger, 1971.

Franko, Lawrence G., "Multinationals in the Middle East", *Journal of World Trade Law*, July-August, 1976.

Franko, Lawrence G., "Use of Minority and 50-50 Joint Ventures by U.S. MNE's During the 1970's: The Interaction of Host country Policies and Corporate Strategies," unpublished manuscript, July, 1987.

Franko, Lawrence G., Heptonstall, John, and Derron, Francoise, "The Automobile Industry: Company and Country Strategies in Latin America and Eastern Europe", CEI, Geneva, 1981.

Fuller, Mark B., and Salter, Malcolm S., "Note on the Auto Sector Policies", Harvard Business School Case Services, Case No. 9-382-121, 1982.

Fuller, Mark B., and Salter, Malcolm S., "Note on the World Auto Industry in Transition", Harvard Business School Case Services, No. 9-382-122, 1982.

Gereffi, Gary, *The Pharmaceutical Industry and Dependency in the Third World*, Princeton, NJ: Princeton University Press, 1983.

"IBM's Mexico Production Plan Back in the Melting Pot", *Financial Times*, January 21, 1985.

Johnson, Jean, "Brazilian Informatics Policy", *The Fletcher Forum*, vol. 9, No. 2, Summer, 1985.

Knickerbocker, Frederick, *Oligopolistic Reaction and Multinational Enterprise*, Harvard Business School, 1983.

Moody's Industrial Manual, May 1984.

New York Times, May 10, 1985.

Sarathy, Ravi, "The Struggle for Technological Independence-Brazil's Industrial Policy", Unpublished article, 1984.

Scrip, June 24, 1984, September 12, 1984.

Stopford, John and Wells, Louis, T. Jo., *Managing the Multinational Enterprise*, London: Longman, 1971.

Stopford, John M., Dunning, John H. and Haberich, Klaus O., *The World Directory of Multinational Enterprises*, Book Tower: Detroit, MI, 1983.

Torrens, Ian M., *Changing Structures in the World Oil Markets*, Paris: The Atlantic Institute for International Affairs, 1980.

IV THE GLOBAL FLOW OF LABOR

7. SETTING THE GLOBAL HUMAN RESOURCE MANAGEMENT AGENDA FOR THE 1990s

NOEL M. TICHY

Introduction

The global playing field of the 1990s is ushering in an era when multinational companies will be divided into two tiers. There will be a small, elite group of true world class companies capable of competing globally in terms of product quality, innovativeness, cost, and distribution and marketing muscle. The second tier will suffer continuous casualties among their ranks as they fail to compete successfully. Our premise is that the key to the success of the first tier MNCs will be leadership and an innovative set of Human Resource Management practices. This "Foreword" spells out the emerging 1990s leadership agenda for attaining the first tier of globally competitive MNCs.

As we enter 1988, the volatility and imbalances of the global economy simultaneously attest to leadership's failure in the 1980s and its agenda for the 1990s. There are no easy solutions for the United States: It must address its budget deficit, live within its means, work harder, be more productive. The U.S. can only reverse its decline with shared equality of sacrifice. Black Monday, the slide of the dollar, the third world debt crisis, and the great trade imbalances have strained many of our global coordination mechanisms beyond their capacity. New shared leadership from Japan, the U.S., and Europe must take bold steps to prevent catastrophe.

A recent global economy forum, '88 Tokyo Forum, with representatives from five of the world's leading economic think tanks—Brookings Institution, IFO, Royal Institute of International Affairs, L'Institat Francais des Relations Internationales, and the Nomura Research Institute—concluded that starting in 1988, the following strategic changes are needed to deal with the global economic uncertainty:

1. U.S. bipartisan long term sustainable actions to reduce the budget deficit
2. Stimulation of both the Japanese and West German domestic economies
3. New capital flows to third world countries, with Japan playing an increased role in both direct investment and in public good aid
4. An international monetary order to stabilize the exchange rate needs to be created. "For the U.S. to try to rely on the exchange rate to fix its trade imbalance is an evasion of the problem," according to Paul Volcker during the '88 Tokyo Forum.
5. A consolidation of free trade, a true opening up of Japan.

From *Human Resource Management* Vol. 27, No. 1 (Spring 1988), pp. 1–18.

These five seemingly common sense recommendations, it was concluded, probably will not happen until there is more trauma in the global economic condition. Possibly, this may be several years in the future: in the U.S., 1988 being an election year, there will be a leadership hiatus. Yet companies will continue to rapidly globalize in this increasingly mercurial environment; become global they must or risk demise. There will be no hiatus for global competitors while political mantles are passed on. Standards are now set globally in industry after industry. Product design, innovation, service, quality and speed of response to changing markets are driven by whoever is best in the world. National boundaries are less and less relevant. The competitive dynamic is self-perpetuating and it daily exacerbates an already overburdened system.

This "Foreword" shares how the *HRM Journal* is evolving a Human Resource agenda for the 1990s. The seeds of this agenda were sown in 1983 with the inaugural issue of a newly focused *Human Resource Management*. The shift took place to foster a dialogue among scholars and executives around strategic Human Resource concerns. At the time, we said:

> The new *Human Resource Management* comes into being at a time when the challenges facing our management of people are monumental. World economic and political systems are in turmoil. There are tugs and pulls on the management of multinational corporations in this area, such as the tension over protecting jobs within national boundaries versus looking offshore for cheaper labor costs so as to remain world competitive. In addition there are important economic policy issues stemming from the transformation of economies and job structures in the industrialized world. The increase in high technology jobs and the service sector and the decrease in the manufacturing sector present many difficult prospects for people. The social and political responses by society to these changes are still being debated with the outcome quite unclear. We will take part in this dialog.
>
> The effort has just begun. There are no easy answers and quick-fix fads come and go. At least a decade of transformation will be required to make the shifts in managing our human resources. The journal intends to contribute to the development of better concepts and tools for successfully managing this transition. (Tichy, 1983a)

At that time there were several themes we focused on as central to the remainder of the 1980s:

Organizational flexibility and adaptability. We outlined the remainder of the decade as witnessing rapid changes in many organizations: changes that would require new organizational forms and management process with greater responsiveness, adaptiveness, and flexibility. The Human Resource function would be required to take the lead in developing these new forms. It would bear the brunt of responsibility for preparing people to operate in them and seeing that they effectively tied into the business strategy of the firm.

Economic performance and productivity. We stated that these two issues would probably be driving most organizations through the 1980s as they tried to stay (or become) world competitive and avoid their own demise. Much more attention would be needed to productively make both qualitative and quantitative links between HR variables and the economic performance or organizations.

By 1985 the move was made to accelerate the journal's global focus.

An Initial Global Agenda

We began the process with a summer symposium held at INSEAD in Fontainebleau, France. From that gathering of HR industry leaders and academics based in Europe, the U.S., and Japan, three major themes for the field emerged:

1. *Leadership*—There was no debate about the demand for future leaders capable of working in multicultural environments both within their companies and across national boundaries. It was felt that much could be learned from examining companies such as Philips, Unilever, Nestle, IBM, McKinsey & Company, and some of the Japanese MNCs.

2. *Culture*—It was debated as to what degree corporate culture can be managed to fit a given multinational corporation's strategy. Revolutionary cultural change, often triggered by a crisis, demands strong line leaders at the forefront. Whereas the other kind of cultural change—incremental—encompasses a more long time horizon, greater reinforcement in the human resources systems, and leadership that is not as visible as in revolutionary change. It is important to make the implicit explicit: to continually examine the culture through a variety of feedback mechanisms, mapping out the culture, assessing where the organization is, where it wants to go, carefully identifying strategies for change which constantly deal with the cultural gaps, and working the organization culture in relationship to the particular national culture in which it is embedded.

3. *New Organizational Forms*—There simply were not as yet clear answers to the many problems of recruiting, selecting, developing, rotating, and managing human resources in the context of the global organization. It may turn out that unless human resource strategies are both redesigned to be more global and are more tightly coupled to business strategies, it will not be possible to create viable global organizations (Schein, 1986). New concepts regarding what is "work" and how to redistribute tasks, redefine roles, authority relationships, and sources of power are already in evidence based on the new models proposed for the study of organizations by conference members.

Hedlund (1986) raised the issue of strategic and structural differences provided by the heterarchical—vs. hierarchical—MNC. Others argued for a different framework, seeing organizations less like two-dimensional photographs and more like holograms with each part of the picture containing all of the information needed to reconstruct the whole. Multigons were proposed—an organizational form in which power perpetually shifts from one part to another as tasks require. We conceptualized organization's common cultural assumptions as possibly functioning like genetic codes, with every member automatically knowing what to do under various conditions.

In thinking about the truly multicultural organization, we talked of how to achieve "controlled diversity," or "decentralization without fragmentation" (Schein, 19860. These ideas inevitably cause the further radical notion to emerge, that lodging accountability in individuals will no longer be possible. When groups and units have the same information for decision making, they will be jointly accountable. This effect, called informating, is perhaps one of the most dramatic (Schein, 1986).

In the Spring 1986 issue of *Human Resource Management,* we noted that, "These issues and the August 1985 symposium set the stage for our next international human resource symposium, which will be held in Japan in the spring of 1987" (Tichy, 1986). That conference served to further our mission to help develop the global Human Resource Management agenda for the 1990s.

Asia-Pacific

The catalyst for much of the world business transformation clearly emanates from this region, with Japan as the center of gravity. Within industries in both Europe and the U.S., Japan's progress toward leadership has triggered massive transformations in automobiles, steel, consumer electronics, commercial aircraft, semiconductors, copiers, watches, and more recently, computers and financial services. We can expect Japan to soon become an industry leader in aerospace and pharmaceuticals (including genetic engineering).

But Japanese firms also face fundamental change, in part as a result of the technological revolution to which they have themselves contributed. Spurred on by mounting political pressures, fast developing competitive forces in NICs (Newly Industrialized Countries, i.e., South Korea and Singapore as well as stronger U.S. and European MNCs), and a plunging dollar, many of the best known of these companies are in the process of radically and rapidly altering their global posture (Bartlett, 1988). The series of economic, political, and cultural forces operating to transform Japanese MNCs' present organizational strategies include:

Economic Forces:
- Yen revaluation
- World competition (U.S., Europe, and Asia-Pacific)
- In balance of payments between the U.S. and Europe
- Unemployment pressures in Japan
- Need for domestic stimulation to shift from totally export driven economy

Political Forces:
- Lack of strong consensus leadership in government
- Tax bill controversy
- Labor disgruntlement
- Aging population

Cultural Forces:
- Quality of life and rising expectations
- Creativity stimulation in education and the workplace
- Job security expectations becoming uncertain for increasing numbers of firms
- Role of women in the workplace showing early signs of change
- Opening up the cultural boundaries of Japan is needed

The Nomura Research Institute offers an interesting analysis of these pressures, arguing that the external forces can be summarized by four key changes:

1. Rapid changes in technology and social systems (e.g., telecommunications);
2. Expanding needs for services designed for both consumers and industry;
3. Tie-ups, collaboration, and realignment of competitive relations all taking place across industrial boundaries because of the development of #1 and #2 above;
4. The need for a new type of international strategy that outgrows the past export-oriented policy.

In response to these changes, the Nomura consulting group proposed that key internal organizational changes will have to be made if Japanese firms are to remain competitive in the global business arena. Their conclusions were quite radical for Japanese companies. They conclude:

- the current emphasis on harmony and consensus within Japanese companies inhibits innovative and strategic action;
- the inordinate emphasis placed on spiritualism, hard work, and perseverance in Japanese firms has a tendency to weaken management's strategic vision;
- the great army of employees hired during the boom years now form the senior ranks within Japanese industry. These people are in need of retraining to prepare them for coping with a changed environment;
- despite the progress in internationalization at local levels, in many Japanese firms, a long term international strategy has yet to be hammered out by headquarters, which retains its domestic orientation.

In February and March of 1987, interviews were conducted by Noel Tichy with senior executives of major Japanese companies, including:

Hitachi—Mr. Mita, President
Canon—Mr. Kaku, President

Toyota—Mr. Ohshima, Executive Vice President
NEC—Mr. Sekimoto, President
Nomura Securities—Mr. Tabuchi, President
Honda—Mr. Okubo, Executive Vice-President
Yokagowa Medical Systems—Mr. Sugeyama, President

Using the three-act transformational leadership framework (Tichy and Devanna, 1986) to organize and format their comments, inferences were made about the organizational dynamics of change in their companies (Figure 1).

Figure 1
TRANSFORMATIONAL LEADERSHIP: A THREE-ACT DRAMA

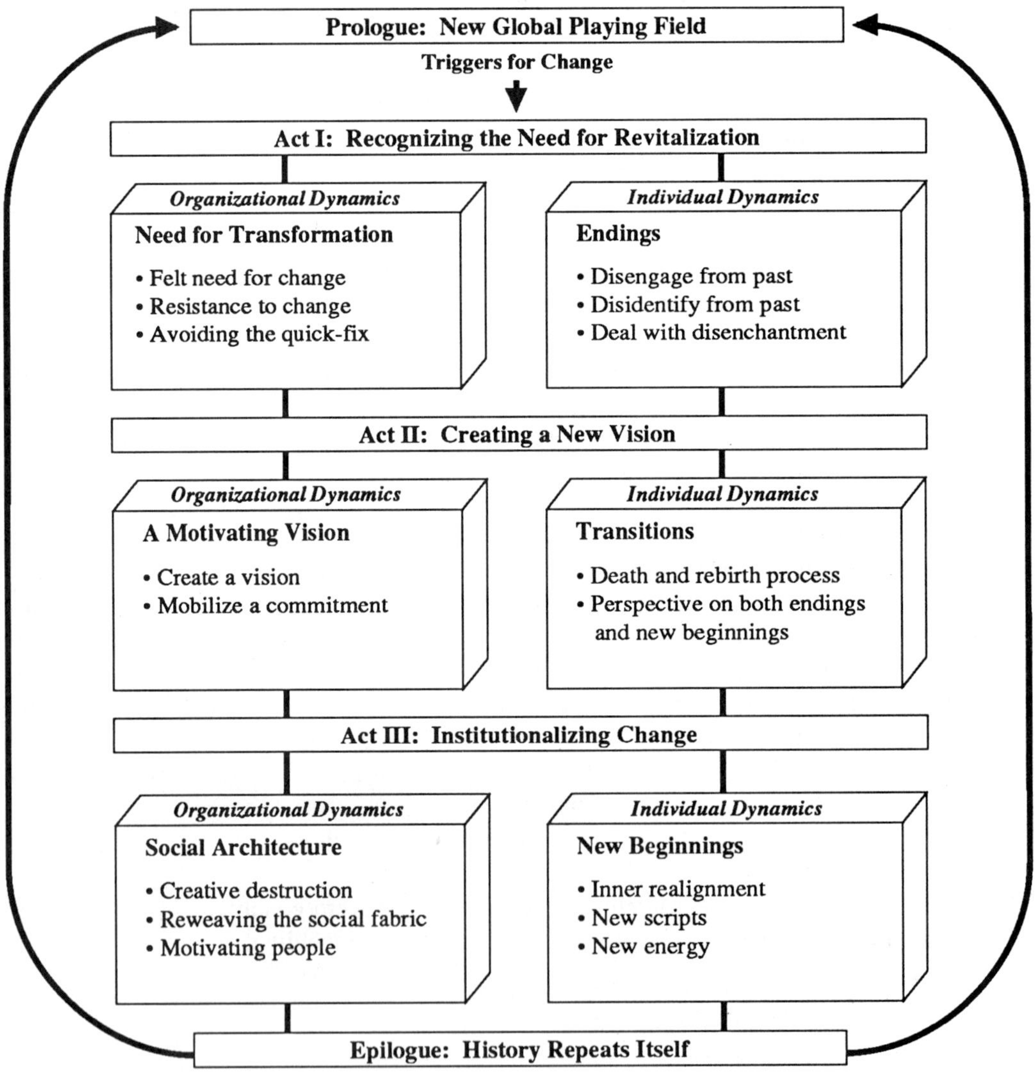

Act I: Recognizing the need for revitalization. It usually takes a strong environmental shock of a technological, economic, or social nature to evoke an awareness of discomfort within organizations, such as Chrysler's imminent bankruptcy in the early 1980s. But in some cases, proactive leadership's sensitivity to developing pressures can wake up the organization and release energy for revitalization.

It is essential for the organization to develop *a felt need for change* to avoid decline. In Japan, the yen revaluation and trade retaliation by the U.S. surprised many. There had been a growing complacency and arrogance within Japanese industry that made it vulnerable to shocks to yen revaluation, trade friction, low cost manufacturing challenges from Korea, and other NICs (Newly Industrialized Countries).

Trigger events, once perceived and interpreted as a need for change, discharge both positive forces driving toward change and *resistance* at both individual and organizational levels. Revitalization will be thwarted unless resistance in managed.

This may become a major problem for Japanese firms, in part due to the harmony and consensus style management they practice. These characteristics, which lead to incremental change, not quantum change, pose no major problem in times of growth. But in times of revolutionary change, they create serious difficulties—older leaders who are resistant to change cannot easily be circumvented due to entrenched seniority systems. One exception to this scenario is Honda, where younger leaders are explicitly supported in the interest of enhancing the innovative capacity of the firm.

A variety of fads may begin to erupt in Japan in order to put bandaids on serious problems that really require more than *quick fix solutions*. However, Japanese mangers don't appear to be as prone to quick fix solutions as are U.S. managers—note the latter's faddish application of quality circles, "Theory Z management," the excellence craze, etc.

Act II: Creating a new vision. It is the *image* of the future desired state that stirs the workforce to relinquish the past and begin to prepare for a new organizational direction. It may evolve slowly and is often the work of many, but it is the key to providing the necessary motivational pull into the future. Creating a motivating vision has little to do with how it is developed and everything to do with how it is responsive to pressures both outside and inside the organization.

This will be the major challenge for each of the Japanese companies observed. The best position appear to be Honda and Nomura, with Hitachi and Canon in the toughest positions, followed by Toyota and NBC. The leadership may not be up to the task in several cases. Garnering support that evolves into commitment to the new vision requires that transformational leaders provide stewardship for the workforce to help people deal with conflicting feelings of fear and hope, anxiety and relief, pressure and stimulation, loss of meaning and challenge of a new meaning, threat to self-esteem, and a renewed sense of personal value. This will take time, a very scarce commodity in today's competitive environment.

Act III: Institutionalizing change—Re-architecting the Organization. Transformation will not be enduring unless the social fabric of the organization is fundamentally altered. Charisma and personal drive on the part of the leaders can, in the short run, bring about change. However, unless the organizational processes, decision making, planning, structure, human resource systems, etc. are re-architected, the change will be transitory.

The institutionalization of a new culture and vision is most dependent on the human resource management systems. The best way to permanently alter the behavior in an organization is to staff with different types of people, appraise them on new criteria, reward new behaviors, and develop them differently. Thus, the challenges for the human resource profession in Japanese companies are immense. There are three primary domains requiring the attention of leaders in these firms:

1. Technical issues
   - Japanese companies need to develop new business strategies dealing with sourcing, localization, and portfolio shifts
   - New global organization design and structural mechanisms are needed for coordination and control
   - New human resource selection, development, and reward systems are needed

2. Political issues
   - More top down change is required
   - New coalitions are impacting the strategies of companies
   - There is union turbulence
   - A rebalancing of power with localization and new ventures and strategic alliances is underway
   - Reward systems are showing signs of stress as growth and profits shrink

3. Cultural systems
   - New value systems are needed for globalization strategies
   - New value systems are needed to integrate more international organization structures
   - New value systems are needed to support quantum change

As a result of these interviews and a survey of business climate, it appears that Japan's fundamental global challenges fall into four areas:

1. A need for new global product and service market strategies;
2. A need for new global coordination and interation mechanisms:
3. A need for developing strategic alliances; and
4. New staffing and development systems.

These transformation problems seem similar to those of IBM, GE, Philips, Siemens, and others. Thus, we decided to organize our symposium in Japan around these four sets of challenges.

The Global HRM Journal Symposium

The symposium participants examined each of the four challenges from three perspectives: (1) the senior line executive, (2) the HRM executive, and (3) the academic. We developed a 1990s agenda for each of the three groups. The participants in the symposium represented line executives, human resources executives, and academics from Japan, the U.S., and Europe (see "List of Participants" at the end of this issue). Four days of intense dialogue resulted in the following 1990s agenda.

1. Global Product and Service Market Strategies

As companies more aggressively look to world markets, they are faced with developing world class products and services at world class costs. This means changes in design, production, distribution, and marketing. The human resource management implications are multifold, including developing new forms of design teams, being better able to use strategic sourcing, and establishing world class standards for design, service, and performance.

As a result of the symposium task force work, we developed the following agendas.

1990s Agenda for Senior Line Executives

- Clearly articulate why going global is needed
  - Determine what is meant by global
  - Carefully identify what products/product lines are global
  - Where possible, avoid going global
- Determine what markets we have to be if we are to be a player, that is, specify what markets we *must* be in order to be in a strong position ten years from now.
- Identify who are our major competitors worldwide, who we need to beat, who we need to join (pre-empt)
- Define the competitive imperatives, i.e., mastering economies of scale, technological advantage, access to markets, distribution, etc.
- Identify what skills are required and where they exist in the organization
- Determine how to create organizational processes that treat globalization as an ongoing experiment with deliberate learnings and redirection

1990 Agenda for Human Resource Management Executives

- Insure that there is HR involvement as an integral partner in formulating the global strategy

- Develop competencies in HR to be a contributing partner
- Take the lead in developing the processes and concepts for top management as they develop global strategy (information scanning processes, information processing, decision making, learning processes)
  - Develop a framework for top management to fully understand the implications on people and organization structure
- Facilitate the implementation phase by identifying key skills required, assessing current competencies, and developing sourcing strategies that may be required

1990 Agenda for Academics

- Develop a clear concept of what global really means (i.e., the following issues need to be debated: integrated markets, just major markets, sources of competitive pressures, degree of interdependence)
- Develop an understanding of the nature of the market pressures for integration and fragmentation (efficiency gains from integration; desire for political and social autonomy; translation into company goal)
- Carry out comparative case studies
  - Identify companies' global strategies and develop classification schemes
  - Comparative case studies across political/social boundaries are needed
- Develop performance measures (if units become integrated and interdependent, how can we measure at unit and individual levels?)
- Develop measures of global integration and competition

2. Global Coordination and Integration

As the boundaries of the organization span wider geopolitical and cultural diversity, so does the difficulty of integrating the organization. Radically improved communication and cultural integration will be required, ultimately altering all of the human resource systems. Organization design concepts such as those discussed in our 1985 symposium (heterarchical vs. hierarchical structures, multigons, and informating) are rapidly emerging as reality. In the Japan symposium, three globalization cases were analyzed to help develop the 1990s agendas. The case, from different industries, driven by different imperatives, illustrate in concrete terms, a variety of solutions to global integration. All three cases show how a set of outside trigger events—driving forces—created a need for global transformation.

Case 1: SKF (Swedish ball bearing manufacturer)

Competitive pressures triggered an intense effort to achieve price competitiveness via new economies of scale across the total European market. This led to a need to reorganize to create worldwide manufacturing units, SKF moved through three phases of globalization:

Phase I: 1970. SKF represented a decentralized group of subsidiary companies (Spain, Italy, Germany, France, and the U.K.) each serving a home market with a strong Swedish headquarters and staff organization with the products development from Sweden.

Phase II: 1980. Two major changes were made: the decentralization of product development centers to each regional market for greater local responsiveness and an additional export responsibility for each regional center. By the mid-1980s it was found that more coordination and integration was needed to insure cutting edge technology across the company as well as coordinating forecasting and supply.

Phase III: Mid-1980s. SKF established a forecasting and supply center in Belgium and an engineering and research center in Holland, both separate from headquarters in Sweden thus decentralizing power and turf issues. This has resulted in much more sharing and integration than a headquarters dominated control center. This polycentrism results in a more effective global company, balancing local market responsiveness with economies of scale.

Case 2: Cathay Pacific Airlines

The challenge was coordinating global cargo/passenger route decision-making. Cathay Pacific blended a set of "hard" integrating mechanisms with a set of "soft" mechanisms. The result has been a rapid and substantial level of global coordination.

	Hard	Soft
Integrating Mechanisms	• Information systems for product planning, routine decisions (on-line; replacing or complementing planning process)	• Training • Communications • Get togethers (meetings, conferences, seminars, etc.)
Unifying Goal	• Moving operational targets • "Coordination Centers" • Neutral location • Neither centralized nor decentralized • International staff • Balancing stability and change	• Selection and promotion ("if not cooperative then moved and not promoted") • Incentives linked to total system goals • Mobility / Rotation • "Matrix mind" • Transfer of expertise

Case 3: NEC

NEC has a long term global strategy called "C and C" ("Computer and Communication") requiring the integration of technologies in the communication and computer worlds. It crosses multiple global markets requiring customization as well as economies of scale. The dilemma for NEC is represented below. (As competitive advantage increases so does the degree of coordination difficulty. Thus, the key constraint is solving the organization's design and management process issues.)

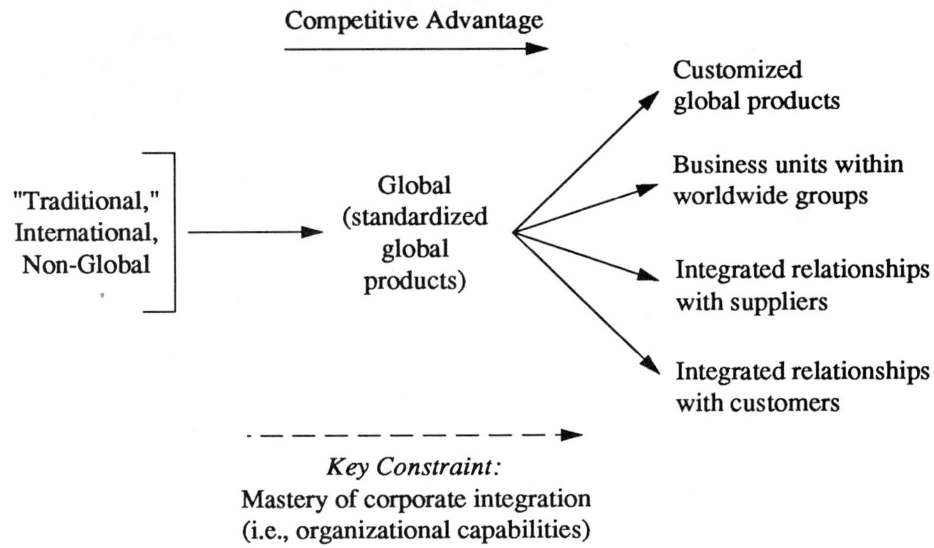

As we look to the 1990s, the core agenda items for each of our groups are as follows.

1990s Agenda for Senior Line Executives

- Determine the balance of local responsiveness to global integration, local adaptation to universal products, local competition to global competition, local manufacturing to world scale factories, low R& D investment to high R&D investment, and local customers to global customers (Galbraith and Kazanjian, 1986), so as to develop the specifications for the global organization.
  - View organization design as a blend of hard and soft mechanisms with special emphasis on process above structure, heterarchy above hierarchy (Hedlund, 1986).

1990s Agenda for Human Resource Management Executives

- Provide the organization with new concepts and paradigms for global organization design—old models lead to traditional hierarchical bureaucratic solutions
- Develop the blend of hard and soft mechanisms; be the process experts
- Provide the action research learning feedback loops for global integration experimentation

1990s Agenda for Academics

- Break the old frames of neo-Weberian structural thinking to begin articulating organic network models of design (Tichy, 1983)
- Develop comparative cross national and cultural longitudinal case studies to learn from practice innovation
- Develop new research methods for global, cross national, and cultural organization studies

3. Strategic Alliances

In order to deliver on global strategies, more and varied alliances are emerging. These are partnerships which are needed to gain market entry, price competitiveness, technology, and to develop new learnings about management. The success of these alliances will be largely determined by a set of human factors, proper pre-screening of partners, proper negotiation, the right conditions for partnering, and good coordination and integration mechanisms. These arrangements are fiendishly difficult to manage, and should be avoided; however, they may be necessary under some circumstances. Thus, we must learn to make them work. This starts with a recognition that there are many variations of alliances; thus definitions and a framework are critical.

1990 Agenda for Senior Line Executives

- Develop clear models of types of alliances and strategic rationales for when to use them (outline the strategic purpose—access to markets, technology access, sourcing best play, management learning, importance of speed, risk diversification, government requirement, etc.)
- Understand the joint venture process: how to find an appropriate partner, the courting and pre-nuptial process, how to arrange the marriage deal, the launching of the venture and honeymoon period, and how to build a successful ongoing relationship

- Design strategic alliance management processes that provide effective means of:
  - Handling joint strategy formulation
  - Developing structural linkages
  - Providing adequate day-to-day coordination and communications
  - Establishing a win/win climate
  - Protecting the bargaining power of each party

1990s Agenda for Human Resource Management Executives

The strategic alliance is an inherently unstable relationship which requires a very delicate set of organizational and management processes to create the necessary levels of trust and ongoing capacity to collaborate. Human Resource Management executives play a critical role in establishing these conditions. Their agenda includes:

- Laying the foundation for the alliance by seeing that a cultural audit of each party is conducted and that there is a clear understanding of each other's intentions and styles
- Selecting the right key people, which is critical to the success of the alliance
- Providing adequate autonomy and maneuvering room for the head of the alliance so that the following can be evolved:
  - The alliance can develop its own shared values and culture
  - Participants can develop their own processes for communication, decision making, and conflict resolution
- Taking the lead in setting up the appropriate monitoring and corrective action mechanisms

1990s Agenda for Academics

The world will be witnessing an unprecedented number of strategic alliances over the next several years. The academics need to take the lead in developing useful typologies of alliances and codifying what is emerging. Over time, they should be in a position to help evaluate the effectiveness of alliances and discern the conditions necessary for success. The proposed agenda is:

- Develop a typology of strategic alliances—from licensing agreements through full joint equity deals, with separate organizations being created (such as Fuji/Xerox)
- Provide analytic frameworks for the systematic study of alliance strategy, structure, and processes

- Develop longitudinal case studies to provide in-depth understanding of alliance dynamics and to develop criteria for evaluating success and failure

4. Global Staffing and Development

Developing leaders with global vision will be the key to world class competitiveness. Japanese corporations' management processes are beginning to feel the strains. Their staffing and development systems will be tested domestically as well as globally. They can no longer afford to relegate second tier managers to international assignments. They must engage in massive localization efforts as well as create new alliances around the globe. U.S. and European organizations are also struggling to find answers. Only those firms that meet the challenge of developing a new breed of global leader will survive.

1990s Agenda for Senior Line Executives

- Honestly assess the depth of commitment to development of global leadership talent for the firm
- Does the company have a culture that truly recognizes the global nature of business? Examples of such commitment can be found in GE's mission: "Number 1 or Number 2 globally in every business or else fix it, close it, or sell the business." Motorola's CEO has committed to the global development of all the top staff; and NEC has invested heavily in a new management development center for its internationalization of managers.
- Top management needs a guiding set of principles for development:
  - What are the leverage points for developing global leaders?
  - What are the critical groups and functions that need to be targeted?
  - How can key managers get bought into the commitment of globalization?
    - They need ways of making them stakeholders (adjust rewards and punishments; encourage active participation)

1990s Agenda for Human Resource Management Executives

- Globalize the Human Resource staff
- Link Human Resource plans to global business plans
- Conduct analyses to determine which key function, key jobs, and job requirements and skills are needed to operate globally
- Develop programs that "internationalize" people, not just operations
- Develop information systems to support global HRM
- Develop a plan for attracting the most capable people in the world: top management, middle management, staff functions, etc.

1990s Agenda for Academics

- Develop valid and effective ways of assessing the competencies required for global staffing
  - Ethnocentrism
  - Flexibility in problem solving
- Identify the best practices in the world—find companies that are doing a better than average job and identify their key success factors
- Look for ways of globalizing the business schools and universities
  - Curriculum and courses
  - Cross-cultural perspectives
  - Students and admissions policies
  - Conferences and events to bring global interests together

Conclusion

The 1987 Japan Symposium was an exciting event because it not only brought into clearer focus a global human resource agenda, but it was itself a model of what the future can bring. The participants represented a wide spectrum of global companies and academics from Europe, the United States, Australia, and Asia-Pacific, all working together to achieve greater understanding and engage in collaborative problem solving. At the end of the week, we felt that as a group we had demonstrated to ourselves the difficulty and challenges of cross-cultural collaboration. But more importantly, we worked through the problems and emerged with a temporary global organization that worked—it was open and communication, problem solving, and conflict resolution processes were exemplary.

The challenge for that group and those of us concerned with the state of our global economy is to recognize that we are entering a period where it is easy to become a victim of forces too great for anyone to control and thus, easy to decide to "wait and see." But the stakes are much too high for this. Global interdependence requires a mobilization of many people, organizations, and nation states. Wherever there is a break in the chain, the repercussions are felt elsewhere down the line. Consistent with our initial intention for the *Human Resource Management* journal "to make a difference," we have begun to increase our commitment to a global agenda. We will take part in the dialogue and events that contribute to shaping the growing global economy. We will be part of the transition and we will chronicle it.

References

Bartlett, C. A., and Yoshihara, H. New challenges for Japanese multinationals: Is organization adaptation this Achilles heel? *Human Resource Management*, Spring 1988, 27(1).

Galbraith, J. R., and Kazanjian, R. K. Organizing to implement strategies of diversity and globalization: The role of matrix designs. *Human Resource Management*, Spring 1986, 25(1).

Hedlund, G. The hypermodern MNC—A heterarchy? *Human Resource Management*, Spring 1986, 25(1).

Schein, E. H. Epilogue. *Human Resource Management*, Spring 1986, 25(1).

Tichy, N. M. Foreword. *Human Resource Management*, Spring 1986, 25(1).

Tichy, N. M., and Devanna, M. A. *The transformational leader*. New York: John Wiley & Sons, Inc., 1986.

Tichy, N. M. Editor's Note. *Human Resource Management*, Spring/Summer 1983a, 22(1/2).

Tichy, N. M. Foreword. *Human Resource Management*, Spring/Summer 1983, Vol. 22, No. 1/2.

Tichy, N. M. Networks in organizations. In P. G. Nystrom and W. Starbuck (Eds.), *Handbook of organization design*. Oxford, UK: Oxford University Press, 1981.

8. GLOBAL MANAGERS FOR GLOBAL CORPORATIONS

PATRICIA SANDERS
Management and Organisation Department, Central Connecticut State University, USA

The evolution of international business into global corporations is breeding a new type of manager: the global manager. A hypothesised emergent global management style (the global business diplomat) uses "geopolitical" concepts as a theoretical foundation for its formulation and describes the reasons why emerging global managers will need to encompass a wider range of attitudes and skills than those held by their inter- or multinational predecessors.

The evolution of international business into global corporations is breeding a new type of manager, the global manager. This article describes a hypothesised emergent global management style, the global business diplomat (GBD), and uses "geopolitical" concepts as a theoretical foundation for its formulation. It describes some reasons why emerging global managers will need to be different from their international or multinational predecessors. It offers a preliminary description of the proposed global management style and includes implications for management educators.

Emergent global management styles have not yet attracted the full attention of management researchers, but appear to be perceived more sharply by management practitioners. Carlo De Benedetti[1], Chairman and CEO of Olivetti SPA, predicts that as ownership of corporations becomes more "grey", leadership will become more critical because wealth will be "spread more to society", and societies will become "more interlocked". Rob Wilmot, the European high tech industry leader, and others, refer to this type of manager as "transnational" or one who has "no national ties".[2]

Changing Context of International Business

Emergent global managers will need to be different from their traditional international or multinational predecessors for two basic reasons. First, the context in which business is conducted worldwide is changing radically, and is creating new types of global business enterprises. Secondly, the changing business context is forcing fundamental shifts in management philosophy and practices of traditional international and multinational businesses. Within the context of this article, the term, "global business enterprise" (GBE) is used as a generic term to describe emerging global business configurations such as "global industries",[3,4,5] "global corporations",[6] "international coalitions",[4] or Global Strategic Partnerships.[7]

Reprinted from the *Journal of Management Development* Vol. 7, No. 1 (1988), pp. 33–44 by permission of the publisher.

GBEs share the following characteristics: they comprise two or more companies or industries, or networks of companies or industries, who co-operate through resource pooling and technological exchange, and who share a long-term global strategic relationship, but all short of mergers and joint ventures.

Emerging GBEs are quite different from their multinational predecessors, and some are predicting the demise of traditional multinational corporations altogether.[6] Traditional multinational corporations are composed of a parent company located in a home country and subsidiaries located in host countries. Multinational corporations (MNCs) operate in many countries to which they customise their products or services, and have international stock ownership.[8] A global corporation operates "with resolute constancy, . . . as if the entire world (or major regions of it) were a single entity; it sells the same things in the same way everywhere".[6]

There are at least four business forces contributing to the creation of emergent types of GBEs. These forces, in turn, are testing traditional MNC management values and practices. Following is a brief description of these forces with implications for global managing.

(1) *Globalisation of markets and production centres.* While systematic assessments of the practicality of developing global markets are few,[9,10] there is a definable and growing trend in this direction. For example, N. V. Philips Gloeilampenfabrieken, the Dutch multinational, in an ongoing restructuring of its worldwide facilities, has established "international production centres" where a given product is made for world markets".[11] George van Houten, the board member for research and development, indicates that at Philips "geographic specialisation, with world matters as its targets, is a trend that will continue" and cites the following advantages: economies of scale, sharing costs and risks of R & D, and achieving product standardisation.[11]

Peter Drucker contends that with some products and services, markets are already global, "with customer values, preferences, and buying habits the same regardless of nation or culture". According to Drucker, if differences do exist, products or services are more apt to be segmented by "life styles rather than by geography".[12] Global corporations will place less emphasis on customising products and offer "globally standardized products that are advanced, functional, reliable, and low priced".[6]

The implication of global markets on management style is that decisions regarding products and services will be made more frequently on a system-wide basis, thus chipping away local autonomy in decision-making by subsidiary and local managers, making their jobs less strategic. Managers will have to know global customer preferences and know how to manage to those preferences. If business moves "too far too fast toward global marketing", the consequences may be "disenchanted" subsidiary managers.[9]

The overall consequences of this loss of local decision autonomy may result in a loss of competent subsidiary managers to less competent successors. This means that managers will need to know more of an entire enterprise system or strategic portfolio rather than a given company, subsidiary, or country.

(2) *Globalisation of communication and telecommunications networks.* Globalisation of industry is becoming possible due to the increased potential for communication centralisation and co-ordination. Telecommunication, with its use of satellites and computer data processing, will enable instant communication on a global scale regarding all aspects of product or service management, financial and cash flow management, global inventories, and management, financial and cash flow management, global inventories, and global R & D management. Dick Tracy's futuristic "2-way wrist computer with a KU-Band satellite uplink" which enabled the international transmission of fingerprints is becoming a reality, rather than a sci-fi high tech gimmick.[14]

The implication of global telecommunication networks for managers is that more information will be generated than can be used at a given time, and at a faster pace. The challenge will be one of how to contribute to such networks and emphasis will be on the entrepreneurial integration of information, rather than on simple use. This will require a form of "high speed management" where decision systems will be integrated into product or service portfolio modelling, technology, and structured innovation.[15]

In formulating policies governing information systems, managers will be faced with two conflicts. First, they will need to resolve tensions between innovation and control, and to resolve conflicts between technical experts and users in "developing skills for dealing with the new technology and in setting priorities".[16]

(3) *Globalisation of capital.* Global strategies go against traditional tests for capital allocation and will require global financing systems.[6] In global markets, capital appropriations will be managed as systems decision, rather than local operating decisions. In addition, debt, capital investment, and dividend policies will vary with the requirements of an integrated investment programme of the whole company or trans-nationally, rather than by subsidiary or local operating unit. While not an overwhelming trend, there seems to be some movement in the direction of using "neutral" currencies, such as the European Currency Unit.[17]

The implication of global financing for management is that once again it will deteriorate subsidiary autonomy in the decision-making process, and particularly in appropriations decisions. This means that managers will have greater need for knowledge and co-ordination skills regarding international monetary systems. "Localized financial management" will be a "prescription for disaster" for businesses operating in the global economy.[13]

(4) *Global competition.* International competition has long been a business reality. What distinguishes the current wave of competition from its

predecessors is the increased intensification of global competition due to slowing or contracting markets, and new competition from established producers, less developed countries, developing nations and newly industrialised nations;[18] global automation and world-class manufacturing;[18,19] and "competitive scope', which refers to the "breadth of activities" an industry must employ to remain competitive.[4]

The implications of global competition for global managing are many and diverse. Two significant implications include the ability of managers to develop global strategies which transcend company or country boundaries, and then to develop and to create innovative organisational structures to implement these strategies. Organisational structures must balance and co-ordinate two competing dimensions: country and global, where "the ultimate authority must represent the global dimension if a global strategy is to prevail".[4]

Self-contradicting as it may seem, intensified global competition will require a fundamental shift in management values from competitive to collaborative thinking, and actions where managerial control is flexible but interdependent. Perlmutter and Heenan advise that "managers who want to implement Global Strategic Partnerships must be ready to make fundamental philosophical changes. Without a new mind-set, GSPs are bound to fail".[7]

Changing International Management Philosophy

During the past two decades a body of research has emerged critical of the global power and influence of large multinational corporation.[20-23] These critics have charged that managers of large MNCs would have more influence over the life-styles and wealth of nations of the world than would sovereign governments. The predicted results were an uneven distribution of wealth and global homogeneity, Western-style. While most of these predictions have failed to materialise, the forces for the globalisation of business require a new management philosophy. The changing, or hopefully simultaneously emergent, management philosophy will refer specifically to changes between traditional MNCs and emergent GBEs brought about as a result of the above mentioned global forces.

(1) *Autonomy v. centralisation.* The traditional multinational corporation is composed of a parent in a home country with subsidiaries or "siblings" in foreign countries. Decision making within an MNC is divided not only functionally, but between parent and subsidiaries.[8] Traditionally, major decisions relative to capital appropriations, business strategy, key personnel, and research and development were centralised in the parent in the home country, but in manufacturing, marketing and finance decisions, usually a great deal of autonomy was granted to subsidiary managers. While some researchers have challenged this traditional balance of autonomy and centralisation in MNCs,[24] the globalisation of markets, capital and

manufacturing is requiring more centralised and interdependent systems decisions within the emergent GBEs.

In terms of a shift in management philosophy, this means that managers, whether in the "parent" or in a "subsidiary" will have to know an entire global system, rather than a given company or country. Knowledge alone, however, is insufficient for effective management. More importantly, this will require a "global systems loyalty" rather than company or country loyalty. To GBE managers the distinctions between parent-home country and subsidiary-foreign country will be irrelevant, if they exist at all, and "loss" of autonomy will not be an issue. By global systems loyalty is meant, a fundamental belief in the efficacy of the set of decisions in the business relationship, irrespective of specific company, country, culture, or degree of autonomy versus centralisation. In the final analysis, perhaps autonomy and centralisation are not mutually exclusive, but simultaneous properties of the systems decision-making process.

(2) *Competition v. collaboration.* The traditional management philosophy of large MNCs is competitive for world markets. In fact, recent publications[3,25] advocate a philosophy of global competitiveness through global strategies where the goal is to "win out" in the competitive game. In a case study of three global competitors, the formula for success was defined as the ability

> to control leverage points, from cross-national production scale economies to the foreign competitors' sources of cash flow. By taking unconventional action, such as lowering prices of an important product or in key markets, the company makes the competitors' response more expensive and difficult. Its main objective is to improve its own effectiveness while eroding that of its competitors.[5]

Others have promoted "readaptive" formuli to make "maturing" American industries less vulnerable to "foreign" competition.[26]

The GBEs of the future will be more similar to global strategic partnerships (GSPs) where co-operation and competition are balanced.[8] Perlmutter and Heenan define six signs of success in GSPs, who learn to share their abilities:

(1) A "win-win" Mission.

(2) A balanced or synergistic strategy of co-operation and competition.

(3) Governance driven by parity rather than power.

(4) Compatible corporate cultures.

(5) New organisational patterns driven by partnership.

(6) Unitary "Management" methods.[7]

According to Perlmutter and Heenan:

> In the traditional view, competitive advantage is a product of a home-country orientation, proprietary technology, centralized decision making, vertical planning systems, and market dominance. The new global model, on the other hand, is more flexible about ownership and managerial control. It encourages joint decision making, vertical and horizontal planning, and fusion of competent allies from around the world despite cultural differences.[7]

Finally, Kenichi Ohmae, a critic of traditional MNC models, concludes that

> traditional multinationals have tried to do everything on their own as they entered each market. They can't do that anymore because the skills and products required to compete worldwide have become more sophisticated and complex.[27] Ohmae indicates that the future success of multinationals "will be their ability to develop and enhance company-to-company relationships, particularly across national and cultural boundaries".[27]

(3) *Parochialism v. Ecumenicism.* An ethnocentric/geocentric model for multinational management has been described.[28,29] This is a well described and accepted model which this writing does not dispute. Ethnocentrism, however, is a social concept and the above dichotomies are more consistent with the hypothesised geopolitical model of the merging global manager. Parochialism and ecumenicism, as used here, imply a way of thinking and influencing, rather than a way of behaving. In this context parochialism refers to narrow thinking and influence, limited to ones' boundaries, whereas ecumenicism refers to worldwide thinking and influence. In German geopolitical writing, two terms may be used to describe the latter type of thinking: *Lebensraum,* or "living space", and *Weltanschauung* or "world view".[30] While it is difficult to translate these terms precisely from the German to English, both are dynamic concepts and may be interpreted here as an ability to balance one's influence between one's own living space and globally. This may be the true challenge to the global management development programmes.

Traditionally MNC subsidiary managers, were given instructions on how to "behave" in host countries; this was generally aimed at sensitising them to the habits, customs, mores and culture of the country to which they were assigned. Loyalties, however, were very clear—to "their" company and country.

Global managers, however, will be required to have more of a "world view" or *Weltanschauung. Weltanschauung,* however, refers not to a set of behaviours, but to a way of thinking. If defined as "a way of thinking", it may be very difficult to "train" global managers. Rather, global corporations may have to seek managers with such an orientation in the first place or, as Drucker puts it, multinationals "increasingly will have to open [their] management jobs everywhere to wherever the talent can be found, regardless of passport".[12]

Some MNCs, such as Philips, IBM, Unilever, and Allegheny International, have had some success with searching out global managers.[31] At Unilever, for example, emphasis is placed on developing a cadre of global managers who can be moved from one country to another. Sir Kenneth Durham, Chairman of Unilever PLC, describes the task of watching "carefully about 200 managers, of whom 25 may be starred", and whose job it is "to balance all these (management) balls in the air".[32] At Philips, international managers are referred to as "displaced persons"—who are truly international staff. Kees Krombeen, managing director of the corporate staff bureau says, "When I took this job ten years ago, less than 5 percent of them (managers) were non-Dutch. Today, 40 per cent are, and we have more than 300 non-Dutch (managers) working in Eindhoven".[11]

(4) *Economic globalisation v. political nationalism.* As ownership of multinational business becomes blurred, and as GBEs increase, at the same time the world is expecting a new wave of nationalism, "neoprotectionism", and in some cases outright chauvinism.[33,27] The global manager will have to learn the political realities of doing business as well as business realities. It is skill in handling this parallel political "game" that most likely will distinguish global managers from their traditional MNC counterparts. Drucker indicates that the "changing" MNC" must succeed in becoming a bridge between both the realities of a rapidly integrating world economy and a splintering world polity".[12]

The Global Business Diplomat

Geopolitical concepts are used as a theoretical foundation for describing the global business diplomat (GBD). Using these concepts, differences and similarities between global and traditional MNC managers are hypothesised.

Geopolitics is a "method of political thought', and may be defined as "political geography applied to national power politics and its actual strategy".[34] The domain of geopolitics is:

> concerned with conflict and change, evolution and revolution, attack and defense, the dynamics of terrestrial space and of the political forces struggling on them for survival".[34]

Geopolitical thought had its beginnings in Germany between the two World Wars, and it is not synonymous with "political geography".[30] Geopolitics represents a method to study political phenomena in relationship to their dependence upon and influence on their physical setting and on cultural factors. As a method, it implies predicting future geopolitical events and developing strategies to manage these events. Geopolitics has been referred to as the "geographical conscience of the State".[34]

Table I compares the formulation of emerging GBDs using geopolitical concepts with traditional MNC managers using traditional sociocultural concepts. It uses seven variables to compare the emergent global business diplomat with traditional MNC managers: primary focus, operating arena, value orientation, role, method of analysis, goal, and time orientation. The intent of Table I is not to dichotomise the two management types. It is used as a method for comparison and to illustrate commonalities between the two styles.

It is hypothesised that the earliest group of geopolitical managers in the U.S. emanated from the military, particularly during and after World War II. The movement of leadership talent at that time was from the government or military to private enterprise. The so called "whiz kids", who went to work for such organisations as the Ford Motor Company, are good examples. Their business skills were important, but probably not as important as their knowledge of, and influence in, political circles.

Currently, the small cadre of experts performing similar roles today continue to come from government positions, and, typically, have been senior government officials, where political astuteness and prowess have been accumulated. The difference, however, is that the latter group tends to practice as private consultants, rather than aligning with a specific global corporation.

Table I
GBD AND MNC MANAGERS COMPARED ON SELECTED VARIABLES

	GBD Managers	MNC Managers
Primary Focus	Geopolitical variables	Sociocultural variables
Operating arena	Worldwide/global	Home/host country
Value Orientation	Lebensraum/ Weltanschauung	Ethnocentric/geocentric
Role	Geopolitical strategist	Socioeconomic strategist
Method of Analysis	Geopolitical/risk analysis political/economic risk analysis	Social cost/benefit analysis Socio-economic analysis
Goal	Prediction of and influence over geopolitical events	Forecast socioeconomic/ market trends
Time Orientation	Present/future	Past/present

It is hypothesised that two characteristics, political influence (rather than competitive game playing) and corporate non-alignment, distinguishes the GBD from traditional MNC managers. In addition, the GBD must be comfortable in working with and exerting influence among non-government agencies, which are not only increasing in number, but are gaining in global political influence. It is predicted that the first generation of GBDs will be independent consultants with international government experience. However, as global business enterprises multiply in number and in influence, it will be incumbent upon these corporations to hire and develop their own GBDs. In any event, development will include the ability to engage in international parallel political analysis.

Henry Kissinger, though an extreme example, is the probable embodiment of the future new breed of the non-aligned global business diplomat. In a recent interview, he described his work as dispensing "geopolitical-economic" advice and helping clients "with their international planning".[35] The GBD engages primarily in political risk analysis for corporate clients, who eagerly seek not only their expertise and insight, but their celebrity. Political risk analysis is aimed at predicting the "fate of the country or region or issue".[35]

The GBD will not only engage in the analysis of world problems, but will also engage in actual acts of diplomacy. Their operating arena is the world, their primary role is a non-aligned analysis of international politics and economic problems as they relate to business activities, and their goal is influence on the one hand, and (often) trouble-shooting on the other. Although some current researchers recommend against using outside experts in the early stages of political analysis in preference to line managers,[36] this writing rejects this notion, favouring both the non-alignment and seasoned influence of the GBD consultant.

A Preliminary Portrait of the Global Business Diplomat

While non-aligned, the GBD works closely with insiders of a corporation. Thus, loyalty is to the business transaction at hand, rather than to a company, industry or country. Obviously, there is a great potential for conflict of interest to occur, but a known track record of integrity and success will make the non-aligned consultant attractive to global corporations. Being non-aligned also increases the potential for collaboration on many diverse levels.

After non-alignment, the second most important characteristic of the GBD is experience with or within a national government (and not only the U.S. government) and that ethnocentric barriers do not exist.

The role of the GBD is not to engage in actual negotiations but to "set up" the negotiating arena where other global managers participate. In this regard they also will need to manage complex and diverse information data bases, and in many instances will have privy to "inside" information or inside sources. They are less concerned about a particular corporation's strategy formulation, but need to understand the compatibility (or incompatibility) of a particular business strategy with political, economic, social and ecological strategies. Likewise, the antagonism between centralisation and autonomy operationally is not relevant to the GBD. Autonomy is a by-product of non-alignment; however it does not give licence to act capriciously. Corporate regulations and constraints apply and must be dealt with creatively. In fact, this model partially emerged from Brooke's research[25] on autonomy and centralisation where he concluded that:

> New styles of management will probably emerge at both ends of the spectrum. At the most integrated, there is likely to be a demand for special skills of diplomacy both within the company and with respect to governments and other interests in the environment. At the decentralised end, there will be greater reliance on the business relationship and less on the structure and the instruction.

The GBD operates more closely to the centralised end of the spectrum, but cannot ignore the decentralised end of the continuum.

Implications for Developing Emergent Global Managers

Perhaps global managers will ultimately be "born" and not made. This is not consolation for management educators. However, the following implications are presented.

Emergent global managers have at least three distinguishing characteristics: the ability to understand and manage a world view in their business relationships as well as to manage their own inner space; the ability to relinquish decision autonomy and at the same time to develop a collaborative approach to business relationships, and to understand their own national heritage, while at the same time understanding global political risks and strategies. Emergent management development programmes for global managers will need to be different from traditional programmes in at least three ways.

First, traditional management development programmes have tended to focus on managing cross-cultural differences in values, customs, and mores, rather than on understanding inner similarities, such as compassion, loyalty, sexuality and fealty. For example, emergent management development programmes will have to include an understanding of how spirituality, superstition, taboo and gender roles affect relationships, including business relationships, among people of varying cultural backgrounds. A focus on differences promotes stereotypes, while a focus on similarities promotes an understanding of relevant differences.

Secondly, traditional MNC management development programmes have tended to focus on cognitive cultural differences, rather than on emotional and intuitive similarities, and methods in approaching similar problems such as death, loss of a job, or child rearing and family life. As a result, the focus of education has been on content and outcomes, and not on similarities in approaching and processing problems, regardless of the content or quality of outcome. Future management development programmes will need to cross over into other disciplines, such as anthropology, archaeology, applied psychology and philosophy, in search of a holistic understanding of how people approach and process similar problems, regardless of national or ethnic origin.

Finally, traditional multinational managers were frequently advised to steer clear of the political realities and analysis in host countries. Today this advice would be naive, where often the economic fate of a country, and the international business community may be tied to the political fate of that country. Iran is a case in point, where in the mid-seventies, U.S. oil companies and other multinational corporations found their economic futures tied to a hostile Ayatollah who had replaced a friendly Shah. Future management development programmes will need to include education and training in diplomacy, political risk analysis and statesmanship. This will require skills that focus on political and geographic analysis which are future orientated and predictive in nature, rather than on skills which seek to develop retrospective socio-economic analyses to understand present or future events.

It is hoped that this presentation will contribute to the growing body of knowledge of the roles and responsibilities governing managerial behaviours in a global setting. Management educators must be concerned about their role in developing and preparing future global managers. Fundamental questions include: can a global management perspective be taught or is providing global awareness a more realistic goal,[31,37] and to what extent are we witnessing the birth of a global management culture and to what extent is it nationally bounded?

A final implication of such theorising for management educators is the search for the development of a global business ethic. Can we possibly imagine a global management morality without a definition of fundamental underlying moral values?

References

1. Piper, A., "Carlo De Benedetti: Facing the Realities of Global Alliances", *International Management,* Vol. 41 No. 4, pp. 22-30.
2. Hill, R., "Personal Profile: Rob Wilmot", *International Management,* Vol. 41 No. 5, 1986, p. 37.
3. Porter, M. E., Competitive Strategy: *Techniques for Analyzing Industries and Competitors,* The Free Press, New York, 1980.
4. Porter, M. E., "Changing Patterns of International Competition", *California Management Review,* Vol. 28 No. 2, 1986, pp. 9-40.
5. Hout, T., Porter, M. and Rudden, E., "How Global Companies Win Out", Harvard Business Review, Vol. 60 No. 5, 1982, pp. 98-108.
6. Levitt, T., "The Globalization of Markets", *Harvard Business Review,* Vol. 61 No. 3, 1983, pp. 92-102.
7. Perlmutter, H. V. and Heenan, D. A., "Co-operate to Compete Globally", *Harvard Business Review,* Vol. 64. No. 2, 1986, pp. 136-52.
8. Schnitzer, M. C., Liebrenz, J. L. and Kubin, K. W., *International Business,* South-Western Publishing Co., Dallas, Texas 1985.
9. Quelch, J. A. and Hoff, E. J., "Customizing Global Marketing", *Harvard Business Review,* Vol. 64 No. 3, 1986, pp. 59-68.
10. Davidson, W. and Haspeslagh, P., "Shaping a Global Product Organization", *Harvard Business Review,* Vol. 61 No. 4, 1982, pp. 125-32.

11. Hill, R., "Philips over the Years: A Model of the Maturing Multinational", *International Management,* Vol. 41 No. 8, 1986, pp. 28-32.
12. Drucker, P., "The Changing Multinational", *The Wall Street Journal,* Wednesday, 15 January, 1986, p. 28.
13. Times-Mirror Inc., "Dick Tracy Comic", *The Hartford Courant,* Sunday, 21 September, 1986.
14. Cushman, D. and King, S., "The Impact of High Technology on International Management", in Shuter, R. and Chatterjea, S., (Eds.), *International Management and Comparative Management Systems,* Cultural Press, Wawatosa, Wisconsin, 1986.
15. McFarlan, F. W. and McKenney, J. L., "The Information Archipelago—Governing the New World", *Harvard Business Review,* Vol. 61 No. 4, 1983, pp. 91-99.
16. Bernier, L., "Here's Why More Companies are Opting for the ECU", *International Management,* Vol. 41 No. 2, 1986, pp. 46-48.
17. Ball, D.A. and McCulloch, W. H., *International Business: Introduction and Essentials,* Business Publications Inc., Texas, 1982.
18. Jelinek, M. and Goldhar, J., "The Strategic Implications of the Factory of the Future", *Sloan Management Review,* Vol. 25 No. 2, 1984, pp. 29-37.
19. Schonberger, R., *World Class Manufacturing,* The Free Press, New York, 1986.
20. Bagley, E., *Beyond the Conglomerates,* AMACOM, New York, 1974.
21. Barnet, R. and Muller, R., *Global Reach: The Power of the Multinational Corporations,* Simon and Schuster, New York, 1974.
22. Scheer, R., *America after Nixon: The Age of the Multinationals,* McGraw-Hill Inc., New York, 1975.
23. Vernon, R., *Storm over the Multinationals: The Real Issues,* Harvard University Press, Cambridge, Massachusetts, 1977.
24. Brooke, M. Z., "Autonomy and Centralization in Multinational Firms", *International Studies of Management and Organization,* Vol. 14 No. 1, 1984, pp. 3-22.
25. Porter, M. E., *Competitive Advantage: Creating and Sustaining Superior Performance,* The Free Press, New York, 1985.
26. Lawrence, P. R. and Dyer, D., *Renewing American Industry: Organizing for Efficiency and Innovation,* The Free Press, New York, 1983.
27. Ohmae, K., Triad Power: *The Coming Shape of Global Competition,* The Free Press, New York, 1985.
28. Perlmutter, H. V., "The Tortuous Evolution of the Multinational Corporation", *Columbia Journal of World Business,* Vol. 2, 1969, pp. 9-18.
29. Heenan, D. A. and Perlmutter, H. V., *Multinational Organizational Development: A Social Architecture Perspective,* Addison-Wesley, Reading, Massachusetts, 1979.

30. Kristof, L. K. D., "The Origins and Evolution of Geopolitics", *Journal of Conflict Resolution*, Vol. 4, 1960, pp. 14-51.
31. Spooner, P., "The Art of Making Global Managers", *Chief Executive* (UK), October, 1984, pp. 20-22.
32. Muson, H., "How Unilever Moves the Earth", *Across the Board*, Vol. 22 No. 9, 1985, pp. 2-23.
33. Barton, J. H., "Coping with Technological Protectionism", *Harvard Business Review*, Vol. 64 No. 6, 1984, pp. 91-97.
34. Weigert, H. W., *Generals and Geographers: The Twilight of Geopolitics*, Oxford University Press, London, 1942.
35. Gelb, L. H., "Kissinger Means Business", *The New York Times Magazine*, Sunday, 20 April, 1986, pp. 28-42.
36. Shreeve, T. W., "Be Prepared for Political Changes Abroad", *Harvard Business Review*, Vol. 62 No. 4, 1984, pp. 111-122.
37. Maisonrouge, J., "The Education of a Modern International Manager", *Journal of International Business Studies*, Vol. 14 No. 1, 1983, pp. 141-146.

V THE GLOBAL FLOW OF INFORMATION

9. TRANSBORDER DATA FLOWS: IMPLICATIONS FOR MULTINATIONAL CORPORATIONS

RAJAN CHANDRAN
Associate professor of marketing, Temple University in Philadelphia

ARVIND PHATAK
Professor of management and international business, Temple University in Philadelphia

RAKESH SAMBHARYA
Assistant professor of management and international business at the University of Kentucky in Lexington.

Transmitting data across national borders is crucial to many multinational corporations' operations, yet the issue is continually clouded by different regulations in different countries as well as the reasons behind them. The authors suggest that MNCs adopt a cooperative approach when dealing with other countries on this issue.

In 1980 Sweden forced Xerox Corp. to change its data-processing operations. Xerox had been processing the payroll for its Swedish employees, among others, at a center in London. The Swedish government forced Xerox to discontinue this transborder processing and hire a Swedish service bureau to process the payroll.[1]

Burroughs, which was developing a centralized personnel-records system in the United States on all its employees around the world, was prevented from completing the project because of West German objections.[2] Like the Swedish government, the West German government did not want sensitive data on West German nationals ending up in a data bank in the United States.

The Bank Act of Canada requires banks operating in that country to process and maintain copies of all data pertaining to Canadian customers only in Canada. Brazil prohibits offshore processing of data and requires companies to maintain copies of computer data bases inside Brazil. France, meanwhile, is considering the assessment of taxes based on transborder-data-flow (TDF) content, as well as a value-added tax on processed software entering the country.[3]

The regulation of TDFs by various means is, obviously, of increasing concern to countries and multinational corporations (MNCs). The increased concern also is evident in the number of recent articles published on TDFs.[4]

This article examines this issue in depth. In the first of four sections, the article defines TDFs, discusses the importance of information for business and government, and deals with the current technology involved in TDFs.

Section two focuses on the underlying conflicts associated with TDFs. While most businesses perceive TDFs as indispensable for day-to-day operations, governments view them as a threat to their interests.

Section three notes on the implications of TDF regulation for MNC operations and states U.S. policy on this issue, while section four offers some guidelines for MNCs and some closing comments.

TDFS: Information, Technology and Networks

The most accepted definition of TDF is the one used by the United Nations Center on Transnational Corporations (UNCTC). Transborder Data Flows are movements of machine-readable data for processing, storage or retrieval across national boundaries.[5] TDF involves point-to-point delivery of messages between nations, between international organizations, and between nations and international organizations.

The importance of information in our world cannot be overemphasized. According to Daniel Bell, the post-industrial society is basically an information society. Bell views the issue as follows:

> The main difference between an industrial and a post-industrial society is that the sources of growth and innovation in a post-industrial society are derived increasingly from the codification of theoretical knowledge, rather than from inventions . . . . Society no longer will be based on a labor theory of value, but on a knowledge theory of value, i.e., value is fundamentally increased, not by labor, but by knowledge.[6]

The information industry has become the prime force for harnessing this knowledge. This industry, which includes hardware, software, and data generation, receiving, and transmission, is a major factor in the industrial structure of developed nations today.

Information is viewed as an essential ingredient in facilitating growth and development and in gaining political and economic power. The importance of the information sector can be seen from the fact that while the combined U.S. market for computer communications was $150 billion in 1979, the total world market in 1990 will be about $560 billion. Total U.S. exports of information and communication services were approximately $30 billion in 1983.[7]

Unlike the traditional assets of labor, capital, and land, information is expandable, transferable, shareable, and diffusable. Information-resource management is widely regarded as critical in the management of an enterprise. TDFs are utilized by MNCs in such diverse areas as finance, marketing, accounting, manufacturing and production planning, strategic planning, and administration.

City planners now think that just as rivers, railroads, and highway interchanges once determined where commercial settlements would occur, access to the latest in information-receiving and transmission technology will determine the next generation's location of commercial settlements. Olympia and York, the Canadian real estate developers, and Tishman Speyer, of New York, are developing buildings and office parks with the latest in information-receiving and transmission technology. Furthermore, The Port Authority of New York and New Jersey, in conjunction with Merrill

Lynch and Western Union, is developing a teleport with all the latest in information-receiving and transmission technology.[8]

Technology

Data transmission across borders is accomplished today through computers and telecommunication links. Current trends indicate a further convergence of development in computer and telecommunications technology. The continuing advances in two-way satellite communication systems, microwave transmission, encryption and filing techniques, terminals, and bandwidth and cellular technology provide an ever-widening variety of transmission, storage, processing, and retrieval services.

Advances in communications technology have made it possible to transmit information in the form of digital signals, which permit higher-volume data communications than analog signals. The use of these digital signals by telecommunication networks has made the whole process of information transfer efficient and cost-effective. Digital logic has blurred the lines between data, telegraph, and voice circuits for computer communications. It is now possible to carry voice and data traffic in a single stream of codes in corporate-communications networks across national boundaries.

International Data Networks

A worldwide network infrastructure has developed to accommodate the increasing volume of data transactions. In the U.S. and many other parts of the world, many private and public networks have been or are being formed. From the United States, for example, private data networks reach into Canada, Europe, Japan, and Australia, covering practically the whole Organization for Economic Co-operation and Development area. Examples include TELENET, TYMNET, CYBERNET and MARK III. There are also special-purpose networks, such as the airline industry's SITA, an inter-airline reservation and ticketing system, and the banking industry's SWIFT, an electronic fund transfer system linking banks all over the world. Most European countries are developing public data networks, including TRANSPAC, EPSS, EURONET and The Nordic Public Data Network. Data traffic volume in Europe increased twelvefold from 1975 to 1985, due to the increasing internationalization of markets and expanding intergovernmental transactions in the areas of defense, administration, taxation, and crime.[9]

Types of Networks

Networks that are used to transmit data flows can be classified as either public or private. Public networks can be further subdivided into two categories:

- Private commercial networks, of which COMSHARE, CYBERNET, and MARK III are examples; and

- State-owned commercial networks, of which EURONET, EPSS and The Nordic Network are examples.

Private corporate networks consist of a central computer in the MNC's home country linked via privately leased telecommunication lines and satellites to its various domestic and international units. An example of this kind of a network would be Satellite Business Systems, a joint venture of Aetna and IBM. MCI and Xerox also operate their systems. Other examples of sophisticated corporate networks are Citibank's Globecom and General Electric's MARK III.

Public networks offer their highly sophisticated systems for two major types of services, time-shared data processing and data-base-information transmission and retrieval. Many organizations find it cheaper to rely on these networks for international data processing than to build and maintain their own private systems.

MNCs are the heaviest users of TDF because of the vast amount of information they need to control and coordinate their subsidiaries. Research done by the authors indicates that the MNC's information needs are positively related to both the number of subsidiaries and percentage of foreign sales. The importance that MNCs attach to TDF can be judged from the fact that by 1985 more than 200 MNCs were operating their own computer-communications systems.

From remote on-line terminals, overseas data are sent to the central computer system in the home country for processing. Return instructions are then sent back to the overseas affiliates. Consequently, neither data-processing capabilities nor analytical expertise is needed at the overseas sites. Their basic tasks there lie in data collection and entry, and in decision implementation. The network permits highly centralized corporate management. The U.S. domination in networks and American MNC's desire for operational control to be located in the U.S. has led to concentration of data in U.S. corporate data banks.

The electronic transmission of data has become imperative for certain MNCs in the financial services and travel industries, as well as for computer service bureaus and news businesses. The Business and Industry Advisory Committee of the OECD pointed out that some MNCs have found it worthwhile to invest large sums of money in private networks, indicating how essential a well-functioning TDF is to modern business.

Areas of Conflict

As ways to use TDFs and networks multiply, conflicts between governments and MNCs that use them arise in several areas.

Economic Issues

American computer-manufacturing firms dominate the computer industry and data networks on a global level and are expected to continue their domination over the next decade. Canadian, European, Japanese, and other governments fear the standard-setting advantages this dominance provides to the American firms in information products and services. These nations anticipate the loss of domestic and foreign markets to American firms offering sophisticated data-processing services via international data networks. This dominance, they feel, represents a direct threat the their economies.

When data-processing services are consistently purchased from outside the country, the development of a domestic information-service industry is stymied. This situation results in a loss of job opportunities to nationals, exacerbates the unemployment problem, and results in a loss of tax revenue. Many countries (Brazil, for example) have passed laws to ensure that data processing is performed inside the country.[10] This guarantees jobs and helps the domestic computer industry grow.

TDFs, which make overseas data processing easier, also result in a currency outflow. Additionally, the use of foreign data-processing services provides an expense screen for transferring funds from the local subsidiaries to the parent company abroad.

Complications have also arisen in the pricing of the data lines and interconnections used to transmit data flows. Companies traditionally have leased lines privately from Post, Telephone and Telegraph Departments (PTTs), which are government-controlled monopolies. These lines have been paid for on a time basis, rather than on a speed, volume, or content basis.[11] In many parts of the world, notably Western Europe and the Eastern-Bloc countries, these government-controlled telecommunication service links are major sources of revenue for their respective PTTs. The proliferation of privately leased lines has been regarded with apprehension by European PTTs, because it affects the load factor and resultant revenue for these public networks.

The Italians have countered with a proposed volume-sensitive pricing scheme. The French have suggested content pricing based on the intrinsic value of data.[12] European PTTs aim to increase the cost of privately leased lines until they became prohibitively expensive. The PTTs hope to force companies to switch to public lines so they can protect their monopolies.

Closely related to the pricing issue is the issue of the taxability of data flows.[13] This involves possibly levying a tariff on both raw data as it electronically leaves the country and value-added data as it enters the country. Presently tax is collected only when data is transferred through some solid medium, such as tape or a disk.

Any attempt to tax data flows, whether to raise revenue or as a means of gaining control, obviously would have grave implications for MNC operations. The imposition of duties and attempts to gain control would undoubtedly lead to "contraband data" and "data havens."[14] The evolution of TDFs challenges the effectiveness and appropriateness of tax structures which were developed primarily for manufacturing economies.

Privacy Protection

Gordon C. Everest defines privacy as:

> . . . the right of the individual to be left alone and to determine what information about oneself to share with others . . . .Whereas privacy relates

> to one individual, data privacy relates to the personal data pertaining to the individual held by organizations. The privacy rights of an individual can be violated when data pertaining to that individual are misused.[15]

Protection of privacy is a major issue in the information-driven society in which we live. The capacity of modern computers to store and retrieve data on individuals creates concern about abuse by those who control the information. Most of the developed nations of the world either have or are writing legislation protecting the privacy of individuals within their own countries. Some countries are imposing regulations on the transfer of personal data across national borders, as well. The fear is that foreign storage and data processing can be used to circumvent national regulations on protection of privacy, or that foreign governments might easily gain access to sensitive data about citizens. The issue of extraterritorial jurisdiction for violation of privacy laws threatens to become a major issue.[16]

Details of legislation vary from country to country, reflecting socio-cultural differences. While in the U.S. there is a tendency to speak of privacy of the individual, Europeans and others prefer to speak of data protection. Differences also exist concerning the definition of "person"—whether it includes both natural and legal persons (associations, corporations and other institutional entities). European countries in the OECD have adopted provisions that would extend protection to all legal persons. This has resulted in the creation of omnibus laws, which are applicable to all sectors of society. These statutes generally require notice, permission, or licensing for files containing personal data. The regulations create government monitoring and enforcement agencies but do not provide effective judicial mechanisms for properly redressing abuses.

Financial services MNCs, such as credit card companies that provide services at the retail level, would feel the effects of these omnibus laws most heavily. Without the ability to check on individuals and companies in European countries, U.S. firms would be restricted in their functioning. The inability to store data about personnel and companies across national boundaries raises serious operational and control problems for multinational companies.

Some progress has, however, been made in easing these restrictions through the OECD, which released in 1980 guidelines governing the Protection and Privacy of TDFs. Many U.S. corporations and industry associations have endorsed these guidelines. Such efforts could be successful in minimizing restrictions in TDF.

Political and National Sovereignty Issues

Control over data flows can provide considerable political and economic power. France's former Minister of Justice, Louis Joinet, addressed this point from the European perspective at a symposium held in Vienna in September 1977:

> Information is power, and economic information is economic power. Information has economic value and the ability to store, process and

> transmit certain types of data may well give one country political and technological advantage over other countries. This in turn, may lead to a loss of national sovereignty.

Various governments have placed restrictions on international transfers of certain types of vital data (for example, transferring data on oil samples for analysis in U.S.) to protect their security and sovereignty.[17]

The growing dependence on international networks for data flows may expose countries to unknown political dangers. Systems failures in the country where the computers are situated could lead to interruption of international data flows, resulting in chaos. Industrial enterprises, airlines, banks, and governmental agencies, to name a few, increase their vulnerability by depending more and more on data bases and computing facilities situated abroad. As a result of the storage of various kinds of vital data in the U.S., some countries fear that the U.S. and its MNCs may know more about them than they know about themselves. This is a distinct disadvantage not only in political and commercial negotiations, but in wartime as well.

Many third-world countries and even some developed nations are alarmed at what they perceive as cultural imperialism practiced by data-rich countries on data-poor countries. John Eger states:

> What many countries fear is cultural inundation or annihilation. They are resisting what they call "electronic colonization" or "electronic imperialism." They do not want their minds, banks, governments, news, literature, music, or any other aspect of their lives to be Americanized. Neither do they want to be Anglicized, Sovietized, or otherwise victimized by advanced technology and information that freely flows across their borders, thus possibly causing their own identities to become extinct.[18]

Modern television transmission, coupled with the computer and satellites, have considerably enlarged the means for transferring data across borders. Countries want to continue to have the means to control the nature of the messages that reach their people, whether through magazines, books, films, or computers. Until recently, computer communications did not appear to pose a threat and were ignored. Countries have now awakened, however, and want to tighten the data flow.

The Impact of TDF Restriction

There have been very few empirical studies measuring the affect of TDF restrictions on MNCs. Business International surveyed 89 companies regarding TDF and concluded that MNCs are already dependent on international data flows for their foreign operations and will become even more so in the future.[19] Kahwaty studied the impact of TDF laws on U.S. banks and reported that these laws create operational inefficiencies, lower competitiveness, and hinder centralization of foreign data.[20] A more recent survey study by Kane, who surveyed 370 service companies, reported that the majority, 63 percent consider TDF regulation to be a serious potential problem, and 28 percent reported current problems.[21] Selig, in his survey of MNC information-systems practices, reported that executives consider TDF to be a major issue facing MNCs.[22] A brief overview of the implications of the restrictions, as envisioned by some leading experts, is given below.

1. Conforming to the myriad TDF laws in every country will result in increased overhead costs. It will also require the creation of additional departments and the assignment of extra personnel, often withdrawing them from revenue-producing activities.
2. Inconsistent tariffs and volume- or content-sensitive pricing will also result in increased costs to MNCs. Prices of products in various countries will increase, since data flows account for an increasing share of the cost of providing goods and services today.
3. TDF legal sanctions, if applied, will hinder operations and may disrupt them completely. In some cases data-protection laws are vague and leave room for discriminatory application. They may therefore discourage TDF use because MNCs may fear the penalties for innocent violations of complex regulations.
4. Given that ready transmission of data across national borders may not be possible, it may be necessary for MNCs to duplicate data files and data bases in foreign countries and to pay for extra hardware and software and the personnel to maintain them.
5. TDF regulation will inhibit the development of international data-processing networks that would offer services at the lowest possible cost.
6. It may be possible to transmit data only to those countries with reciprocal data protection laws, as there may be conflicts of jurisdiction between the MNC's home country and the subsidiary's host country.
7. United States time-sharing suppliers (TELENET, for example), may be effectively priced out of the market by PTT tariff escalations. Many U.S. MNCs rely upon these suppliers to a significant degree.

Similarly, TDF barriers can have harmful effects on home and host countries as follows:

1. There is the danger that the countries regulating TDFs may be creating a patchwork of contradictory national laws and taxes that ultimately could cause worldwide confusion in communications.
2. There is also the possibility that in a world where TDF laws are not standardized, data havens will spring up in countries with few or no laws. Data and data-processing investments would tend to dry up in the regulating countries and move into these haven countries.
3. Such a move could thwart the advancement of computer hardware and software technology in those regulating countries.
4. Data-protection legislation may lead to another information-services war, which could have disastrous consequences.

We have summarized in the **Table** some of the key issues and barriers related to TDF and the consequent implications for MNCs and countries.

Table
MAJOR TDF ISSUES AND CONSEQUENT IMPLICATIONS

Issues/Barriers	Implications for Countries	Implications for MNCs
Restrictions on the availability of PTT-owned leased lines to private companies and the availability of interconnections	Increasing revenues for local PTTs by diverting traffic to their public lines	Increases costs to large users MNCs may be forced to rely on an inferior system, thereby affecting efficiency
Imposition of technical standards on computer and telecommunications hardware unilaterally	Protects and promotes local computer and telecommunications hardware May also improve export potential of country, especially with nations with which they have close economic and defense ties	Prohibits and/or limits the opportunity of foreign vendors to provide compatible hardware and software systems to users in the country Barrier may also inhibit quality
Denial of access to Euronet to companies using computers located outside Europe	Promotes local information industries	Denies access to lucrative European market
Requirement that data-processing functions be performed within a country	Provides "infant industry" protection for local data-processing service industries TDFs are subject to approval by government Opens employment of local nationals in a new field	Increases costs to both MNCs and users. As local industry capability grows, the MNC market share will drop Governments will further deny international data links to MNCs
Restrictions on foreign direct investment in the local information industry	Develops and protects local computer industry	Discriminates against foreign investors and eliminates the manufacturing and/or marketing of certain equipment
Controls over imports of computer and telecommunications hardware	Provides infant-industry protection for computer industry Also protects the local labor market	Restricts foreign manufacturers from access to European and other markets Increases cost and operational efficiency of users
Unconventional pricing of data, such as volume and content pricing of information	Promotes public networks and in-country data processing by giving them a competitive edge	Stymies growth of private networks Increases costs to users
Restrictions on commercial visas for personal of MNCs	Promotes local information industry and increases employment	Stymies expansion of MNC operation in those countries
Concern over protection and control of privacy	Requires enactment of numerous national privacy and data protection laws ensuring that privacy of individuals and corporations is maintained	Creates day-to-day operational and control problems
Concerns about national sovereignty and cultural identity	Raises fear of getting swamped by U.S. dominance in computer and telecommunications industry	Promotes further restrictions on foreign direct investment, operations, control of MNCs in DCs and LDCs Rise of nationalism and protectionism

Source: Adapted from "International Telecommunications and Information Policy," Hearings Before a Subcommittee of the Committee on Government Operations, House of Representatives, Ninety-Seventh Congress (Washington: U.S. Government Printing Office, 1982).

U.S. Position and Policy

The U.S. views many TDF barriers as being motivated mainly by economic considerations. W. Michael Blumenthal, the chairman of Burroughs Corporation and former secretary of commerce in President Carter's Cabinet, observes that the worldwide rise in nationalism and its economic sidekick, protectionism, are the causes of the TDF problem.[23] With barriers to trade of goods eased through the General Agreement on Tariffs and Trade and other trade liberalization agreements, barriers to trade of services have stepped into the international limelight. The new protectionism manifests itself in the service sector, with restrictions on TDF being one such area.

The situation with regard to developing nations is somewhat different. John Eger, a consultant on communications law and regulatory policy and former telecommunications advisor to Presidents Nixon and Ford, states that many of the countries resisting or blocking data flows are not concerned with economic competition in any literal sense. They have no information technology of their own and therefore cannot hope presently to compete with technologically rich nations. This possibly causes their opposition and apprehension.[24]

The U.S. seeks to explain its case by pointing out the benefits of unrestricted TDFs. TDFs will be beneficial to developed and developing countries.[25] Some of these benefits are stated below.

1. TDFs will make it possible to coordinate the management and research skills of one geographic area with the production and natural resources of another more efficiently. The MNCs' use of distributed computer networks will allow them to avoid duplication and to ease coordination of resources.
2. TDFs will enable MNCs to manage global operations more effectively. Response time to situations that arise will be shortened.
3. Knowledge, technology, and culture originating in one country can be made available almost immediately via telecommunications networks to most other countries. Time delays between have and have-not countries will be diminished.
4. The development costs of originating new technological applications can be spread over a broader base of users. Telecommunication networks enable any originating country to undertake a larger development effort because of economies of scale than could be justified on a home-country-only basis.

To date, U.S. policy has been articulated clearly in a report prepared under the direction of Senator Robert Packwood (R-Ore.).[26] This document states the long-range telecommunications and information-policy goals as defined by constitutional, legislative, executive and national-security parameters are based on two clear and guiding principles:

- To enhance the free flow of information across national boundaries; and
- To promote an environment for the provision of telecommunications and information facilities service, and the production and dissemination of information itself, in which maximum reliance is placed on free enterprise,

open and complete markets, and free trade and investment, with minimum direct government involvement or regulation.

The policymaking apparatus regarding telecommunications and information matters is vested in three major agencies. The Assistant Secretary of State and Coordinator for International Communication and Information Policy with the rank of ambassador, Diana Dougan, is a key policymaker. The Department of Commerce, with David Markey heading the National Telecommunications and Information Administration, plays an equally important role. The third major agency is the Federal Communications Commission, under the tutelage of Mark Fowler. Collectively they have become the Reagan administration's voice in dealing with telecommunications, an area whose exports are beginning to challenge arms and agriculture.[27]

The MNCs should recognize the legitimate concerns other nations have regarding TDFs. Despite the current U.S. lead in information-networking technology, this issue is too fundamental to the future of the world's economy for the U.S. to expect to hold such a dominant position indefinitely. The fears expressed by other nations about their dependence on U.S. networking technology are rational, and we must recognize these concerns. As W. Michael Blumenthal[28] stated:

> The protectionist barriers will not fall until other countries feel they are not threatened by America's 'information' gap' . . . . Our dealings abroad, then, must be cooperative ones, creating partnerships with companies in developed nations and established technology transfers in the Third World.

MNCs should encourage multinational trade negotiations and bilateral agreements between the U.S. and its trading partners among both the developed and developing nations. MNCs should actively support U.S. government efforts as well as those of international bodies to achieve this spirit of mutual cooperation.

MNCs must promote the need for data-protection regulation (and tariffs) on a worldwide scale and the establishment of uniform standards for communications equipment and technology, so there can be a predictable legal, economic, and technological environment in which to operate.

In host countries, MNCs should attempt to voluntarily conform as fully as possible to TDF guidelines in order to assuage foreign-government fears about data abuse, diffuse the privacy issue, and eliminate the need for further restrictions.

MNCs should assess how TDF regulations will effect their operations. They may have to examine the impact of TDF restrictions on hardware and software as well as on compatibility with each host country's regulations.

Operationally, MNCs should maximize flexibility in their data-base management structure so they can adapt to changing TDF regulations. Where possible, MNCs should maximize what can be stored and processed within regional boundaries. There will then be less need for TDF regulation as well as a lower network cost. Such an operations structure would reassure host governments that decisions affecting their economies would not be made beyond their regional borders, as well as allowing flexibility within the MNC's structure.

It is clear that the emerging issues related to TDF cannot be separated from the larger phenomenon of the nature of the relationship between MNCs and individual countries. This problem is just another manifestation of an inherently conflictual relationship between the two entities. Although TDF regulation is a new development, it falls into a pattern similar to that by which MNCs and countries have tried to find accommodations with one another in the past. Finding avenues for accommodation seems to be a more realistic solution than confrontation. The conditions are still favorable for a cooperative approach that balances the legitimate claims for national sovereignty and development with the very real need for TDFs.

References

1. "Transborder Rules Irk U.S. Firms," *Data Communications,* July 1980, p. 40.
2. W. Michael Blumenthal, "Transborder Data Flow and the New Protectionism," *Vital Speeches of the Day,* 47 (1981): 550-555.
3. David E. Sanger, "Waging a Trade War Over Data," *New York Times* March 13, 1983, pp. 1, 26.
4. In addition to the articles cited above, see, K. Kreyfack, "Europeans Tighten Data Flow," *Electronics,* February 10, 1981, p. 106; D. E. Sanger, "Multinational Worry As Countries Regulate Data Crossing Borders," *Wall Street Journal,* April 26, 1981, p. 1; and Martin B. J. Buss, "Legislative Threat to Transportive Data Flow," *Harvard Business Review* March/April 1984; pp. 111-18.
5. "Transnational Corporations and Transborder Data Flows: A Technical Paper" (New York: United Nations, 1982).
6. Daniel Bell, "Communications Technology For Better Or For Worse," *Harvard Business Review* 57 (May/June 1979): 20-42.
7. "International Communications and Information Policy," Hearings before the Subcommittee on Arms Control, Oceans, International Operations and Environment of the Committee on Foreign Relations of the United States Senate, (Washington, D.C.: United States Government Printing Office 1983).
8. A. Pollack, "Business Planners Look to Telecommunications," *New York Times,* May 2, 1983, p. xx.
9. "Transnational Corporations and Transborder Data Flows: A Technical Paper" (New York: United States Center on Transnational Corporations, 1982).
10. "Waging a Trade War Over Data," *New York Times* March 13, 1983, p. 1.
11. Frederick W. Honduis, *Emerging Data Protection in Europe* (New York: American Elsevier Publishing Company, 1975).
12. "Waging a Trade War Over Data," *New York Times* March 13, 1983, p. 1.
13. David Hebditch, "Will Data Flow Be Stemmed?" *Telecommunications* 13 (May 1979): 75-82.
14. Harry Katzan, Jr., *Multinational Computer Systems* (New York: Van Nostrand Reinhold Company, 1980).

15. Gordon C. Everest, "Non-uniform Privacy Laws: Implications and Attempts at Uniformity," *Computers and Privacy in the Next Decade* (Ed. by Lance J. Hoffman, Academic Press, 1980).
16. "Transborder Data Flows and the Protection of Privacy" Proceedings of a Symposium held in Vienna, Austria, Sept., 1977 (Paris: OECD, 1979).
17. "National Barriers To Data Flow," *Dun's Review*, July 1978, pp. 93-97.
18. John Eger, "Transborder Data Flow," *Datamation*, November 1978, pp. 50-54.
19. *Transborder Data Flows: Issues, Barriers and Corporate Responses* (New York: Business International, 1983).
20. John Kahwaty, "Transborder Data Flow and Its Impact upon International Banking" Thesis done at Rutgers University, N.J.: American Bankers Association, June 1982.
21. Michael J. Kane, "The Impact of TDF on Large U.S. Corporations," *International Information Economy Handbook* (Springfield, VA: Transnational Data Reporting Service Inc., 1985).
22. Gad J. Selig, *Strategic Planning for Information Resources Management: A Multinational Perspective* (Ann Arbor, MI: UMI Research Press, 1983).
23. Blumenthal, pp. 550-555.
24. John Eger, "U.S. Proposals Through Negotiations," *Journal of Communication*, 29 1979: 29-30.
25. Alden Heintz, "The Dangers of Regulation," *Journal of Communication*, 29 1979: 129-134.
26. *Long Range Goals in International Telecommunications and Information: An Outline for United States Policy* (Washington: U.S. Government Printing Office, 1983).
27. Reginald Stuart, "A Tale of Three Great Communicators," *New York Times*, August 27, 1985, p. A-18.
28. Blumenthal, "Transborder Data Flows and the New Protectionism," pp. 550-555.

ANNOTATED BIBLIOGRAPHY

ANNOTATED BIBLIOGRAPHY

I. THE GLOBAL FLOW OF GOODS

Briggs, Jean A. "Back to Barter?" *Forbes* 133.6 (March 12, 1984): 40–42.

This article examines the increasing popularity of countertrading in international trade. Issues such as bilateral trade versus multilateral trade are reviewed as the author expresses fears on the effects of increased barter activity.

Buckley, Peter J., and Robert D. Pearce. "Exports in the Strategy of Multinational Enterprises." *Journal of Business Research* 12.2 (June 1984): 209–225.

The effects on the multinational parent firm are examined when foreign production is expanded. The article suggests that a firm's international competitiveness is increased when foreign production is increased.

Dyment, John J. "Strategies and Management Controls for Global Corporations." *Journal of Business Strategy* 7.4 (Spring 1987): 20–26.

As corporations evolve into global firms, the management control systems must also change to reflect the new requirements of the global firm. These companies must be centrally managed, and strategic objectives need to cross national borders. The new control system should address data on the objectives, financial control, tax, legal and administrative compliance, tactical information, and management accounts.

Hazelton, Walter A. "The Ins and Outs of Foreign Trade." *Management Accounting* 69.6 (December 1987): 53–58.

Trading and Value-added requirements of foreign countries should be understood before a U.S. firm conducts business in those countries. The value-added components and trading requirement options are identified.

Mefford, Robert N. "The Effects of Unions on Productivity in a Multinational Manufacturing Firm." *Industrial and Labor Relations Review* 40.1 (October 1986): 105–114.

Unionization results in increased productivity in the multinational firm. The results may be due to improved labor relations or better quality workers.

Munkirs, John R. "Technological Change: Disaggregation and Overseas Production." *Journal of Economic Issues* 22.2 (June 1988): 469-475.

Economic indexes used to evaluate the economy of a nation may no longer be appropriate due to the emergence of world markets and economic interdependence. These indexes reveal little about firms that are transnational, supranational, or anational. Public policy and economic theory are examined.

Steck, Robert N. "Export Trading Companies." *D&B Reports* 22.3 (May/June 1984): 42–43.

As a result of U.S. world trade share decline from 1970 to 1981, the Export Trading Company Act of 1982 was passed. The intent of the act is to assist U.S. firms by eliminating some anti-trust restrictions, allowing the development of exporting companies.

II. THE GLOBAL FLOW OF LABOR

Alogoskoufis, George, and Alan Manning. "Wage Setting and Unemployment Persistence in Europe, Japan and the USA." *European Economic Review (Netherlands)* 32.2, 32.3 (March 1988): 698–706.

An analysis of the differences in the levels of unemployment between the principle European markets and those of Japan and the United States.

Bar-Haim, Aviad. "Workers' Participation and Personnel Policies in Israel." *International Labour Review* 127.3 (1988): 381–397.

An analysis of the decline of worker participation levels in personnel policy, recruitment, selection, wages and benefits determination as a result of recent economic stabilization agreements despite the presence of strong shop-floor committees and a highly unionized workforce.

Brander, James A., and Barbara J. Spencer. "Unionized Oligopoly and International Trade Policy." *Journal of International Economics (Netherlands)* 24.3, 24.4 (May 1988): 217–234.

The effects of unionization upon firms in an international market are studied. The trade policy consequences as a result of unionization are examined.

Green, Francis, and Michael J. Potepan. "Vacation Time and Unionism in the U.S. and Europe." *Industrial Relations* 27.2 (Spring 1988): 180–194.

An examination of the lesser amounts of vacation time in the United States in relation to their European counterparts. Unions are important in determining vacation amounts. In the United States, vacation time is given as a seniority reward.

Hansen, Gary B. "Creating a Future for Workers Displaced by Foreign Competition." *Business Forum* 13.1 (Winter 1988): 16-21.

American workers are being displaced because of international market competition, resulting in labor and management calling for restrictions on foreign goods through legislation and other trade barriers. New approaches to supporting and training displaced workers are mentioned.

Hundley, Greg. "Taxation and Strikes: The Post-War Experience in Three Countries." *British Journal of Industrial Relations* (UK) 26.1 (March 1988): 57–61.

An examination of the effects of tax changes on the number of strikes in the United Kingdom, Australia, and the United States. There appears to be evidence that taxation does affect the number of strikes in the United Kingdom and Australia, while there is no evidence that taxation affects strike rates in the United States. The levels of state intervention as a cause of the results is examined.

Kruse, Douglas L. "International Trade and the Labor Market Experience of Displaced Workers." *Industrial & Labor Relations Review* 41.3 (April 1988): 402–417.

The length of time that displaced workers remain jobless is examined. Two possible reasons for increased joblessness are demographic characteristics associated with high import/change industries, and the tendency of high-import industries to be in a state decline.

Kupfer, Andrew. "How to Be a Global Manager." *Fortune* 117.6 (March 14, 1988): 52–58.

Strategies used by some large international corporations to compete in international markets are presented. Additional suggestions for multinational management are given.

Kurtenbach, Elaine. "Labour: The Door Creaks Open." *International Management (UK)* 43.9 (September 1988): 49–53.

An examination of the increasing levels of legal and illegal aliens in the Japanese labor market. Japanese firms attempt to attract professionals from other nations for their growing international operations even though they are regarded as outsiders to both the company and Japanese society.

Mendenhall, Mark E., and Gary Oddou. "The Overseas Assignment: A Practical Look." *Business Horizons* 31.5 (September/October 1988): 78–84.

Twenty percent of overseas assignments end prematurely, and still others are completed by unhappy or ineffective personnel. Culture shock is one explanation for these occurrences. Elements leading to the success of an overseas assignment are reviewed.

Pucik, Vladimir. "Strategic Alliances, Organizational Learning, and Competitive Advantage: The HRM Agenda." *Human Resources Management* 27.1 (Spring 1988): 77–93.

A study of the strategic duty of organizational learning for Human Resources in international cooperative enterprises. Organizational learning impairments and HR agenda points are presented.

Schneider, Susan C. "National vs. Corporate Culture: Implications for Human Resource Management." *Human Resource Management* 27.2 (Summer 1988): 231–246.

Corporate culture is determined by Human Resource practices. The effects of corporate culture on the foreign subsidiary of a multinational corporation may present problems due to clashing of beliefs, values, and the subsidiary's national culture. National cultures and the role of the corporate culture should be considered when making Human Resource decisions.

Staiger, Robert W. "Organized Labor and the Scope of International Specialization." *Journal of Political Economy* 96.5 (October 1988): 1022–1047.

A model of the effects of unionization in an import-competing sector on trade, union wages, and shifting international production patterns.

Vineall, Tony. "Creating a Multinational Management Team." *Personnel Management (UK)* 20.10 (October 1988): 44–47.

Personnel management will become increasingly important to the multinational firm for recruitment in international markets, relocation solutions, and training and leadership in setting an organization's culture, climate, and style.

Volard, Sam V., Dennis M. Francis and Frank W. Wagner III. "Underperforming U.S. Expatriate Managers: A Study of Problems and Solutions." *Practising Manager (Australia)* 9.1 (Spring 1988): 37–40.

Expatriate managers in the multinational corporations have performed relatively ineffectively; as a result, the U.S. Economy has suffered. The selection process for expatriate managers is examined. Also introduced are recommendations for expatriate manager acculturation to be introduced into the selecting/training program.

III. THE GLOBAL FLOW OF CAPITAL

Anvari, M. "Efficient Scheduling of Cross-Border Cash Transfers." *Financial Management* 15.2 (Summer 1986): 40–49.

An examination of the costs associated with intra-multinational corporation transactions across borders. A mathematical program is provided to help identify the optimal transfer schedule.

Baker, James C. "The Cost of Capital of Multinational Companies: Facts and Fallacies." *Managerial Finance (UK)* 13.1 (1987): 12–17.

Methods employed for capital budgeting by many of the largest U.S. and European multinational firms. An examination of the alternative methods, and some of the inherent problems associated with them.

Defusco, Richard A., George C. Philippatos and Choi Dosoung. "Risk, Return, and International Investment by U.S. Corporations." *Applied Economics (UK)* 20.9 (September 1988): 1199–1209.

A model to examine whether market power as a result of foreign operations is priced as an additional dimension of asset valuation, and the resulting variations in the expected returns of the common stock of the multinational firm.

Dotan, Amihud, and Arie Ovadia. "A Capital Budgeting Decision — The Case of a Multinational Corporation Operating in High-Inflation Countries." *Journal of Business Research* 14.5 (October 1986): 403–410.

An examination of the difficulties associated with capital budgeting for a subsidiary of a multinational corporation operating in a high-inflation country.

Eaker, Mary R., and Joan Lenowitz. "Multinational Borrowing Decisions and the Empirical Exchange Rate Evidence." *Management International Review* 26.1 (1st Quarter 1986): 24–32.

An empirical study of borrowing in different currencies by a multinational. The use of a simple decision rule may lead to lower borrowing costs.

Flamm, Kenneth. "The Volatility of Offshore Investment." *Journal of Development Economics* 16.3 (December 1984): 231–248.

A study of the semiconductor industry was performed in order that new modeling methods be developed for direct foreign investment where risk diversification is used for plant site determination.

Gershenberg, Irving. "Labor, Capital, and Management Slack in Multinational and Local Firms in Kenyan Manufacturing." *Economic Development and Cultural Change* 35.1 (October 1986): 163–178.

As management resources have shown to be an operational constraint on production in less developed countries, the expansion of employment opportunities in these countries may require the establishment of new firms rather than the continued training of management students.

Lee, Kwang Chul, and Chuck C.Y. Kwok. "Multinational Corporations vs. Domestic Corporations: International Environmental Factors and Determinants of Capital Structure." *Journal of International Business Studies* 19.2 (Summer 1988): 195–217.

A comparison of bankruptcy costs and debt ratios between multinational corporations and domestic corporations. The initial indications are that multinational firms do not have lower bankruptcy costs, but do tend to have lesser debt ratios than domestic corporations.

Lee, Boyden E., and Ronald R. Bloom. "Transfer Pricing as a Tool of Funds Management." *Southwest Journal of Business and Economics* 3.1 (Fall 1985): 11–18.

Transfer pricing as a means of management of working capital for the multinational is an effective method. The accounting risk, transition risk, economic risk, and political risk of working capital decisions are examined. Four methods of setting transfer prices as a means to minimize foreign exposure are introduced.

Lee, William. "1992: Promise or Problems for Non-EC Companies?" *International Financial Law Review (UK)* 7.9 (September 1988): 18–19.

As the European Community trade agreement approaches (1992), concerns are being expressed by non-European Community countries regarding a free flow of goods, people, services, and capital with their countries. There are unclear positions resulting from the Treaty of Rome, and new international agreements may be necessary to clarify trade issues for companies in nonEuropean Community countries.

Reitzes, James D., and Donald J. Rousslang. "Domestic Versus International Capital Mobility: Some Empirical Evidence." *Canadian Journal of Economics* 21.2 (May 1988): 312–323.

A test to determine whether capital moves more easily between industries within the same country or between countries within the same industry has indicated that the tendency is for greater ease of capital movement for different industries within the same country. This is a change from prior data, where international mobility was more likely.

Ruffin, Roy J., and Fahad Rassekh. "The Role of Foreign Direct Investment in U.S. Capital Outflows." *American Economic Review* 76.5 (December 1986): 1126–1130.

The effects of U.S. foreign direct investment versus foreign portfolio investments are studied. The results indicate that it is possible that foreign direct investment displaces an equal amount of portfolio investment, resulting in little effect on net capital flows.

Zink, William J., and Susan H. Griffiths. "Establishing Overseas Operations: Tax and Treasury Considerations." *Cash Flow* 8.1 (January 1987): 46–50.

Tax and treasury concerns should be considered before a small or medium-sized company establishes overseas operations. Foreign tax structures, domestic tax liabilities, and treasury decisions for organizational structure are examined.

IV. THE GLOBAL FLOW OF INFORMATION

Dingwall, James. "In Canada — International Data Flow." *D&B Reports* 22.1 (January/February 1984): 56–57.

Canada is very dependent upon information, and the free flow of information across the Canadian-U.S. border has become very important. There is a fear that unilateral barriers will be established by some countries to restrict information flow.

Moore, Steve. "Information Managers Must Face the International Communications Web." *Data Management* 22.6 (June 1984): 30–32.

While many countries regulate the flow of information, many have been pressuring the General Agreement of Tariffs and Trade to include information trade issues into its policy deliberations. There is concern over economic and social control over communications networks.

Pucik, Vladimir, and Jan Hack Katz. "Information, Control, and Human Resource Management in Multinational Firms." *Human Resource Management* 25.1 (Spring 1986): 121–132.

It is important for Human Resource Management to establish a control system to manage the technical and social information systems in the multinational firm. The information network is vital for effective global competitiveness, and it needs to be decentralized. The Human Resource Management system to control it must be flexible and predictable.

Rankin, T. Murray. "Business Secrets Across International Borders: One Aspect of the Transborder Data Flow Debate." *Canadian Business Law Journal* 10.2 (May 1985): 213–246.

The technological ability to transfer data rapidly across national borders has many people concerned. While the flow of data is important to Canada and Canada's trade partners, efforts must be made to hinder the flow of business secrets. Governments need information flow policies, while the citizens must monitor the government regulations.

V. THE GLOBAL FLOW OF TECHNOLOGY

Atak, Osman A. "International Experience Theory and Global Strategy." *International Marketing Review* 3.4 (Winter 1986): 52–61.

Newly industrialized countries are finding themselves with strategic advantages in industrial markets. The experience theory and the effects on the labor share, market expansion rate, and the ease of technology adaptation are examined.

Chaushuri, Adhip. "Multinational Corporations in Less-Developed Countries: What is in Store?" *Columbia Journal of World Business* 23.1 (Spring 1988): 57–63.

Due to the increased number of multinational firms competing in less developed countries, as well as the less developed countries learning to deal with the multinationals, has given the less developed countries a stronger bargaining position. The transfer of technology will become an important factor in determining policy issues.

Performance criteria and investment incentives will become more common in policy packages offered to the multinationals.

Dunning, John H. "Market Power of the Firm and International Transfer of Technology: A Historical Excursion." *International Journal of Industrial Organization* 1.4 (1983): 333–351.

The economic power of the multinational corporation affects how it transfers technology internationally. The international technology transfers for the past 150 years are examined.

Engel, Alan K. "How to Profit from Japanese Technology." *Directors & Boards* 12.4 (Summer 1988): 14–17.

As Japan increasingly becomes a technology exporter, it becomes more important for U.S. companies to gain ties to Japanese firms. Certain cultural and strategic barriers will continue to hinder U.S. companies in the future when dealing with the Japanese in domestic and international markets.

Etemad, Hamid, G.S. Kindra, and Jean-Louis Schaan. "World Product Mandates and Technology Transfer." *Industrial Marketing and Purchasing* 1.1 (1986): 42–58.

The use of international trading companies and world product mandating are methods for becoming an international competitor. Advantages of using these methods are examined, with specific references to Canadian manufacturers.

Ghoshal, Sumantra, and Christopher A. Bartlett. "Creation, Adoption, and Diffusion of Innovations by Subsidiaries of Multinational Corporations." *Journal of International Business Studies* 19.3 (Fall 1988): 365–388.

The ability of the subsidiary of the multinational corporation to communicate throughout the organization could enable it to make a positive impact on innovation activities. Organizational communication and integration play a role in the effects of local resources and local autonomy.

Harvey, Michael G. "Application of Technology Life Cycles to Technology Transfers." *Journal of Business Strategy* 5.2 (Fall 1984): 51–58.

Proposed steps for the transfer of technology by the multinational corporation to the less developed nation. Analysis is required of technology, competition, and the technology's impact on the receiving country.

Lasserre, Philippe. "Selecting a Foreign Partner for Technology Transfer." *Long Range Planning* 17.6 (December 1984): 43–49.

Increasingly, joint ventures and licensing contracts between the multinational corporation and local firms are becoming effective means of entry into Third World markets. Both firms can benefit through the use of the expertise and resources that each party has.

Looney, Robert E. "The Impact of Technology Transfer on the Structure of the Saudi Arabian Labor Force." *Journal of Economic Issues* 22.2 (June 1988): 485–492.

The employment changes that have taken place to date as a result of industrialization have become nonbeneficial as the changes have not reflected the true economic needs. There is a shortage of local labor and skilled workers to run the new industries.

Madeuf, Bernadette. "International Technology Transfers and International Technology Payments: Definitions, Measurement and Firms' Behaviour." *Research Policy* 13.3 (June 1984): 125–140.

Issues related to the definition, interpretation, measurement, and recording of international technology transfers are examined. The balance of payments in relation to the amount of technology transferred is also reviewed.

Meyer, Peter B. "Combining New Job Creation with Advanced Technology Adoptions: British Innovative Local Economic Efforts." *Journal of Economic Issues* 22.2 (June 1988): 443–449.

A study of British attempts to use advanced technology to improve local labor and economic conditions. Local authorities have met resistance from the Thatcher Administration as they attempt to use technology to help their constituents.

Prasad, S. Benjamin. "Technology Transfer: The Approach of a Dutch Multinational." *Technovation* 4.1 (January 1986): 3–15.

In response to the claims that much of the technology transferred to less developed countries is not suited for the production that it is to be employed in, N.V. Philips has established a pilot plant in the Netherlands. The goal was to keep the plant simple, adapt to small series, have the required tools available, and keep the amount of capital in use low. The plan has now been expanded to include 20 new plants.

Taylor, Michael B. "Technology Can Be Marketed to Less-Developed Nations." *Marketing News* 22.19 (September 12, 1988): 23.

U.S. firms have failed to recognize that when dealing with developing countries, the technology is the salable item not the resulting goods or services. Pricing and repeat business problems result from this failure.

Zuscovitch, Ehud, Jean-Alain Heraud, and Patrick Cohendet. "Innovation Diffusion From a Qualitative Standpoint." *Futures* 20.3 (June 1988): 266–306.

The effects of the diffusion of material on technoeconomic change creates a new logic of evolution. Change is shown to be an evolutionary process rather than a sudden event.